A Place to Remember

About the Series
The American Association for State and Local History Book Series publishes technical and professional information for those who practice and support history, and addresses issues critical to the field of state and local history. To submit a proposal or manuscript to the series, please request proposal guidelines from AASLH headquarters: AASLH Book Series, 1717 Church St., Nashville, Tennessee 37203. Telephone: (615) 320-3203. Fax: (615) 327-9013. Web site: **www.aaslh.org**.

About the Organization
The American Association for State and Local History (AASLH) is a nonprofit educational organization dedicated to advancing knowledge, understanding, and appreciation of local history in the United States and Canada. In addition to sponsorship of this book series, the Association publishes the periodical *History News*, a newsletter, technical leaflets and reports, and other materials; confers prizes and awards in recognition of outstanding achievement in the field; and supports a broad educational program and other activities designed to help members work more effectively. To join the organization, contact: Membership Director, AASLH, 1717 Church St., Nashville, Tennessee 37203.

A Place to Remember
Using History to Build Community

Robert R. Archibald

ALTAMIRA
PRESS
A Division of Sage Publications, Inc.
Walnut Creek · London · New Delhi

Copyright ©1999 by AltaMira Press, A Division of Sage Publications, Inc.

For information address:
AltaMira Press
A Division of Sage Publications, Inc.
1630 North Main Street, Suite 367
Walnut Creek, California 94596 U.S.A.

Sage Publications Ltd.
6 Bonhill Street
London EC2A 4PU
United Kingdom

Sage Publications India Pvt. Ltd.
M-32 Market
Greater Kailash 1
New Delhi 110 048 India

Library of Congress Cataloguing-in-Publication Data

Archibald, Robert, 1948-
    A place to remember : using history to build community / Robert Archibald.
        p. cm. — (American association for state and local history book series)

Includes bibliographical references (p.) and index.
ISBN 0-7619-8942-0
ISBN 0-7619-8943-9
    1. United States—History, Local—Philosophy. 2. Community life—United States Case studies. 3. City and town life—United States Case studies. 4. Archibald, Robert, 1948- 5. Historians—United States Biography. 6. Public history—United States. I. Title. II. Series.
    E180.5 .A73 1999
    973—dc21
                            99-6261   CIP

99   00   01   02   03   04   7   6   5   4   3   2   1
PRINTED IN THE UNITED STATES OF AMERICA99

Editorial Management: Pam Lucas
Editorial Production: Virginia Alderson Hoffman
Cover Design: Joanna Ebenstein
Typesetting: ibid, northwest

Excerpt from "The Dry Salvages" in FOUR QUARTETS, copyright 1941 by T.S. Eliot and renewed in 1969 by Esme Valerie Eliot, reprinted by permission of Harcourt Brace & Company. Excerpt from "Burnt Norton" in FOUR QUARTETS, copyright 1943 by T.S. Eliot and renewed in 1971 by Esme Valerie Eliot, reprinted by permission of Harcourt Brace & Company.

～ **Table of Contents** ～

Acknowledgments

This book has been in production for a long, long time—in some sense, it has been in progress for as long as I myself have been (and so it isn't really finished). Similarly, this book is the work of not just Rob Archibald but a work that has drawn on the experience, the expertise, and indeed the patience of many people. From Michael Quinn and his wives to my youngest grandchildren, I thank them all.

More specifically, I acknowledge some particular assistance in this effort.

The staff of the Missouri Historical Society are a talented and dedicated group of people. In the midst of an enormous renovation and expansion of our museum (including the capital campaign and plans for ambitious new exhibitions), they have worked diligently and faithfully to insure continuity and adherence to our mission. In my absence on this writing sabbatical, I had every confidence that the Missouri Historical Society, including the President's Office, would continue to function at its best because of all these people.

Kathy Petersen, my research and writing assistant, was truly my wise and patient collaborator. If there are merits in this book, many are because of her. And especially, among other MHS colleagues, I am grateful to: Karen M. Goering, MHS Executive Vice President, who both saw and oversaw the fertilizations of many of these ideas and whose talents, dedication, and support are indefatigable; Lee Ann Sandweiss, MHS Director of Publications, who contributed a steady supply of encouragement and support throughout this past summer; and Pattie Pinter Hartmann, my executive assistant, whose professional capability is superlative and whose personal quality is a joy.

Many people in and of Michigan's Upper Peninsula will see themselves in this work. Their hospitality, good nature, and willingness to share even the pain of the past were evident in all my days of this sojourn. And especially my family, most notably my sister Anne Archibald and her husband David Dill, my cousins Rhena Grazier and Rhett Dulany and Rhett's family; Sue Frisk, who showed me the U.P. in old and new ways; Elizabeth Delene, research associate extraordinaire and friend as well; Russell M. Magnaghi of Northern Michigan University and Sandra Clark of the Michigan Bureau of History, whose advice and encouragement are much appreciated; and Terry Davis, who is not of Michigan but who as friend, colleague, and woman both smart and wise had a strong effect on this project.

AltaMira Press surely has some of the most cooperative yet exacting staff in the business, especially Mitch Allen and Pam Lucas. Our questions and concerns were always met with patience, promptness, and excellent discussion.

I believe this is indeed a place to remember, and all of you have contributed to the community of this place. Many thanks.

To Sue
Past, Present, and Future

~1~

Facing the Past

History is not disembodied. The past is implicit in the present, in each of us, and in the places we inhabit. This is why I went to my first home in the Upper Peninsula of Michigan to write. It was an opportunity to measure myself, to see how I have changed and how this place changed. To what extent are my memories of this place related to new meanings, new stories I have ascribed to people, places, and events in light of my subsequent experience? Has my memory served simply as a record of the past? I left this place when I was twenty-one and have returned infrequently, too often for funerals of loved ones, and always on quick trips. So this has been my first opportunity to reacquaint myself with the place that is the crucible of my formative memories. My memory recalls specific places, people, and interactions, but it has also re-interpreted and assigned new meanings to the interactions. Here in Ishpeming, Marquette, and other once-familiar places in the U.P., I can compare how I once remembered with how I remember now.

Theresa sits hunched over on the brown painted board balanced on top of the radiator in the shop window on Division Street. She is ninety-six years old. From the street I see her diminutive silhouette framed through the window beneath the green and yellow sign that spells *Andriacchi's* in cursive letters over the building facade. Dominic, her father, immigrated with her mother and three small children from Italy at the turn of the century to this neighborhood, then an enclave of earlier Irish immigrants—Ryans, Hickeys, Collins, Gleasons, and others, gradually being replaced by Andriacchis, Bonettis, Gagliardis, Ombrellos, Bertuccis, and Tassons. Several of Dominic Andriacchi's children were born in Italy, but Theresa was born here. As I drive from Marquette to Ishpeming, my apprehension mounts that I might find the store closed and Theresa gone like so much of this once-thriving iron mining town on Michigan's Upper Peninsula. But no, one more time she is there as she always has been. I take one

9

step up to the door, open it, and enter. Theresa turns, looks at me, and greets me with a noncommittal hello. "Hi, I am Rob Archibald," I say, to save her from struggling with her memory. "Oh yes, I remember you," she says. But she doesn't get up from her backless radiator seat, newspapers strewn beside her and a stout cane leaning against the wall to her right. She wears a black dress. Usually I remember faces, not clothes. But for Theresa the clothes are as constant as her hair in a tight bun and the wrinkled outlines of her face. She wears only black dresses.

"How are you?" I ask. "Fine," she says. "You know in my whole life I have never even had a headache. God has been very good to me." The store is even more bereft and barren than when I last visited three years ago. I hear the Regulator clock still ticking from its spot

"I have come to think of time as extending out from me in all directions connecting me to everything that was, is, and will be . . . Time is a variable and can move in multiple directions." (The Regulator clock in Theresa Andriacchi's store. Photo by Sue Frisk, 1998.)

on the wall behind the rolltop desk which sits up high on a platform. That desk is evidence of a time past when Theresa's father and then Theresa herself could keep eyes on the store while seated at the desk placing orders, keeping accounts, and paying bills. The dressing rooms along the back wall remain intact. Clothing racks are lined up at right angles in front of the dressing rooms' disheveled beige curtains. I wonder about the length of time since Theresa ordered new clothing stock. Judging from the styles I can see on the racks, it is twenty-five years, maybe longer.

I can only discern partially decayed remains of what is in my memory luminous and alive. Only the shadowy outlines of my childhood memories are confirmed in this place. Clothing, bolts of cloth, and dry goods were displayed to the rear, with cookies and candies and pasta in tilted bins, salamis, flour, condiments, and sundries in front. Now, only a few Hershey and Kit-Kat bars and sparse packages of pasta survive on the shelves of the once densely stocked store. The now-silent front door clanged as it frequently opened and closed. Customers bantered with Theresa and her sister Rose, and my mother browsed through dress racks and looked at winter clothes for me while waiting her turn with the Andriacchi women. The U-shaped counter, adorned with brown wrapping paper, string dispenser, and scales, is still there, confirming my recollections of forty years ago.

"Where's Anthony?" I ask, referring to her brother who was here on my last visit. "Anthony died a long time ago," she replies. I hold my tongue and do not say that Anthony must have died just within the past three years. I know what she means. When Anthony died doesn't matter. Confronted, as she is, with eternity, time is insignificant. For Theresa, Anthony is gone forever. At her age so much is gone forever. She is only sustained now by an unshakable faith, nurtured by her family's unwavering Catholicism that was transplanted from Italy by her parents' generation within St. John's Church two blocks away as the new arrivals supplanted the dwindling Irish congregation. "If God wishes, I will live to be one hundred," she says.

We talk about dramatic changes in the neighborhood. When I ask what she thinks of these changes, she dismisses them, again leaving all in the hands of her God and abiding faith. Theresa is an endearing relic. This store, built by her father, is at once a means to a living and a familial obligation. Through this store Theresa entered into those bonds that united her with family, neighbors, and community in a dense thicket of intricate relationships encompassing the store, the church, and the neighborhood, and the entire community of Ishpeming. The store was more than marketplace; it was also a place where relationships were initiated, reinforced, and buttressed by life on Division Street, the values of church, the parish school, and a shared ethnicity. It was a place like the ones Ray Oldenburg terms "third places" to distinguish them from work and home.[1]

Theresa does not believe in progress in the contemporary American sense of economic growth, advertising, and escalating mass consumption. What many call progress she calls change, and she does not judge whether it is good or bad. It's just change. The truth is apparent in her old age. She does not open the store every day to make a profit, for there is nothing to sell. She opens it out of a larger sense of her place in life, obligation to family—especially to its deceased members—and duty to her God, values that are eternal for her and unaffected by the marketplace. She opens every morning because people expect it and because during each day an occasional visitor will still stop in, continuing in a limited way the social function the store has always served. It is how she keeps in touch. She does not even keep a radio for company in the store. While many people might judge that the world has passed her by, Theresa does not see it that way. She is finishing her job with fidelity, doing what she was intended to do on this earth. She sits in the window, head bowed, perhaps asleep, until someone enters and speaks. Theresa knows her duty. She is constant. For her, there is no progression of past, present, and future, only eternity and present. Eternity is where Anthony, Rose, and the others have gone. Now is where she is just for the moment.

But the dusty, decayed vestiges of the store I remember are not remarkable in this downtown. Instead, they are representative of the widespread abandonment of business, entertainment, civic, and neighborhood institutions that once sustained daily life here. The railroad tracks are torn up and ironically replaced by a new street for inexorably diminishing traffic. The underground mine shafts that once surrounded the town are sealed with massive concrete caps. The two downtown theaters are gone, one shuttered and the other demolished for a parking lot. Most of the businesses that once provided life's necessities are closed. And our house at 551 South Pine Street is decaying from the outside in, a reversal of the town's order of decline which proceeds from the inside out, downtown first. Once neighborhoods encircled the looming shafts where men were lowered in primitive elevator-cages and red-stained skips of iron ore were hauled up in the same cages. Now the mines and the neighborhoods are remembered only in the street names: Barnum, Excelsior, Winthrop, Lake Angeline, Cleveland, Superior. Yet it's not that the town is dying. Its population has dropped since its heyday fifty years ago, but substantial numbers of people still claim they live in Ishpeming, although they often mean the sprawling township extending miles beyond the old city limits. It is the physical arrangement of people that has changed. Theresa now sits with her back to the street, for the street is now less interesting than the store's barren interior. "Everyone has cars now," she explains.

Ishpeming, like most American towns and cities, has been eviscerated by cars that, while they promoted mobility and individualism, have undermined those very structures that nurtured community and encouraged informal relationships through a spatial proximity and mixed or multiple use. Hence, in Theresa's old neighborhood, residence—houses of different sizes, apartments for new families and some for elderly people, rooming houses for bachelor miners—were interspersed with stores like Andriacchi's and Ombrello's, neighborhood bars like the Venice, schools like St. John's, barbershops like Pete's, churches, social halls, coffee shops—all within walking distance of the towering Cliffs Shaft Mine where most of the men from her neighborhood worked. Once most Ishpeming residents walked to any corner of town in under a half hour, nodding, chatting, watching and watched as they moved about town. But cars delivered speeds that diminished distance. Now residents of the area can travel nearly thirty miles in the same thirty minutes, but they are enclosed in a wheeled box insulated from people and places and with diminished opportunity for casual acquaintance and informal familiarity. The result is the Ishpeming version of the national post-World War II exodus to the good life: houses separated from non-residential functions by zoning laws, a new "downtown" stretching for twenty miles along the highway, modern commercial buildings in the middle of acres of parking. My own city of St. Louis is a big-city example: the population has increased 34 percent since 1950 but the land area that population occupies has soared 355 percent. People in such places live isolated and segregated lives, and those relationships upon which community and civic life depend wilt and wither. And the community disintegrates.

Certainly these radical changes are nascent environmental disasters because they consume enormous quantities of resources. And they are the cause of enormous future tax burdens because they depend upon construction of more infrastructure such as roads and sewers and an increased number of facilities such as schools and libraries. But these new arrangements of space are also the catalysts for a community memory lapse that is not so obvious but even more threatening. Familiar places are repositories of memory both personal and communal. My mother took me to Andriacchi's Store, where she bought clothes for me, and Theresa, or her sister Rose, gave me cookies. Even now Theresa remembers me. We are fixed in each other's minds. Theresa is a repository of my memories, and I hers, so long as we both live. But so is Division Street, the store, the counter, the pressed tin ceiling, the string dispenser, and the Regulator clock. I am pleased to still hear the tick of that clock but I am appalled at the unrelenting decimation of the once-vibrant downtown. I am dismayed at what is happening to our house, and at the disappearance of St. John's School which I attended for eight years. The decay and disappearance of the touchstones of my own formative memories that attach me to my own childhood and to the town of Ishpeming on the Upper Peninsula of Michigan are my personal agony. For those who never left or who left only for a short while, these changes are incremental and thus barely noticed. I visited with an Ishpeming friend who had stayed, and she said she thought nothing had changed much. Her comment is reminiscent of the lobster who, as the pot of water was brought to a gradual boil, ignored the slowly escalating temperature until too late and thus became dinner.

A "home town" remains a special place for a lifetime. It has something to do with a first exposure to life, the place where we first come to know the world. Such places are deeply imprinted in our brains and become the irreplaceable measurement of all other places. Perhaps it is related to the instinct that draws salmon thousands of miles from the ocean to spawn in the same streams where they first lived. Ishpeming is such a place for me. I am pulled to it while simultaneously trying to draw away because there are so many places in Ishpeming that are memory places, some joyous and others reminders of sorrow. Here I cannot escape my present or past self. Here my own aging is apparent and I mourn my very own lost boy. And here I assess the proud successes and dismal failures of my own life.

The landscapes and places of childhood are the sensory implants through which we view the rest of the world forever. I know that I am not alone in such feelings. Many others have spoken and written of such special formative places, none more eloquently than Barry Lopez in *About This Life: Journeys on the Threshold of Memory.* "We turned around and headed north on Wilbur, windows open to

"The landscapes and places of childhood are the sensory implants through which we view the rest of the world forever." (Lake Superior, near Ishpeming, Michigan. Photo by Sue Frisk, 1998.)

the fresh breeze," he writes. "We drove past the house where my friend Leon had lived, where I had first bitten into the flesh of a pomegranate, and then slowly past other places that I knew but could not recognize. The air all around was brilliant."[2]

My long absence from the place that was and is Ishpeming creates dramatic contrast. I mourn the tragedy of the loss. But for my friend who stayed in Ishpeming something is lost, too. Parts of her identity are made less distinct. Her memory has lost its moorings in the physical environment of the town. The memories still exist but their confirmation is obscured by the destruction of physical referents. This town barely exists for my children because I left and seldom visited. At most we drove through and I said, "This is where I grew up." My friend raised her children near here but the places she knew and remembers must be foreign to them because those places are no longer there. Not only are her memories and mine sundered from what anchored, confirmed, and symbolized them, but an intergenerational connection is severed. Yet even more is lost. Change certainly occurred in the past but at a slower pace that made adaptation possible. Hence it was less bewildering, confusing, and disorienting. Now however, not only do businesses quickly come and go but houses, neighborhoods, entire communities are transitional and the built environment has a short life expectancy. This process is an "un-remembering" through which the places and the memories that they sustain are obscured, as if immersed in impenetrable and unhealthy fog. Although I cannot precisely specify the limits, there is some subjective equation that stipulates the relationship between rate of change and individual and community health.

I find confirmation of change even among Ishpeming's neighborhood of the dead. I only visited the Ishpeming Cemetery as an altar boy who volunteered for funerals as a ploy to get out of school. Now I stroll through the cemetery looking for names, relationships, birth dates, death dates, and quiet. I begin in the older sections of the cemetery. In the Catholic portion I can see the transition on tombstones from Irish to Italian names; this city of dead mimics the changes wrought in the community of the living. Coming upon the graves of people I had known is startling, but what strikes me most as I move into the newer sections is the disappearance of family plots. With the nineteenth-century urban cemetery movement, it became customary even for people who died far from the family home to be returned in death to the family burial plot. Although he lived elsewhere at the end of his life, Thomas McKittrick, the builder of my century-old house in St. Louis, chose to be buried in his family's plot in Bellefountaine Cemetery, St. Louis' great "city of the dead." But now people buy their own single or double burial plots, not lots for their entire families. Many factors may have contributed to the change but among them must be the declining importance of extended families and, since family plots are a long-range purchase, the end of the notion that a family is likely to stay put for several generations. The decline of family plots not only reflects a diminished cohesion in extended families, but their disappearance deprives people of visible symbols of attachment and continuity, for cemeteries are in themselves powerful places of remembrance incorporating tangible evidence of a vital community cornerstone. So not only have neighborhoods and communities been pried loose from ties that bind, but families too have lost their connection to a place.

The places that people make can never be static, but change must not overwhelm continuity. If we allow that, we imperil the bonds of civic life, impoverish relationships with people and places, and endanger democratic institutions and the very foundations of this civilization. Civic, neighborhood, and familial life all depend upon shared places that are repositories of common memories and shared experiences. These are the places that Ray Oldenburg terms "third places" to distinguish them from work and home. The absence of such spaces creates what Oldenburg calls "the problem of place in America" which is manifested in a "sorely deficient public life." "The structure of shared experience beyond that offered by family, job, and passive consumerism is small and dwindling. The essential group experience is being replaced by the exaggerated self-consciousness of individuals. American lifestyles, for all the material acquisition and the seeking after comforts and pleasures, are plagued by boredom, loneliness, alienation, and a high price tag."[3]

Common aspirations can only be formed in "third places" where shared memories grow. More than one hundred fifty years ago Alexis de Tocqueville, the insightful French observer of American life, was struck by the necessity of informal association to democratic life. "Among the laws that rule human societies," he observed, "there is one which seems to be more precise and clear than all the others. If men are to remain civilized or to become so, the art of associating together must grow and improve in the same ratio in which the equality of conditions is increased."[4] But where now are the places where we will practice the art of "associating together"?

Some things change so slowly that alterations are imperceptible in one lifetime. I sit on a huge, rough boulder, part of the breakwater that juts out from Marquette's upper harbor into the frigid, clear waters of Lake Superior. An ore boat, the *Alcorail*, rides low in the water after taking on a load of iron ore and prepares to set sail. But it is not the huge ore boat that engages me. It is the water, the smooth, round, multi-colored rocks that roll forward and back with the waves, the rugged coast, and this lake that you cannot see across. I have sat here countless times to get my moorings. From this rock salty tears have dropped from my eyes into the lake, and youthful sighs have rolled over its waters. I remember being here as a child, and it is the same now as then. Here I find myself. I am moored here because it is beautiful, but even more because it eases the inexorable passages of a lifetime. There is more than one kind of time. There is the time that measures a life in precise, one-directional measurements on a line, like the Regulator clock on Theresa's wall; then there is Lake Superior time, or even Theresa's time, that scarcely exists at all. I have come to think of time as extending out from me in all directions connecting me to everything that was, is, and will be. It occurs to me that all English verbs that imply past, present, and future are forms of the verb "to be." Time is a variable and can move in multiple directions. Quantum mechanics and particle physics confirm the bizarre. We really knew this already.

I am reluctant to use the word history anymore because it is loaded with meanings I do not intend to express. I do not mean names, dates, and places nor a text on a shelf: History is neither a reference book nor a scholarly historical monograph. I do not want to convey a process of scholarly objective inquiry in which the historian struggles to maintain objective distance from the subject matter:

Squishing emotions out of our work is misguided. I certainly do not mean a discipline that relies exclusively on written records, and I am not interested in any history that never reaches a useful conclusion.

History is not disembodied. I can re-remember my earliest "history" in Andriacchi's Store.

I went there with my mother reluctantly. The store after all did not sell toys. I thought that Theresa and Rose dressed strangely, and they spoke with thick accents that were, to my young and uninitiated ears, intimidating and almost unintelligible. Even then the store seemed old fashioned and out-of-date. The fixtures were antiquated. The sisters did not do things the way more up-to-date stores like the Miracle Market did. I was always eager to leave. Even after mother had decided on her purchases, I knew that we were not finished. They talked interminably and instead of slipping merchandise into a paper sack, Theresa and Rose laboriously wrapped mother's purchases in brown paper cleanly torn from a huge roll and then meticulously tied the package with string from the dispenser that still sits on the counter. Andriacchi's Store was my least favorite excursion. Once I no longer had to accompany mother on errands, I did not go back into the store until just three years ago. I returned for several reasons. First, despite the profound changes in Ishpeming, this store had not changed, and unexpectedly Theresa and her brother Anthony were still there. Second, the store now had symbolic meanings for me as an adult but especially as an historian. It was a relic of what the community once was, an extraordinary barometer of change. Not only was the store a part of my own past, but the family's perseverance created an important counterpoint to change and remains for now a fading symbol of loss. Andriacchi's and its style of business are barren anachronisms, a stark symbol of what has been obliterated not only in Ishpeming but in St. Louis and in towns all over this land. When it is gone, we will have lost one more of the fading signposts that bear witness to other ways of living and to what we have both gained and lost in the last fifty years. Meanings, feelings, and memories change, too.

I now think that my decision to be a historian was a result of growing up in Ishpeming, where post-World War II changes in America were accentuated by excruciating economic dislocation. I witnessed this process of abandonment and job loss which only hastened the decline of the downtown. The underground iron mines which reached their zenith of production with the war effort gradually closed until by the time I left Ishpeming none were left. I did not view these changes objectively. They adversely affected my own family and my neighbors. When I entered college I was not nostalgic; I was angry. Not only was my town in decline but the place itself had been ravaged by rapacious mining techniques. As the mines closed, whole chunks of land were fenced off where mine shafts and pits had once been or where land was allowed to cave in. My aged grandparents were forced from their home, and both ends of the main street in the neighboring town of Negaunee disappeared behind chain link fences and warning signs. It is as if somebody took a live thing, chopped both ends off, and hoped it would survive. I realized that living next to old dangerous mine pits in a town that shook with daily dynamite blasts was not normal. I was appalled at the daily dousing of red ore dust that covered even the winter snow, turning crystal white into dirty pink. After my senior year in high school I worked in the local hospital as an orderly. One of my most vivid recollections of that summer is of sick miners coughing and hacking and spitting up bowlfuls of red sputum. It looked like the dirty pink snow as it melted. Both came from the bowels of the earth, an image of my place that I still carry.

My dismay blended easily into naive sixties activism. This activism was a convenient outlet for the dismay I felt about what was happening to my place. Something was wrong with the "system," in sixties parlance. In my junior year at Northern Michigan University I chose history as my major, not because I was interested in scholarly discipline, nor because I wanted to retreat, but rather because I sought explanations that would give me better tools for change. From the outset I embraced history as an activist discipline, not an ivory-towered scholarly pursuit. The past does have implications. It is not enough to study and explicate the past. We must do something about it. In the words of anthropologist Claude Levi-Strauss, "History may lead to anything, provided you get out of it."[5]

But graduate school lasts a long time. I spent five years getting Master's and Doctor's degrees. (Either you get into it or you never get out of it.) I learned to be a scholar and experimented with the mantle of objective distance from subject matter that was demanded. I enjoyed the discipline, the opportunity to read, archival research, and finally the challenge of writing an acceptable dissertation. I was seduced by the idea of becoming a professor; however, I did take several courses in museum studies to enhance job possibilities, but only grudgingly at my major professor's insistence.

The seventies' job market for history professors was dismal. I was fortunate to get a job as curator of history at the Albuquerque Museum; second-rate employment compared to the scholar's life, I thought. "I hope you will be able to get a real history job soon," one former professor said earnestly. At one museum conference I listened to a seasoned museum person decry the invasion of paper-credentialed Ph.D.s into the history museum world. I was a pariah of sorts in both academe and the museum world.

Eventually I began to make sense of the three-dimensional and representational remains of the past. It took me a long time. I tried objective analysis; it only took me so far and stopped short of something else I was seeking. I could squeeze the same sort of evidentiary meanings out of objects and images as I could out of documents. This required research to provide context, analysis to set the object in that context, and finally interpretation of the artifact in light of its context and related assemblages of artifacts. For example, I once took a course at the Museum of New Mexico in which I was assigned the task of interpreting a furniture collection that had belonged to a prominent Santa Fe family. Seemed simple to me. They were just antiques. I checked out all the books I could find on nineteenth-century Victorian furniture and identified the styles and turned in my paper. What a bore! You can see how much I had yet to learn. The professor gave me the paper back and told me to redo it. Finally I got it. This collection of expensive, high-style furniture was symbolic. It was a barometer of the wealth and social status of the family that purchased it. It demonstrated that Santa Fe families reflected class distinctions in their choice of home decor. It reflected trade patterns, since it was manufactured in the east. It proved that Santa Fe was not insular and that its residents emulated the same social values that prevailed in the rest of the nation. But so what? This exercise put the objects in the context of regional and national history, but it really did not add much to my understanding of that history except that now we could exhibit it as well as read about it.

Gradually my personal feelings about Ishpeming and my youth on Michigan's Upper Peninsula and my professional work with symbolic objects merged. Previously I kept my poignant personal feelings about places like Ishpeming and Andriacchi's store that symbolized my own past separated from my professional work as a public historian. For a long time the division seemed distinct, perhaps because the personal is emotional and the emotional is suspect as a source of knowledge and in our culture it smacks of non-professionalism. But if history does not encourage us to care, what is the point? In the absence of empathy, emotion, concern, and caring, history becomes an exercise in nostalgia or an academic sidebar of limited use in a real world. If we do not care, we will not be motivated to take action. I often have this conversation with a friend who is a pre-eminent international advocate for biodiversity and global sustainability. He is convinced, as are all reputable scientists, that human population, resource consumption, and planetary degradation require prompt action if humanity is to survive the consequences of its prodigal binge. "Why don't people get it?" he wonders. "The scientific evidence is clear." Scientific evidence is objective and rational, but in that stark form it is not compelling. Why don't people get it? Why don't we repair our communities, fix our schools, seek economic and social justice for all, and conduct our lives in an environmentally responsible manner? Perhaps because people must learn to care in the contexts of their own lives, and they must believe that their actions can be effective. This requires a process distinct from the format of a scientific paper.

Now my reading stretched into fields foreign to traditional history. I needed to know about memory, the evolution of the human brain, linguistics, neurology, and psychology in order to better understand how our minds work. Most specifically I wanted to know about the relationship between senses, the interplay between emotion and reason, and how we create a functional understanding of world. What I discovered is that it is incorrect to talk about emotion and reason as if they are separate ways of thinking. Emotion is at the very center of human rationality, not distinct from it. Fortunately there are now scientists who understand this and write for lay people. One such writer is Antonio Demasio, author of *Descartes' Error: Emotion, Reason, and the Human Brain.* Demasio argues that we are incapable of making choices without the use of emotion. I think of this when I visit the grocery store to select ingredients for a meal. There I am confronted with dozens of cuts of meat, hundreds of choices of vegetables, fruit, lettuce, and seasonings, comprising hundreds of thousands of possible choices. Imagine weighing the pros and cons of every choice, not to mention considering the infinity of possible combinations of ingredients. If I did that, I would be in the grocery store forever. No, instead I say to myself, "I like steak, I feel like some soup, maybe tomorrow I will eat salad, but tonight I feel like a slice of chocolate cheesecake." I look at the pig brain in the freezer section and ask myself, "How in the world could anyone eat that awful, disgusting looking thing?" Directed by likes, dislikes, mood, and impulse, I buy the steak and ignore the pig brain and get out of the store in twenty minutes. Demasio concludes that this is not to say

> . . . that when feelings have a positive action they do the deciding for us; or that we are not rational beings. I suggest only that certain aspects of the process of emotion and feeling are indispensable for rationality. At their best, feelings point us in the proper direction, take us to the appropriate place in a decision-making space, where we may put the instruments of logic to good use. We are faced by uncertainty when we have to make a moral judgment, decide on the course of a personal relationship, choose some means to prevent our being penniless in old age, or plan for the life that lies ahead. Emotion and feeling, along with the covert physiological machinery underlying them, assist us with the daunting task of predicting an uncertain future and planning our actions accordingly."[6]

Emotion must be part of our work for the most profound impact of objects is emotional, their ability to make us feel what others before us have felt, their power to inculcate habits of empathy and sympathy for diverse points of view and make us feel part of the human drama on this planet. I have a pantheon of favorite museum objects, but for several months I have been obsessed with Emily. Emily was Emily Stine, the daughter of Emily Miller and Jacob Stine, a glazier who lived in what was then the village of Carondelet, now part of the southside of the City of St. Louis. I have held the smudged plaster cast of the peaceful face of this beautiful infant who died in St. Louis in 1841, the year of her birth, as I stand before small groups of people, guests in our collections area. My own emotions nearly sidetrack the telling of the story. "This mask," I say, "was made by Emily's mother." Silence. A woman in front of me looks steadily at the white mask cradled gently in both my hands and speaks in a hushed but firm tone. "I know," she says, "why Emily's mother made the mask." We all know, if we want to, why Emily's mother made the mask. Tragedy, beauty, love, remembrance, and the withering bereavement at a child's death evoke empathy in all of us. These are the most powerful ties of shared humanity. Emily is a message of memory, of a love that transcends time, of maternal bond. This plaster face is a timeless symbol of common concern, a profoundly powerful symbol of what we all share, past, present, and future. In this face, those things that divide us are diminished to pettiness. This is a story to retell, a story to cherish, a story that can heal.

We know that objects, whether built environments or small personal effects, are symbolic memory devices; that is, they stimulate remembering. As public historians we understand that memory is an ongoing process through which we create usable narratives that explain the world in which we live, stories that inevitably connect us to each other, history that builds community. The community we create is founded in shared remembrance and grounded in place, especially those places that are conducive to the casual associations necessary for emergence of shared memory, common ground, and commitment to the common good. Places, memories, and stories are inextricably connected, and we cannot create a real community without these elements.

So there is a point to history, for history is a process of facilitating conversations in which we consider what we have done well, what we have done poorly, and how we can do better, conversations that are a prelude to action. If the past has enduring meaning and implications, then we as historians must become active conservators: of artifacts and stories and community, of life on this earth and thus implicitly of this earth that sustains life. As we face the past, we are also facing the future.

NOTES

[1] Ray Oldenburg, *The Great Good Place: Cafes, Coffee Shops, Community Centers, Beauty Parlors, General Stores, Bars, Hangouts and How They Get You Through the Day* (New York: Paragon House, 1989), passim.

[2] Barry Lopez, *About This Life: Journeys on the Threshold of Memory* (New York: Alfred A Knopf, Inc.—Distributed by Random House, 1998), p. 210.

[3] Oldenburg, p. 13.

[4] Alexis de Toqueville, *Democracy in America, vol. II* (New York: Random House, Inc., 1990), p. 110.

[5] Claude Levi-Strauss, *The Savage Mind* (Chicago: The University of Chicago Press, 1966), p. 262.

[6] Antonio Damasio, *Descartes' Error: Emotion, Reason, and the Human Brain* (New York: G P. Putnam's Sons, 1994), p. xiii.

2

Remembrance

My sister Anne was born six years before me but as siblings our childhood overlapped. We shared a household, and we shared Ishpeming. Place is a powerful stimulus to memory. The best places to conduct oral history interviews, for example, are where the events to be discussed actually occurred. Thus in July Anne and I hiked up the hill from Marquette to Ishpeming for a day of remembrance. We walked down streets once so familiar that we knew the cracks in sidewalks, but now prolonged separation has blurred the outlines. So we give ourselves complete license to reminisce. The power of the place generates memory cascades as we both rediscover forgotten portions of ourselves.

As defined in psychology, neurobiology, anthropology, and linguistics, memory is recall and interpretation of what we have experienced. How do we remember, and what is the elusive, mysterious relationship between memory and history? Exactly what is consciousness? Investigation of human memory is now a popular field of research. Despite modern inquiry and debate, St. Augustine's ancient musings on his own memory, now more than sixteen hundred years old, are among the most satisfying, perceptive, and beautiful speculations on the mysteries of memory. Augustine understood so long ago that memory was a perplexing but defining characteristic of our species. To remember in our own distinctive way is to be human. His *Confessions* is an ageless memoir of an inward journey. Because he wrote with extraordinary sensitivity and introspection, serendipitously anticipating modern investigations of memory, he is a rejoinder to our obsession with the notion that to be "modern" is to be wiser, more advanced, possessing better explanations for existence. In Augustine's thought we discover an inquisitive mind that projects doubt about what we "moderns" mean by "progress." When I read Augustine's words and retrace his thoughts, time is irrelevant.

His words persist timelessly because they examine enduring concerns of humanity. Thus I comprehend what he means when he writes:

> And I come to the fields and spacious palaces of my memory, where are the treasure of innumerable images, brought into it from things of all sorts perceived by the senses. . . . When I enter there, I require what I will, to be brought forth, and something instantly comes; others must be longer sought after, which are fetched, as it were, out of some inner receptacle. . . .[1]

Neurologist Antonio Damasio analyzes the relationship between body and brain this way: "When I say that body and brain form an indissociable organism, I am not exaggerating. In fact, I am oversimplifying. Consider that the brain receives signals not only from the body but, in some of its sectors, from the parts of itself that receive signals from the body! The organism constituted by the brain-body partnership interacts with the environment as an ensemble, the interaction being of neither the body nor the brain alone."[2]

While I appreciate Damasio's scientific approach, I treasure St. Augustine's words:

> There are all things preserved distinctly and under general heads, each having entered by its own avenue: as light, and all colours and forms of bodies, by the eyes; by the ears all sorts of sounds; all smells by the avenue of the nostrils; all tastes by the mouth; and by the sensation of the whole body, what is hard or soft; hot or cold; smooth or rugged; heavy or light; whether outwardly or inwardly to the body. . . . Nor yet do the things themselves enter in; only the images of the things perceived, are there in readiness, for thought to recall. . . . For even while I dwell in darkness and silence, in my memory I can produce colours, if I will, and discern between black and white, and what others I will: nor yet do sounds break in, and disturb the image drawn in by my eyes, which I am reviewing, though they also are there, lying dormant, and laid up, as it were apart. For these too I call for, and forthwith they appear. And though my tongue be still, and my throat mute, so can I sing as much as I will; nor do those images of colours, which notwithstanding be there, intrude themselves and interrupt, when another store is called

for, which flowed in by the ears. . . . Yea, I discern the breath of lilies from violets, though smelling nothing; and I prefer honey to sweet wine, smooth before rugged, at the time neither tasting, nor handling, but remembering only.[3]

But Augustine understood that remembering is not passive; that in fact in the process of remembering we construct new realities. "These things," he writes exquisitely, "I do within, in that vast court of my memory. For there are present with me, heaven, earth, sea, and whatever I could think on therein, besides what I have forgotten. There also meet I with myself, and recall myself, and when, where, and what I have done, and under what feelings." And then in a flash of brilliance critically germane to our work, Augustine describes how he creates the future from memory:

> Out of the same store do I myself with the past continually combine fresh and fresh likenesses of things, which I have experienced, or, from what I have experienced, I have believed: and thence again infer future actions, events, hopes, and all these again I reflect on, as present. "I will do this or that," say I to myself, in that great receptacle of my mind, stored with the images of things so many and so great, "and this or that will follow." . . . So speak I to myself: and when I speak, the images I speak of are all present, out of the same treasury of memory; nor would I speak of and thereof were the images wanting.[4]

St. Augustine's description of how memory works was on the mark and accordingly substantiated by our scientific evidence. Memory is not a dead letter file. Memory is intimately and intricately connected to senses. Through our senses our brain makes a working map of the world, a story that explains the world in usable terms. Our bodies, our brains, and our memories seek to create a dream, a myth, a map that allows us to survive and to function throughout our lives. We are story makers. This is how we make sense of our world. In *The Remembered Self: Emotion and Memory in Personality*, author-psychologists Jefferson Singer and Peter Salovey put a modern spin on St. Augustine's "Court of Memory." They say that "if we want to know how the story ends, we have only what we know of the story thus far to inform our speculation. One of life's ironies, of course, is that how we interpret the story, how we feel about the past incidents of our lives, will influence the story still to come. In the act of looking back as a means to anticipate the future, we change the future. In the act of looking forward as a means to escape the past we inevitably run into the past."[5]

Our stories are narratives with beginnings, middles, and ends connected by causation. Stories are how our minds, bodies, and senses work in concert to make sense of things. Yet there is no evidence that the universe we live in adheres to such principles. We impose narratives on our world and universe as a survival technique that has so far been successful. The question of where narrative comes from, whether it is a feature of how our minds work or whether it reflects the design of the universe, is critical for those who practice history, for history is a process of narrative creation. I have come to view history as the construction of useful narrative, not the discovery of universal truth. What happens when our narratives no longer work? How do we know when our narratives are no longer in the long-term best interest of humanity?

Other societies construct useful explanations of the world in patterns and forms other than chronological narrative based on knowable facts about the past. We dismiss such tales as legend, myth, or fairy tale, but they serve the same function as history. They are a form of explanation of persistent truth, a form of remembering that creates individual and group identity and moderates behavior while simultaneously defining relationships with the world. Whether the story is Homer's *Odyssey* in ancient Greece or a nineteenth-century Ojibwa Indian narrative, such stories tell truth because they perpetuate narratives that provide usable explanations for life. These stories are usually timeless; that is, they are located at some indeterminate time in the past. In fact, history as narrative linked to precise time, committed to objective analysis of past events so as to explain the present, is relatively novel and is especially imbedded in western tradition. It is predicated on the assumption that time is worth measuring and upon the invention of accurate calendars and measuring devices.

Although first published over fifty years ago, R. G. Collingwood's *The Idea of History* persists as probably the finest investigation of the history of history. Collingwood outlines the evolution of "scientific history" from myth, theocratic history, and Christian history. An apologist for scientific and professional history, Collingwood considers history a science and its practice limited to professionals. Just as science developed quantitative and analytical tools, history also advanced as it developed "more sophisticated" rules of investigation. History "progressed" as historians embraced the quest for causal relationships in precise sequences of time. As the search for truth became equated with the use of scientific methodology, every discipline sought legitimacy and professional recognition in the adaptation of scientific principles. All professions create secular priesthoods as a means of defining and protecting their disciplines. Thus Collingwood defines the historian as the authority; that is, only the professional historian is qualified to interpret the past. In defining his profession Collingwood asserts that while all educated persons have had some exposure to history, this does not qualify them to "give an opinion about the nature, object, method, and value of historical thinking." He continues his argument by saying that while we may all have a smattering of historical knowledge, it is a very superficial understanding and "the opinions based on it are therefore no better grounded than a man's opinion of the French people based on a single week-end visit to Paris."[6] I concur that my knowledge of French culture based on a whirlwind tour would be deficient; however, my knowledge of my own place is expert. My experiences in my places, based on my own experience and memories, do have validity despite Collingwood's theories of history that disenfranchise all but academically trained historians. In fact, history is a process that all humans use expertly in their daily lives. To be human is to struggle to make sense of our own pasts as a means of establishing identity and forming relationships with the world we inhabit. This undermines the self-proclaimed exclusive authority of the historian and thus the task of the historical practitioner, as defined by Collingwood. The debate is not esoteric but rather causes frequent tension between the public historian and many academic historians.

Who can practice history?

Collingwood does provide invaluable insights into the character of history. History is a form of self-knowledge that we learn by re-enacting past thoughts in our minds. Thus Collingwood concludes that Newton is implicit in Einstein: Albert Einstein was more than just aware of Isaac Newton; he re-enacted Newton's thought processes in order to develop his theories of relativity which were after all dramatic refinements of Newton's theories.[7] Here Collingwood implies a different type of memory peculiar to humans: artificial memory. Einstein did not know Newton, for they lived in different centuries. Rather, his knowledge of Newton depended upon written or artificial records of what Newton thought. A three-dimensional model of Newton's theories about gravity and the solar system, or illustrations, or oral traditions passed through generations of intermediaries would also serve.

By re-thinking what I was thinking yesterday, I can understand once more why I acted in a specific manner. Likewise if you explain for me why you did what you did yesterday, I can re-enact your thought processes and gain empathy for your point of view. Only in this way can we come to know and understand ourselves and each other. We can use the same process for humans who lived before our times. With the historical evidence before us we can rethink what long-dead humans thought. This process is of vital importance because it inculcates empathy, creates an expanded knowledge of what it is to be human, but also emancipates humanity from the need to re-discover all knowledge over and over again every generation. This process accounts for our amazing ability to accumulate and build upon our knowledge of ourselves and the world around us, no matter whether our explanations are oral and mythic or written and scientific. Symbolism, language, and writing are the vehicles for communication among the living and also the means of transmission of knowledge—accumulated memory—between generations that are disconnected from each other in time.

Collingwood's interpretation aside, every human must be a practicing historian because our species is defined by its ability to remember, learn, and interpret. Without historical reasoning we would not have identities and we would be incapable of any action that required the use of precedent. Neurologist Oliver Sacks describes the case of a patient he calls "the Last Hippie" in his book *An Anthropologist on Mars.* The patient had a tumor surgically removed from his brain. As a result he sustained damage to his frontal and temporal lobes. He was left living absolutely in the present. The growth of the tumor and subsequent surgery prevented his brain from remembering new events. Sacks observed that the man's consciousness, and hence his identity, was radically altered. He could no longer function in the world. Sacks says that "I already had some sense of this when testing his memory, finding his confinement, in effect, to a single moment—'the present'—uninformed by any sense of a past (or a future). Given this radical lack of connection and continuity in his inner life, I got the feeling, indeed, that he might not have an independent inner life to speak of, that he lacked that constant dialogue of past and present, of experience and meaning, which constitutes consciousness and inner life for the rest of us."[8] Sacks observes that not only did the young man have no sense of the past, he also had no sense of "next." All that I am is based on my historical knowledge of my own past experience blended with future expectations. We all must use history; the Last Hippie could not.

We also have persistent civic myths to live by, although historians question them because they cannot be documented. But they possess a reality despite their suspect authenticity just because they are believed and can influence events in the present. The unauthenticated tale of the cherry tree symbolizes George Washington's veracity. St. Louisans cherish the story that the ice cream cone was serendipitously invented at our 1904 World's Fair. The capacity of technological innovation to solve all problems and the ultimate ability of science to explain the workings of the universe are broadly shared myths of twentieth-century Americans. Assumptions that are not provable still exert profound influence in the affairs of humanity.

Although iron mining was its support, Ishpeming's downtown was centered on railroad tracks until the years after World War II when cars, trucks, and planes replaced passenger and freight trains as primary carriers of commerce. The major relic of the era is the Mather Inn, located one block from the railroad station. Built of brick with white wood trim and columns, once surrounded by expertly tended gardens, with plush interior decor and furnishings, Mather Inn is now closed and derelict, its windows covered with black plastic. Anne and I nervously walk around the building, peering in windows at the once beautiful interior. We recall shivering in the cold as we waited near the back door for Jimmy Stewart, who was in town for the making of the movie version of *Anatomy of a Murder*. And on that blustery, dark night we did get his autograph. Anne recalls high school proms and her senior party. I slowly recall dinners in the dining room with grandparents. We look through the shattered pane of the kitchen window. Old shadows of memory move forward into consciousness, assume shape, dimension, sound, smell, and color. Cooking utensils are in place; dishes are still in metal racks as if fresh from the dishwasher, but there is a moldy, mildew scent wafting through the broken glass pane. I remember when this hotel was the grandest place I knew. Now, bedroom furniture is piled high in the once posh lobby. Part of the formerly gorgeous grounds is now a parking lot.

While Anne and I have resurgent memories of the Mather Inn, we are not alone. This place contains memories for everyone who lived in the community prior to the hotel's closing more than twenty-five years ago. The hulking building is still generating memories for more recent residents and visitors, but now only of an abandoned building with a forlorn restoration effort in progress that only nibbles at the advancing edges of decay. At best the building is the occasion for the resurrection of musty memories, the telling of old stories, but not as the locus of new ones. Because so many individual memories are attached to this place, it has broader significance than memories that are only personal. For example, there is a small granite rock on the bluff overlooking our town that reminded me of a bed with a pillow on it when I was a child. When I look at that rock, I am reminded of the solitary times I as a child spent sitting on it. I am not aware of shared memories encompassing that rock. But because of Mather Inn's visual prominence in Ishpeming, and as the site of major events like the making of *Anatomy of a Murder* combined with thousands of shared memories of proms, parties, visiting friends and relatives, dinners, and receptions, as well as more private memories of honeymoons, meetings, and partings, this building is a

repository of civic memory that accords it a community-wide significance. The Mather Inn is a powerful stimulus of common memory.
It demonstrates the importance of such places to community life. Its
closure and probable loss is not analogous to the decay of my house
or even the loss of less prominent business blocks. This building's
decay represents the disappearance of a chunk of something vital
for sustenance of community: shared civic memory. Places like the
Mather Inn exist or once existed in every community and cannot be
replaced by a Motel 6 on the highway, even though I am certain that
some people in Ishpeming would claim that now there are more
motel/hotel rooms than ever before and hence that progress has
been made. The loss of the Mather Inn would be more acceptable
if it were not illustrative of a nationwide decline in places that are
so vital for the perpetuation of distinct community identity, as
opposed to the homogenous strip development on the edges of nearly
every town.

St. Louis's Municipal Auditorium opened on April 14, 1934,
funded by a voter-approved bond issue passed in 1923. The front
facade of limestone and Corinthian columns faces the civic mall,
and the vista extends past the Soldiers Memorial to the Public Library. The words of Carl Schurz are on the east facade: "Democratic
Government will be the more successful the more public opinion is
enlightened and inspired by full and thorough discussion." When
the auditorium opened, then-Mayor Bernard Dickman observed,
"Two panels by a young St. Louis sculptor, Robert Cronback, typify
the activities to which the auditorium is dedicated: 'Discussion' and
'Recreation.'" It was a place for citizens to celebrate their city and
each other. This was a center for civic life, a center that both reflected and enhanced the community's sense of itself. The Municipal Auditorium closed in 1991.

Although the Mather Inn was privately owned, it too was a civic
icon in our small town. When I peer in its windows, I think of the
Municipal Auditorium, now derelict with an uncertain future, as an
analogous memory place. Last spring in St. Louis I sat on the edge
of the forlorn gargantuan stage of the auditorium's 3,500-seat opera
house, looking out in hazy, dim light over the symbolic deterioration
of civic life and the demeaning of the intent of those who ordered

Schurz's words inscribed at its entrance. Once this stage backed up to a moveable wall. Behind the wall was an auditorium with more than ten thousand seats. When the wall was opened, the stage could face in two directions. The auditorium was sawed off and demolished to make way for the construction of a professional hockey arena with high-priced seats.

This building symbolizes civic values certainly, but it is also a repository of communal memory. Columnist Greg Freeman wrote about it in the February 22, 1966, edition of the St. Louis *Post-Dispatch*: "It's a special place," he wrote, "that holds a spot in the hearts of many. Mikhail Baryshnikov danced there. Peter, Paul and Mary sang 'Puff the Magic Dragon' there. Diana Ross and the Supremes urged St. Louisans to 'Stop in the Name of Love' there. Countless high school students held their graduation ceremonies there. Until 1968, the St. Louis Symphony Orchestra performed there. For many of us," he concluded, "the opera house remains a special place."[9] To Greg Freeman's list, I would add war bond rallies, Carol Channing, John Gielgud, Count Basie, Judy Garland, and even Mötley Crüe. So the opera house is not only a symbol of the civic ideal, it stores shared memory, the very raw materials of community. Like the rotting portico of the Mather Inn, the dusty, disheveled stage of the Municipal Auditorium is another form of un-remembering, a civic forgetting of what we are and can aspire to be together. I speculate that if I could find the formula I could equate the loss of such places in communities large and small with a decline in civic engagement, that sense of common purpose that compels us to consider the common welfare in our daily actions and at the ballot box.

The issue is not only debasement of civic life but also depreciated quality of life for all. Without formal and informal gathering places where we share experience and make common memories, and thus establish a common identity buttressed with familiarity, community is devalued and only individualism remains. In *The Geography of Nowhere: The Rise and Decline of America's Man-Made Landscape*, James Howard Kunstler put it like this: "There is a reason that human beings long for a sense of permanence. This longing is not limited to children, for it touches the profoundest aspects of our existence: that life is short, fraught with uncertainty, and sometimes tragic. We know not where we come from, still less where we are going, and to keep from going crazy while we are here, we want to feel that we truly belong to a specific part of the world."[10]

In the past three years I have spoken to dozens of state history groups all over the United States. In preparing for each presentation I have struggled to find a sense of the place I am visiting, particularly identifying those qualities that make that place distinctive. I review historical works and literary expressions of the place. And then, from the time my airplane touches down until I check into a hotel, I search for visible identifying characteristics. Would someone please tell me where I am? Built environments all over this land have assumed a bland sameness. I now must investigate the past to find stories that define places with patterns of life that distinguish it from all others. This evidence of increasing homogeneity suggests that places were more heterogeneous in the past. It is the difference between the Mather Inn and the Comfort Inn on the highway that could be anywhere and is in fact everywhere. It is the difference between St. Louis's Municipal Auditorium and the cookie-cutter Convention Center and Football Stadium not meant to last or to be distinguishable from others like it in dozens of other cities.

Recently I told an audience of hundreds in Des Moines that in one sense Iowa no longer exists. I could have said the same anywhere. Much of the Iowa that writers about Iowa describe is relics and remnants, little pieces of living prairie, a few Indian mounds, festivals that celebrate what was, vestiges of old ways, obsolete silo and barn types, ghost towns, and antiques. Perhaps this bothers me too much. The past is all we can know and it is different from the present. So it is not the *normal* disappearance of the past that is my concern but the wrenching disjuncture I see now between past and present and my profound suspicion that what we are replacing it with will not be good for us or our children. When I look to the past I can find Iowa, or any other place, but I don't think that's enough. I think that when I travel to America's small towns and cities there should be enough persistence of the past in the present so that I know I am someplace not like St. Louis, Missouri, or Des Moines, Iowa, or Ishpeming. Of course I can get off the highway and sometimes find vestiges of the past, or I can seek out a museum of history. But should it be that shrouded and concealed?

The house that Anne and I grew up in is perched on the shoulder of a bluff on the south side of Ishpeming. After a short hike up the bluff to the granite outcroppings that provide good places to sit, you can see the entire town down in front shrinking north to the bluffs on the other side. Anne and I hiked up. We searched for the rocks remembered by both of us in the now tangled overgrowth that proved in three-dimensional form the time that has lapsed since childhood. We could cut down a tree that grew since we last sat here and find tangible, concentric proof in the rings of how many seasons had passed. We did not speak much. I think we were both overwhelmed by the vista over Ishpeming and the recollections of the number of times we each had privately sought refuge in this place, escaping from childhood troubles or simply seeking the solitude of an empty place. St. Augustine was correct. My memory floods me with sights, smells, sounds, and sensations. I can hear mine whistles blow at the end of shifts. I can smell Sweet Williams. I see the umber reds and yellows of Indian Paintbrush. The bells of St. John's call out the Angelus at noon. I can hear mother's voice faintly calling to me from our house below. I can trace my way through the town below knowing instantly each street and each house. I remember crying on this spot. But I also remember picking wildflowers, and wonderful moments of childhood and reverie on this spot. This was nearly my whole world then and in some ways it still is. I return to this bluff even now in those weightless, delicious moments between awake and sleep in the second-floor bedroom of my house in St. Louis nearly seven hundred miles from here.

Magically eliminate Ishpeming from the scene and the rugged land forms remain. The craggy bluffs still surround the site. Look from the south bluffs; Lake Bancroft is to the left in the foreground of Pilot's Knob. Between the bluffs the land is low but still hilly with rock outcroppings on all sides. Little of the land is open. It is thick with cedar in the low, moist areas with a mixture of birch, maple, pine, poplar, and dark spruce scattered throughout. The place is still recognizable even though the streets, the downtown, the homes, churches, and schools are gone. The arrangement of the bluffs cannot be camouflaged. If I could survive on the bluff for a full round of seasons, I would know the place for certain. This place, combined with short summers and their fierce insects, resplendent autumns that can first be felt in the late days of August, early cold winters with below-zero temperatures and sometimes hundreds of inches of snow, and springs that explode in a rush of water and brilliant but fragile wildflowers, cannot be confused with any other place. I would know this place even if no human had been here before me to leave marks. What I could not know is that deposits of millions of tons of hematite iron ore lie shallow but extend down thousands of feet under all the land I can see. These land forms and the riches underneath are responsible for the physical structure of my town. The towering mine shafts that still stand, the tangled street layout that reflects the first mining locations, and the weaving of streets around rocky bluffs and lakes persists. Construction methods that often made use of local stone but by necessity accommodated the harsh climate are apparent from any overlook.

John Voelker, author of *Anatomy of a Murder*, is one of Ishpeming's few notables. Although best known for the movie adaptation of his one bestseller, he was a prolific author rooted in the Upper Peninsula. In an unpublished manuscript entitled *Burning Earth*, he described our hometown. The work is autobiographical, although the author veiled his story within Chippewa, a transparent pseudonym for Ishpeming. So he describes my place fifty years before I arrived.

> The town lay in a broad, undulant valley between serpentine chains of ancient iron bluffs. Some of these bluffs were covered with thick maple groves which flamed into color each fall, but most of the hills near town were virtually bald save for low bushes and occasional patches of gnarled, wind-scarred pines. So irregular was the topography of the country that some of these hills erupted in the town itself, giving it Badger Hill and Grammar School Hill and Blueberry Hill among many others. . . .
>
> In truth the town was just one hill after the other, in turn surrounded by still more hills. . . . It seemed the town had simply grown haphazardly around the iron mines. It was all

sheer accident. If the ore had instead been found under a flat plain, then Chippewa would have been a flat plain.[11]

I was raised within this bowl between bluffs. I am a product of this place. If I was raised somewhere else, I would be someone else. But all places have such genesis. My city of St. Louis has a powerful one; it is located at the confluence of this continent's great rivers. The Mississippi and Missouri Rivers are overpowering influences and, just as the iron ore attracted settlement in Ishpeming, so the commercial potential of trade on the mid-continent's rivers attracted settlers to the great intersection that became St. Louis. T.S. Eliot, a native St. Louisan, expressed a powerful sense of the river in *The Dry Salvages*:

> *I do not know much about gods; but I think that the river*
> *Is a strong brown god—sullen, untamed and intractable,*
> *Patient to some degree, at first recognized as frontier;*
> *Useful, untrustworthy, as a conveyor of commerce;*
> *Then only a problem confronting the builder of bridges.*
> *The problem once solved, the brown god is almost forgotten*
> *By the dwellers in cities—ever, however, implacable,*
> *Keeping his seasons and rages, destroyer, reminder*
> *Of what men choose to forget. Unhonoured, unpropitiated*
> *By worshippers of the machine, but waiting, watching and*
> *   waiting.*
> *His rhythm was present in the nursery bedroom,*
> *In the rank ailanthus of the April dooryard,*
> *In the smell of grapes on the autumn table,*
> *And the evening circle in the winter gaslight.*[12]

The River conditioned and shaped the lives of those who choose to live here. Landscape is a determinant of the places we live and hence a mold into which we pour our lives. Eddy Harris writes in *Mississippi Solo*:

> The Mississippi River is laden with the burdens of a nation. Wide at St. Louis where I grew up, the river in my memory flows brown and heavy and slow seemingly lazy but always busy with barges and tugs, always working—like my father— always traveling, always awesome and intimidating. I have watched this river since I was small, too young to realize that

the burdens the Mississippi carries are more than barges
loaded with grain and coal, that the river carries as well sins
and salvation, dreams and adventure and destiny. As a child
I feared this river and respected it more than I feared God.
As an adult now I fear it even more.[13]

Anne and I leave our bluff perch and circle round to its shoulder but to the north side. We stand at the foot of the path that slinks
up the hill to our house, a trail that we traversed everyday on our way
to and from school, two round trips each day including a rush home
for lunch. The path is overgrown and the lilac hedge along its east
border is nearly lost in the tangle that has advanced since we were
last here. Anne searches for a special tree that she climbed as a girl,
where she relished the delight of a rope swing. I look for rocks and
flowers on the other border of the path. I remember the Sweet
Williams, planted long before our day, perhaps by the family that
first occupied the place, and the rocks. I don't know whether the
rocks were placed deliberately in what were once elaborate grounds
or whether they were stubborn outcroppings of the hill. I know that
I sat on them, lay on them, licked them, and ran my hands over them
almost daily in the good weather days. I found them. The portions
nearest the ground are covered with lichens that merge into "fairy
moss" where the rocks submerge into earth. I imagined that little
people lived in the moss that for such diminutives are spruce trees.

We find the rocks and the Sweet Williams which seem more
prodigious than before. Is it so that Sweet Williams from nineteenth-
century stock have a perfume that exceeds all others? And is it true
that, left to themselves, they fertilize each other and generate unimaginable variegated colors in this process of transforming domes-
ticated to wild flowers? They are as resplendent as ever. I smell, I
touch, and I pick one, a beautiful, deep, delectable lavender that
fades to tinted ivory in the center. And I remember summer, childhood, and Anne when she was eleven. She is transformed before
me. In this flower I find proof positive that, even if only in your
memory and only for a short while, you can go home again. A few
feet away we find a patch of Forget-Me-Nots. They were not here
then. I cannot imagine how they got here.

But the meanings of the past are not always so clear. As Anne and I walk in the midst of these memory places and as we recollect with each other, we find noncongruent memories. First, there are events and places that Anne remembers and insists that I must also, but I just do not; and vice versa. Then there are points where we agree that something took place but each of us has remembered or interpreted it very differently. We agree to not agree. Yet here we are, birds from the same nest with a shared past, disagreeing sometimes on the events of that past and often on the meaning of the events even when we recall them similarly.

The existence of multiple perspectives on the past is commonsensical. Most contemporary historians acknowledge that such perspectives can conflict and nevertheless be accorded validity and respect. Scientists who investigate the human brain agree. Science writer Joel Davis observes that "each of us experiences the world from a unique vantage point. We see the world through our eyes, hear the world through our ears, smell and taste and touch the world through our other senses. No one else occupies our body. No one else occupies the space and time that we occupy. So consciousness," he concludes, "is singular and essentially subjective."[14]

The Ishpeming City Council is debating over a new image for the city seal. Early in this century the Cleveland Cliffs Iron Company constructed two obelisks, elongated pyramidal cast concrete head frames. Head frames are the structures that stand atop the vertical shafts that descend into the earth. Ore was lifted up into the head frames and then dumped in huge piles prior to rail shipment to the ore docks in Marquette, fifteen miles away. Similarly, miners also rode cages down from the head frames into the dank depths and back up at the end of their shifts. The Mayor and City Council deliberate whether or not a rendering of these head frames would be an appropriate symbol for the city seal. This proposal precipitated debate over the city's image and future. No one disagreed that the head frames were prominent and recognizable structures in the town. The question was whether they were the right symbols for the town. Some said that the head frames reflected a backward look and hence were not suitable because Ishpeming is "a city on the move." There is disagreement about both how the town should regard its past and how it should anticipate its future. The head frames are the ambiguous symbols of the debate.

As we plan the exhibitions at the Missouri Historical Society, we engage in ongoing conversations about community symbols. We are using the grand entry area as a space in which to encourage visitors to think about community identity. Several symbols, recognizable to most St. Louisans, were immediately identified. The mighty Mississippi and Missouri Rivers are obvious in our old river town. We contracted with artists to create a river mosaic in the floor. We have a replica of Charles Lindbergh's *Spirit of St. Louis* used in the Jimmy Stewart movie, so we will hang the plane from the ceiling. Forest Park, where our museum facility is located, is the site of the Louisiana Purchase Exposition, the 1904 World's Fair. This fair still stands in the minds of many St. Louisans as the apogee of our city's history. Finally, there is no escaping the dominating icon of the Jefferson National Expansion Memorial—the Gateway Arch. These symbols are broadly recognized by citizens of the region, but they hold different meanings, and there are missing symbols in our pantheon. The absence of symbols that incorporate my city's vibrant African-American culture is excruciatingly obvious. Yet our selections were based on random surveys of residents about community symbols. We included the favorites.

St. Louis has largely turned its back on its rivers. Because St. Louis is no longer a river town, the riverfront is no longer a center of community social and economic activity. Now it is a haven for casino gambling, tourism, and fast food restaurants. Simultaneously the river is a geographic division between Missouri and Illinois that has made it easy to forget that both sides belong to the same metropolitan region, easy to ignore East St. Louis. The Missouri River splits the core of the region from its sprawling suburban hinterlands and has become a geographic demarcation of divided civic interests. The Lindbergh plane is likewise ambiguous. Like all heroes, Lindbergh was flawed. It is difficult for Jewish St. Louisans to regard this man who consorted with Nazis as a positive symbol for St. Louis. No question, the 1904 World's Fair was a grand event that spotlighted St. Louis for the world to see. Yet the fair conveyed a message of progress that was both racist and now obsolete. Despite the fascination with the fair in contemporary St. Louis, the fair builders inhabited a world that is not one that we would find to our liking, especially if we were poor, black, female, a recent immigrant, or in need of health care. The construction of the Gateway Arch required the destruction of most of the nineteenth-century waterfront, and the arch itself is a monument to those thousands of people who migrated through St. Louis for parts west. What of those of us who stayed? Yet it is useful to begin with these symbols, for in their ambiguity they raise all the essential questions about community identity and stimulate healthy discussions about how we differ but more importantly what we share.

But what of the symbols that are not included because they are not broadly identified and commonly shared? The absence of symbols of African-American achievement is symptomatic of my community's most intractable problem: the persistence of segregation even in how we remember ourselves. St. Louisans who are not African-American display a general amnesia about issues that confront African-American residents. A residue of slavery and a legacy of racism still circumscribe opportunity in many areas and painfully limit economic possibilities at enormous personal, commercial, and social cost. This amnesia prevents many white St. Louisans from even glancing at our community from the perspective of African-American citizens.

Odester and Jack Saunders and St. Louis Alderman Mike Mitchell meet us at the chain-linked gate of a boarded-up hospital at noon. Marsha Jordan, program director of the Missouri Historical Society's "Exploring the 'Hood," and Myron Freedman, director of our exhibits and design department, accompany me. Mike has keys. Mike's mother, Bertha, served many years as alderman, and her son now fills the seat. We cautiously walk through the dark, musty lobby of the derelict building, aiming flashlights to make ovals of light near our feet. The hallways are strewn with a decayed pattern of sodden insulation, peeled paint, and broken glass. Glass shards crunch underfoot. We bump abandoned gurneys, wheelchairs, crutches, I.V. stands, suction machines, and boxes of dressings. One nursing station was abandoned in the middle of a shift. Charts, forms, and records of patients are still here. We walk through operating rooms

A, B, C, and D. The surgery schedule for the last day is still posted. The green chalkboard with pre-printed columns for patient names, diagnoses, and surgeons dangles on the wall. We turn left into the huge pink-tiled recovery room. I warily bend to pick up a broken tile from the floor and cram it into the pocket of my coat. I sense Marsha's heightened emotions from the quick, excited movement of her body and the accelerated cadence of her speech. She explains that her older sister was born here. Jack whispers that he was born here, too, and grew up in the neighborhood. The alderman adds that he, too, was born here and that his first job was as a deputy sheriff guarding prisoners brought for treatment. For them, African-American St. Louisans, this is an emotional homecoming to a place of nativity, a hall of hope, a promise broken, a place defiled, a legacy lost, a future imperiled.

We make our way through corridors of offices, classrooms, laboratories, emergency rooms, patient wards, supply rooms, treatment rooms, bathrooms, kitchens, one hall that leads to the nurses' residence, another that goes to the separate laundry building and the power plant. In one corridor, we meet a pack of wild dogs. Odester is frightened. The dogs are the present. Her husband grabs an I.V. stand. I take a thick piece of angle iron from the floor. But the dogs disappear in flashlight gloom. We hurry by the administrator's office, with unspoken eagerness to get down the stairs and out.

A few minutes later we sit at "Fat Mat's," a microbusiness started by parishioners of St. Matthew's Church across the street. The parish priest joins us. We talk about the past of this place, and the plans to renovate the hospital for apartments and a cultural center. We tell stories and eat mounds of spicy barbecue and cole slaw and potato salad with plenty of soda and white bread.

This is Homer G. Phillips Hospital in the center of St. Louis's historic African-American neighborhood, the Ville. This hospital is an omnipresent symbol of achievement in adversity. Opened in 1939, it was a center of extraordinary excellence in a segregated city. It is a symbol unshared. White St. Louisans neither commemorate nor even remember what happened here. I am here because I want to commemorate and because I am involved with Jack and Odester in an effort to redevelop the Ville, but also because our city cannot heal until this place, its people, and its surroundings become a symbol shared by all St. Louisans. This hospital was an anchor of the Ville neighborhood, a point of great pride for African Americans. By 1944 "Homer G." ranked in the top third of the largest general hospitals in the nation. By 1948 this hospital trained over one-third of the graduates of the two black medical schools in the country. Dr. John Gladney, a member of my board, tells me that Homer G. had a national reputation for treatment of the acutely injured and that techniques for intravenous protein feeding and treatment of burns and bleeding ulcers were pioneered here. But that is not all. This hospital also ran schools for nurses and x-ray and laboratory technicians, and a medical record library service. This place casts long, enduring, and nurturing shadows.

"This is Homer G. Phillips Hospital in the center of St. Louis's historic African-American neighborhood. . . an omnipresent symbol of achievement in adversity." (W. C. Persons, c. 1936, courtesy of the Missouri Historical Society.)

But Homer G. was not a solitary neighborhood anchor. Standing on the roof of the hospital, looking a block west I could see Sumner High School, an icon of educational excellence in a segregated place. This school opened in 1875 as the first African-American high school west of the Mississippi. Its alumni excelled in every field. Some became household names: opera singers Grace Bumbry and Robert McFerrin, Tina Turner, Dick Gregory, Lester Walton, and Arthur Ashe. Friends tell me that this school attracted an extraordinary faculty; most white institutions would not hire African-American scholars. They tell me that families came from all over the United States to this neighborhood so their children could attend Sumner High School.

And I see even more. Just behind Sumner and a little south is the site of Annie Turnbo Pope Malone's Poro College. Her hair care and beauty products business grew into a multi-million-dollar nationwide industry. Later her school housed Lincoln University Law School. And she gave money to establish the still-operating Annie Malone Home, initially an orphanage, now a home for girls, located just west of Homer G. I could describe the churches, Tandy Community Center, and the neat bungalows and shotgun houses. This is an extraordinary place, not because it is a nice story but because it is an important one for this city now.

This story has a potential to heal but only if it is remembered, shared, and celebrated. It is a story of extraordinary achievement in a segregated and racist place. It is a story that embodies what we are all capable of at our best. It is a story that presumes people are entitled to health care and good education. Most of all, however, it is a story of how narratives firmly rooted in place bind people to each other through a shared past, pride in mutual accomplishment, imbued with an understanding of their place as an inter-generational work in progress. Among the factors that produced this remarkable story is the structure of the place itself: community institutions, places of worship, businesses large and small, surrounded by and mixed in with the houses of the people; gathering places, mingling places, talking places, walking places; places conducive to the creation of those informal bonds that are the bedrock of community and the foundation of democracy. This neighborhood still works because of the present value of these enduring legacies. This is a place that must be remembered for our sakes, and for the sakes of our children.

Community symbols reflect our collective identity, incorporate our aspirations, and in their ambiguity can be focal points of discussion through which we confront each other, acknowledge difference, and define common ground upon which the civic enterprise must rest. I wonder. How would St. Louis change if the Ville and the legacies and the burdens that it represents were a symbol shared and celebrated by the entire community? What if we could add the Ville, represented by a replicated cornerstone of Homer G. Phillips Hospital, to our hall of symbols? And what if all of us recognized it as readily as we do the Gateway Arch? If this were so, we would make great progress in overcoming our burdens of division, racism, and promises unkept.

Although I know Ishpeming intimately, there are many things I did not know about it at all. My personal memories of mine closures and wrenching impacts of unemployment upon people I knew did not include an understanding of the post-World War II economy and the adjustments that took place all over America. My anger at land despoliation as ground caved in and was fenced off with chain link and barbed wire was not informed by any knowledge of global consequences of human resource consumption. Now I return and connect the dots; I discover the intersection of personal memory and what we call history. I work to reconcile the two into a consistent narrative. I broaden the story to include hitherto unknown information. I understand that the perspectives of mine owners and union leaders differ dramatically. I know that for housewives who listened to rattling dishes at afternoon blasting time and for the husbands who daily descended into the depths, closure of the underground mines caused worried ambivalence. My story must include my memories and those of others; it must tolerate ambiguity, and it must join me with the past before my own time. And it must include the experiences of those who, like the people of St. Louis's Ville, have been written out of the old stories. This must be an inclusive story that acknowledges others whose points of view vary from my own, a story in which all who participate can find themselves and thus assume ownership of what is an inter-generational work in progress. One of the primary obligations of the public historian is to facilitate the public process of remembrance and the creation of an inclusive narrative, and always to "connect the dots."

NOTES

[1] St. Augustine, *Confessions* (New York: Book-of-the-Month Club, 1996), p. 230–31.

[2] Antonio Damasio, *Descartes' Error: Emotion, Reason, and the Human Brain* (New York: G. P. Putnam's Sons, 1994), p. 88.

[3] *Confessions*, p. 231–32

[4] *ibid.*, p. 232.

[5] Jefferson A. Singer, and Peter Salovey, *The Remembered Self: Emotion and Memory in Personality* (New York: The Free Press, 1993), p. 80.

[6] R. G. Collingwood, *The Idea of History* (London: Oxford University Press, 1956), p. 7.

[7] ibid., p. 333.

[8] Oliver Sacks, *An Anthropologist on Mars* (New York: Alfred A. Knopf Inc., 1995), p. 49–50.

[9] Greg Freeman, "Memories of Opera House Are Too Precious To Lose," *St. Louis Post-Dispatch*, February 22, 1996.

[10] James Howard Kunstler, *The Geography of Nowhere: The Rise and Decline of America's Man-Made Landscape* (New York: Simon & Schuster, 1993), p. 275.

[11] John Voelker, unpublished manuscript, 1943, copy in possession of the author.

[12] T.S. Eliot, "The Dry Salvages" from *Four Quartets* (New York: Harcourt, Brace and Company,1943), p. 21.

[13] Eddy L. Harris, *Mississippi Solo: A River Quest* (New York: Nick Lyons Books, 1988), p. 1.

[14] Joel Davis, *Mapping the Mind: The Secrets of the Human Brain and How It Works* (Secaucus, N.J.: Birch Lane Press, 1997), p. 241.

⁓ 3 ⸙

Somewhere in Time

I stand at his grave in the Negaunee Cemetery a few miles from Ishpeming, but I can see him standing in the backyard of his house in Negaunee—tall, erect, white shirt and tie, with a pipe in his hand. This is my great-grandfather, Michael Quinn, born in small-town frontier Wisconsin, a baby when the Civil War began. He died when I was seven, so much of what I know of his life is hearsay. But I knew his house well, a gaudy yellow and brown gingerbreaded relic of the nineteenth century with a graceful porch swept around the front facing Main Street. My family lived there while contractors tore our house apart in a major remodeling and Michael visited his son in California, escaping the worst of an Upper Peninsula winter. Yet my memory of his house is just snippets, as distant remembrances often are. For instance, the ice man still came; I remember how he wrapped the huge tongs around blocks of sawdust-encrusted ice and lugged them to the antiquated kitchen, for Michael refused to replace the ice box that had served so well for so long. A wood-fired, water-jacketed laundry stove squatted against a basement wall, a vestige of those years before a central hot water heater. And then I remember his funeral in 1956, my first bewildering confrontation with death. I do not think my memory of that year has much to do with Michael Quinn's death, although my memories are punctuated by the sight of his body; but in 1956 I was of an age when I became conscious of time and the author of my own stories that linked moment to moment in sequence and causation.

Cemeteries are not morbid places for me, and they were not for Great-grandfather Quinn, who outlived three wives—Emma ("Mama"), Delia, and Mary—and frequently visited their graves. Emma was the mother of his children and died young, shortly after her namesake, my grandmother, was born. I recall the hushed family debate when

49

concerned relatives decided that Michael, then in his nineties, should no longer drive. But he only used his car for weekly drives to the Negaunee Cemetery. No family member wanted to break the decision to him, not because he was given to anger but because they anticipated his distress. By then his life was mostly poignant memory in which he sought solace and comfort. Graveyards are special memory places. They contain the final memory confirming physical evidence of bygone lives. So in a break from writing I go to Michael's grave. A beautiful young woman walks in the family plot next to ours. It, too, is a Quinn plot. These Quinns are relatives but I cannot recall enough of family stories to know the relationships.

"Cemeteries are not morbid places for me. . . . They contain the final memory confirming physical evidence of bygone lives." (Michael Quinn's plot, Negaunee [Michigan] Cemetery. Photo by Sue Frisk, 1998.)

I walk up to her. "Are these yours?" I ask, pointing at the headstones. "Yes," she replies, "here are my grandfather and grandmother." She points at the grave of Morgan Quinn. I knew him. While we discuss the dead, both hers and mine, we tacitly acknowledge in our unguarded conversation that we are distant relatives, and we do not behave as strangers. We remember together, long ago conjoined in a shared inheritance of blood by the people whose remains are buried at our feet. I show her Michael Quinn's grave and tell her some of my stories. I chuckle as I recall the stories told me by his daughter, my grandmother, as we once visited his grave together, but I recognize the tragedy implicit in the three wives buried alongside him. My new cousin Kay and I leave together, having both received an unanticipated gift from the dead.

Although I knew Michael Quinn and am his linear descendant with one-eighth of his genes, most of his life is a mystery to me. I have a hard time imagining his birth before the Civil War in a country very unlike the one that we inhabit. As a young man he headed north to the Upper Peninsula seeking opportunity, I presume, in the hardscrabble booming copper and iron mining towns scrunched against the granite of Lake Superior's southern shore. Eventually he settled in Negaunee, running general stores there and in other mining towns. I knew him only as an elderly man with his life circumscribed by his choices; nearly everything except the circumstances of his death was settled. I did not know him when his life held infinite possibilities, including me, but before he had made those choices that led to my birth. Several years ago I acquired a microfilm run of the *Ishpeming Iron Ore* and its predecessor papers from 1879 through World War I. I searched through microfilmed pages for Michael in my hometown newspaper of seventy-five years before I was born. I found him, young man on the make, first in business with his brother in Ishpeming, and then with his main store and home in neighboring Negaunee.

I am not a genealogist. I have searched the pasts of others, but not my own. This was the first time I had looked for people and events in the past that directly connected to my own life. I was unprepared for my reaction. It is difficult for me to accept that I am the result of an infinity of miscellaneous, perhaps accidental choices, and that no one before my birth had me in mind. History has always seemed inevitable, although intellectually I know that this is not so. Seen from the past, the future has an abundance of possible choices and no foreordained path ahead. Michael cleared his own trail, not certain where it might lead, while to me his path is obvious. From the perspective of the present we, as we look back, are the only possible future of the past, but from the perspective of the past we are but one of many possible futures.

Yet here projected onto the screen of the microfilm reader is Michael, not yet married, contemplating his own future and considering his options, not aware of me. The year for my own grandmother's birth approaches but Michael has not yet found his bride who is to be my great-grandmother. In the small-town, gossipy nineteenth-century newspaper I am sucked into the past, transfixed and engaged in Michael's time while planted in the present, simultaneously knowing he will make the choices necessary to let me live far in his future but wondering all the same. I understand in startling emotional flashes the contingency of the past. It did not have to turn out this way and from Michael's perspective an infinity of futures are possible. I am startled by a relieved sigh, my own, expelled into the hood of the microfilm reader when at last Michael meets Emma, his bride-to-be, and at least one enormous contingency upon which my own existence depends is eliminated, although Michael does not yet know.

The odds that my ancestors would make the choices that led to my life were actually rather remote. We view the past as inevitable only because it is done and now cannot be altered. Yet if we transpose this thought to our own lives, we know that we made choices in the past that we now live with, but we know that at the time we had a variety of possible choices. Likewise I know that we inhabit one of uncounted possible worlds; there is no inevitability about the world we live in. It is the result of random choices made through all time. It is not the working out of some plot known in advance. There is no predetermined path from past to future; we create the way through story and choice. The narratives we impose only work in reverse. We reflect upon what we know and shuffle it together in our minds into some reasonable explanatory facsimile of the world we inhabit. This is hindsight. This is history.

In recent years scientists have developed theories about chaos. When I first became aware of "chaos research," the notion seemed an oxymoron to me. How could science develop theories about phenomena that were intrinsically unpredictable? Then I realized after some reading on the subject that scientists did not really mean chaos. The example popularly used to illustrate the principle of chaos is the inexact science of weather prediction, especially long-term forecast. It is not that weather and climate change are inherently unpredictable, but rather that weather and climate changes depend upon such a seemingly infinite number of unidentified variables that the system appears to be unpredictable and therefore chaotic. This weird but sensible theory simply says that systems in the universe tend toward complexity on the verge of chaos, which tends to insure that all possible outcomes will occur—in ecology, biology, chemistry, climatology, and physics. I am interested in how this idea of chaos might be applied to history.[1] History, too, consists of an infinity of variables and is further complicated because so much of the past is not knowable. All we can know about the past is what has survived, and what has survived is just an infinitesimally small portion of the evidence. So I conclude that human affairs through time are chaotic, or might as well be given the constraints of the complexity of events, the limitations of our own minds to cope with infinite variables, and the lack of surviving evidence. Hence history, or the narratives that we impose on the past, is evidence of the fundamental way in which our minds seek to make sense of what we know, rather than the discovery of a pre-existing story.

The universe may be more bizarre than we can ever imagine, more extreme than even the science fiction writers can create. All historians must grasp at least the rudimentary implications of both relativity theory and quantum physics. We cannot say that it is not our field because scientists in these related disciplines are examining the boundaries of time and reality—which is our business. So unless we wish to divorce history from reality and time, we need to know how our colleagues in the sciences are redefining these concepts. Einstein's theory of relativity overturned the presumption that time is absolute, that it ticks away at the same pace everywhere all the time. Einstein posited that time is relative, that each observer measures it differently. There is no indication in the universe for the existence of time as we define it, nor is our definition of time evidence of how the universe works. Instead, it is evidence of how our minds work.

Even Einstein's brilliant brain balked at the conclusions of quantum mechanics. The great physicist Niels Bohr observed that "anyone who is not shocked by quantum theory has not understood it."[2] I am shocked and I cannot claim to understand. On the far edges of this theory is the view that everything that can happen does happen. Think of that for a moment. All possible histories, all conceivable narratives happen. Physicist Paul Davies says that "the existence of an infinite collection of universes and an infinity of times means that anything that is allowed to happen within the wide scope of quantum fuzziness does happen in at least one of the universes."[3] And this can be applied, he observes, "to the entire Universe, if we are prepared to accept the rather fantastic notion that the whole Universe is continually splitting into countless copies, each in a slightly different state, one for every possible outcome of every possible quantum interaction."[4] In this world past, present, and future are all mixed up. This is not science fiction but it is where the future may occur before the events that appear to have caused it. This has profound implications for our narratives. It upends the structure that we inherited from the primeval origins of life on our planet and that has evolved over millions of years. Thus it violates how our brains work. We must think about these things because they are the intersection of science, philosophy, and narrative. The edges of modern science do subvert the concept of linear history that is wed to predictable time flowing in one direction and to the presumption that through an examination of past events we can make sense of the world. It is not my intent to undermine my own discipline but rather to put it in perspective and to elucidate that, while history is crucial to us, it is a function of how we evolved, not a reflection of the realities of the universe.

I do not find relative time and the multiple universes of quantum physics entirely disconcerting. Really I find some aspects consoling because they confirm some of my own instincts. Humans are not separate from this universe. We are made of the same atoms and other much smaller particles. In this sense the universe and all of its properties are implicit in us, just as human history is embodied in the present. It is just our finite thinking abilities that lead us to the incorrect perception that while we are in this world, somehow we are not of it. In one sense, delving into the past or exploring the nature of matter or the attributes of the universe are just ways of examining the insides of ourselves. Collingwood was absolutely correct when he observed that history was the only means to self-knowledge. We are peeling the onion of our self, not digging up old bones.

We all experience times of reverie when the present yields to a profound sense of timelessness. It is what I call transcendence. I have felt it while sitting on the rock bluffs overlooking Lake Superior, by the Little Blackfoot River in Montana, on cold crisp nights in the Sangre De Cristo Mountains of New Mexico, or by the ocean, or in listening in solitude to the lapping wave sounds pierced by the raucous laughter of loons in the dark of night. Sometimes music, poetry, flowers, art, or a quiet corner bring it to me. For you it may be a cathedral, a church, or another special place or experience that draws you outside the confines of your life and into contemplation. Here we transcend ourselves and cross into that space in our minds where we intuitively know that everything in the universe, including ourselves, is a part of everything else. Here past, present, and future overlap, just as the physicists claim.

I understand this even more when I read the *Ishpeming Iron Ore*. It is not a rational understanding because it is not explainable in objective terms. It is my body speaking to me; a quick heartbeat, damp palms, goose bumps, raised hair on my arms, tears in my eyes, and an uncomfortable feeling in my stomach. The place is so intimately familiar but I am not there. I read about familiar places, streets, buildings, people, but I am not born yet. Yet I know that I am reading about myself. It is as if the past is a puzzle and the pieces fit neatly into the present. Sometimes I am changed because it expands my own knowledge of myself. So the past is not past but continues its work in the present, modifying me and thus altering the future.

In this process I am not conscious of the distinction between past, present, and future. I am not finding bones in these newspaper pages. I am peeling my own onion. I discover pieces of myself. Here is Great-great-grandfather Kruse, the father of Emma, my great-grandmother, who married Michael Quinn, the first person in this story that I knew. His daughter Emma Quinn married Ralph Archibald, and then my own father was born in this place. The names of everything are familiar—the lakes, the bluffs, the buildings, and the streets; even the extreme weather does not surprise me. Although I am not in this story yet, I know that if I keep reading I will find myself, for this is my story, my place.

And then I find a story that joins me to the newspaper's publisher in one of those experiences so typical of the place and so absolutely timeless. I have felt precisely what he expressed. On September 11, 1881, George Newitt wrote in the Saturday edition with unusual eloquence:

> A more beautiful spectacle than that presented [by the Northern Lights] between the hours of 12 and 1 on Tuesday night cannot be imagined. . . . The heavens seemed to have been converted into an immense hollow cone, the apex of which appeared particularly light. The bright white lights, intermingled with a light touch of pale green, chased each other up by thousands from all points in view, traveling toward the top of the cone where they would sink from view as suddenly as they had risen. The scene recalled vividly the beautiful simile written by the poet Burns in his tale of Tam O'Shanter:
>
> > *But pleasures are like poppies spread—*
> > *You seize the flower, the bloom is shed,*
> > *Just as the snow falls in the river—*
> > *A moment white then melts forever;*
> > *Or like the borealis race—*
> > *that flit ere you can point their place.*

Adobe Walls is far from the Northern Lights, on the plains of far west Texas, a dry, baked land north of Amarillo where human existence has always been incidental and tenuous. One hundred and thirty years ago this area was the buffalo hunting grounds of the

Comanche People, who equipped with horses descended from the Rocky Mountains and became the pre-eminent hunters and warriors of the southern plains. In the years immediately after the Civil War the traditional ways of the Comanche were undermined as the buffalo were systematically slaughtered by hide hunters who abandoned one and a quarter million skinned buffalo carcasses to rot on the plains. The prodigal destruction of the principle source of food, clothing, and shelter, combined with pressure from relentless settlement and the United States Army, made the situation life-threatening for the Comanche, and they lashed out in a furious futile final effort to survive on the plains. On June 24, 1874, the Comanche struck at the crude hide-hunter village at Adobe Walls. Hunters with high-powered rifles inflicted heavy losses on the desperate Comanches who were humiliated by defeat and subsequently scattered. By the end of 1875 armed resistance was over and so was any possibility of traditional life for the Comanche.

The Missouri Historical Society has a Comanche Shield. Little was known about its provenance, for it arrived with only this information: "An Indian shield captured from the Comanches by the 10th U.S. Cavalry in 1874. Presented by Major (Brigadier General) S. L. Woodward, U.S.A." The shield with the jagged bullet holes is alive. It belonged to Old Man Yahvana-a; it was the spirit that protected him in battle. Evelyne Voelker, one of my mothers who is a full blood Comanche, gave me her permission to repeat this story.

Yahvana-a's shield rested respectfully revealed on a cloth-covered table in one of our museum collections storage areas, its soft leather cover removed, eagle feathers spread in a circle, bullet holes conspicuous, hard rawhide rimmed with red cloth and decorated with a bull buffalo and a human figure. I remember the incongruity of us on our knees, men and women, adults and children, in a museum storage room, under fluorescent lights, on a hard bare concrete floor, listening to the song sung more than a century ago at Adobe Walls by Yahvana-a, now in a singing reiteration in the voices of his male descendants. We knelt because the Old People came and in their presence we were not worthy to stand. This was a ceremony of mental and physical healing. The shield brought the Old Ones into the present, and the people remembered and sang the song, honored the past and the deeds of ancestors who were present on an autumn Saturday afternoon. I could move outside of the event, speak to you as a historian or an anthropologist and deconstruct the event in order to explain, but it would be inadequate and disrespectful. The event must be felt to be understood. We were humbled in the presence of the past and overcome with the strength and sacredness and the intimate immediacy of the connection. The men burned cedar, and the eagle feathers cleansed us with cedar smoke and made the world right. The children watched in awe of their own past. We embraced and left in silence that afternoon.

The boundaries between past, present, and future are fluid, malleable, and transparent. The past is active in the present determining the future. There are no bygones. Although incorrect in his pessimistic suggestion that the past is "unredeemable," T.S. Eliot's poem *Burnt Norton* expresses extraordinary truth.

> *Time present and time past*
> *Are both perhaps present in time future,*
> *And time future contained in time past.*
> *If all time is eternally present*
> *All time is unredeemable.*
> *What might have been is an abstraction*
> *Remaining a perpetual possibility*
> *Only in a world of speculation.*
> *What might have been and what has been*
> *Point to one end, which is always present.*
> *Footfalls echo in the memory*
> *Down the passage which we did not take*
> *Towards the door we never opened*
> *Into the rose-garden. My words echo*
> *Thus in your mind.*[5]

So while the past is always implicit in the present, interpretation of the past varies with succeeding generations. The present meanings of the past evolve to reflect the concerns of each living generation. Thus although the meanings of specific events of the past may have had one set of meanings for the generation in the decades after the American Revolution, those same events may have very different meanings now. If I could transpose myself to the 1880s when Great-grandfather Quinn was a young man and if I could discuss with him the great continental crossing of Meriwether Lewis and William Clark we might have agreed on the facts of the expedition—when they left, the route they followed, when they returned—but disagreed on significance of the expedition and its legacies for succeeding generations.

Several years ago I was invited to give a dinner speech at the annual meeting of the Lewis and Clark Trail Heritage Foundation. I considered the kind request with trepidation. This is a group of Lewis and Clark aficionados with a detailed knowledge of the expedition. I am no Lewis and Clark scholar and hence knew nothing that would contribute to this group's knowledge of the "Corps of Discovery." But I agreed to take the assignment. I had in mind a survey of changing interpretations of the expedition through time and hoped that the literature would support my hunch that the significance of the expedition was not static but instead evolved with the needs of succeeding generations to seek new meanings in the past through a prism of concerns of their own time. My hunch was correct; the expedition proved to be an ideal subject for my experiment. Sometimes, of course, interpretations change because information is found that alters our understanding of events, but not so in the case of Lewis and Clark. Their journals and correspondence with Thomas Jefferson constitute the majority of what is known even now, and these sources were available to all of the historians I reviewed.

In 1836 when William Grimshaw wrote his *History of the United States from Their First Settlement to 1830,* America was enjoying the first industrial revolution. This was a time of unbounded optimism, confidence in the future. Americans held a conviction that their country possessed unlimited resources to sustain growth so far into the future that no American need be concerned about depletion. Andrew Jackson's presidency was an age of ambivalence about the "wild" western empire earlier traversed by Lewis and Clark. While there were those who romanticized wilderness and Rosseau's "state of nature," most Euro-Americans were not romantic about nature, wilderness, or native people. Indians were removed, trees cut down, rivers dammed, canals constructed, and the land brought under the plow. This land only awaited a "civilized hand" in order to fulfill its ordained destiny for man. Grimshaw's history gives scant attention to the expedition by later standards. For him as for the majority of his countrymen the Captains had accomplished two things on behalf of the nation: they had discovered and cataloged new resources, providentially provided by the hand of a benevolent God, that awaited exploitation to fulfill their purpose; and they had discovered a land route to the Pacific Ocean that buttressed America's claims to the Pacific Northwest. Nature in its wild state was of no appeal to Grimshaw. Bears were dangerous enemies to be eliminated as soon as practicable. Indians were savages incapable of putting the land to its best use and furthermore were "martial or ludicrous, or voluptuous and indecent."[6] Uncultivated and unexploited land was just potential. The enormous expanse of unexploited land justified its prodigal use. Lewis and Clark were merely vanguards who confirmed the assumption that land was limitless.

The common wisdom that the land was limitless persisted through much of the century. Immigrants poured into the land in the years after the Civil War, eased into land ownership by the liberal provisions of the Homestead Act and with the way cleared by the "Indian Wars." So when Henry Adams wrote his *History of the United States during the Second Administration of Thomas Jefferson* in 1890, he too tersely dismissed the expedition of Lewis and Clark. "They were forced to spend the winter," he observed, "in extreme discomfort, among thievish and flea-bitten Indians, until March 26, 1807, they could retrace their steps. Creditable as these expeditions were to American energy and enterprise, they added little to the stock of science or wealth." And he concluded, "Many years must elapse before the vast region west of the Mississippi could be brought within reach of civilization."[7] In Scribner's *Popular History of the United States* published in 1898, William Cullen Bryant devoted only one paragraph to the Lewis and Clark Expedition. He concluded that it was irrelevant to American history except for the weight of argument it added to America's claims to the Pacific Northwest.

In this same decade Frederick Jackson Turner, a young historian from Wisconsin, proclaimed that on the basis of the 1890 census there was no more unsettled territory, no more frontier. This news was slow to impress popular attitudes. In the new century the United States became a world power. Ours became an increasingly urban nation. Indian people, confined to reservations, were viewed as romantic curiosities by non-Indians, and early conservationists, including Theodore Roosevelt, pointed to what was lost. Now that it was gone, Americans waxed nostalgic for what had been consumed. American confidence in the ability of American institutions, science, and technology to solve humanity's ills was shattered in the bloody trenches of World War I. These changes were exacerbated by reform movements lumped within the rubric "progressive." Americans recognized the inequities of an increasingly urban and industrialized nation as depression simultaneously undermined the agrarian economy that was no longer self-sufficient but rather linked to the urban economy and international markets. Women's suffrage succeeded at long last, and the role of government expanded in an attempt to ameliorate the worst excesses of unfettered capitalism. Many Americans looked backward in search of a time when the nation was a simpler, better place.

Historian Ralph Henry Gabriel reflected this cross-current when he published his *Lure of the Frontier* in 1929. Even the title conveys changed bias. No nineteenth-century historian would have chosen such a title. "Lure" implies attractive qualities and intrinsic value, a reversal of the earlier presumption that frontier was just potential with value proportional to land fertility, natural resources, and water. Gabriel elevated Lewis and Clark to heroic stature. He included reproductions of Charles M. Russell's wistfully romantic paintings of Indians and western scenes. For the first time his volume included a biographical sketch of Sacajawea, now a heroine instrumental to the success of the expedition. Indians were not "vermin" in Gabriel's treatment but rather denizens in a simpler, more honest, romantic world. Nature now acquires value not just a repository for potential. Gabriel finds value in an unsullied natural world and the flora and fauna that inhabit it. It is enough that it exists.

Now as we approach the bicentennary of the Lewis and Clark Expedition we find a multiplicity of values in the exploit. Now we are concerned with global environmental problems; we are warned by pre-eminent scientists that current population and rates of resource consumption cannot be sustained by the planet. We have become a danger to ourselves. Confidence that science and technology will compensate for prodigal behavior has diminished, and our self-confidence has eroded. Our expectations for the future are circumscribed for the first time in our national history. Now we insist that wilderness be a museum, protected and preserved from our rapacious species. "New Age" Indians seek solace in a romanticized simpler life and mysticism.

Now we imbue the Lewis and Clark Expedition with values that represent some of our deepest yearnings. In a world that often seems out of control and unfathomable in its complexity, we seek refuge and solace in the singular accomplishments of these men unfettered and unaided by the sophisticated and bewildering technologies of our own time. We compare the achievements and bravery of these men with the exploration of outer space that requires technology so sophisticated that humans are unnecessary to the achievement. We transfer our environmental concerns to these intrepid men and see in their detailed observation and description of the natural world a nascent emergence of our own worries. Some view Lewis and Clark as proto-environmentalists. We romanticize Indian life in this bygone world and even suspect that theirs was a better time and place.

In the preface to his *America, a History*, published in 1968, Oscar Handlin, a pre-eminent historian of our century, wrote that "new conditions call for a fresh understanding of the past."[8] The past is not a museum, and history is not a musty book. History is the process through which we create narratives that elucidate present concerns. Thus for nearly two centuries generations of Americans have reinterpreted the Corps of Discovery in light of contemporary concerns. Debates about the significance of the Lewis and Clark Expedition, the interpretation of the *Enola Gay*, or the roles of gays and lesbians in American history have less to do with the past than with the values we hold in the present. However, the narrative framework of the past creates our identity in the present and consequently the debates are often contentious because the stakes are the kind of people we will be in the future and the values we will embrace. The outcomes of the struggles for memory always decide the future.

Imagine the ultimate history warehouse. We have assembled within its gigantic walls and ultimate super computers every piece of evidence that reflects every thought and action of every human who has ever lived. I say, "History is finished except for ongoing contemporary collecting to keep the warehouse up-to-date. I have it all and now we know everything. I have every arrow point, every piece of fire-cracked rock, every piece of furniture and every article of clothing, every letter and diary and document and absolutely everything else. Nothing is missing. All we have to do now is arrange this stuff chronologically and let people see it." You say, "Some of this stuff is meaningless junk. This is not history. This is just random facts, curious yes, but not meaningful." I say, "All right, what should we eliminate and what will we keep? Who will decide?" I can tell that we are going to have a long conversation. The outcome will depend upon who is involved in that conversation and obviously will be a series of compromises that produces a narrative in which all participants can find themselves, with perspectives determined by personal histories and the values they uphold. This process is history.

Suspend incredulity again. Imagine that this conversation about what we should eliminate and what we should keep is inter-generational. Not only are representatives of living generations seated around our discussion table in my imaginary warehouse, but also invited are, among others, Jonathan Edwards, Phillis Wheatley, Thomas Jefferson, William Tecumseh Sherman, Mary Chestnut, Frederick Douglass, Lucretia Mott, Marcus Garvey, Eleanor Roosevelt, and their contemporaries. We are looking at everything in the warehouse that has a relationship to the Civil War, discussing we how should remember the war. Two of the participants are shocked to learn that there was a civil war—Edwards and Wheatley died long before the shots at Fort Sumter—while Jefferson reminds everyone of his warning about the "fire bell in the night." General Sherman and Mrs. Chestnut seem to be talking about entirely different events, places, and cultures, while Mrs. Mott in her Quaker bonnet is both saddened and angered all over again.

Douglass' vision of a healed America is shattered when he learns that racism and injustice persist nearly 140 years after the war. "Was it for this," he asks, "that three quarters of a million men died on and off the battlefields of the Civil War?" The perspectives of our particular times are so very different that we cannot find common ground. Jefferson's worst doubts seem to be confirmed, and he even expresses regret at his role in the creation of the nation. He is appalled at the extension of government into the affairs of citizens and at odds with Mrs. Roosevelt over the proper role and scope of government. Jonathan Edwards is appalled at the moral weakness and godlessness of the living generation, while Phillis Wheatley is gently disappointed in our neglect of both religion and classical education. Marcus Garvey is severely critical of the lack of progress, by his definition, of his race and the world in general. We finally manage to agree on one thing—our inter-generational experiment was an ineffective idea. The experiences of past and future are so vastly different as to make consensus impossible. "The past is a foreign country; they do things differently there."[9] To be from a different time is to be from a different place.

But we also agree that each generation must interpret the past and create narratives that are useful for its present and for the future. As we stand and say our polite good-byes Mr. Douglass rises to his distinguished height and admonishes us to remember that for every living generation including our own, there are no bygones. Despite our sense of time passages and the extremity of our differences, the past is present and will not go away.

But there are successful ways of transporting the past into the present so that in one sense all time can be time is present time confirming both the speculations of scientists and of poets and the stern insistence of Mr. Douglass. I have done it with Great-Grandfather Quinn and the newspaper microfilm. I have observed the reappearance of old man Yahvana-a in the hearts of his descendants as they sang his shield song. I am the beneficiary of legacies from a long line of thousands of ancestors I cannot know, and the commingled genes of all humanity live in my body. Thus encoded in my body is a genetic memory of the past from first living cell to now. But I have a conscious memory too. I know that it is possible to make the past present because I do it all day long as I compare the events and feelings that each day brings with what I have experienced before, as my brain and your brain have evolved to do. Our need to create ever-changing stories of ourselves is predetermined in our genes.

Narratives, stories, always have beginnings, middles, and ends. They almost inevitably exhibit a progression, a plot that is worked out in the course of the narrative. Those who study such things insist that humans live historically. Speaking both for the individual and the community, David Carr writes in *Time, Narrative and History* that "narrative, far from originating externally and imposing a story on what was previously a mass of unrelated facts, is inherent in the process in the first place—in this case, the experiences, actions and lives of communities. For the *we*, no less than for the *I*, reflectively structuring time in narrative form is just our way of living in time."[10]

The idea of progress is inherent in this narrative form. While history as a story of progress has gone out of vogue in the twentieth century, it is actually just submerged, still creating the underwater currents where we live. What is the point in chronologically investigating the past if not to demonstrate the process of change and the consequences of decision-making? I think that most who study the past would admit, if pressed, that we have made progress. But I wonder what kind of progress we have made. Are we wiser, have we become more just in our dealings with each other? Can we identify improvement in the moral condition of humanity? Are we having a more positive impact on the planet and hence improving the prospects of those who will follow? These questions have only ambivalent answers. Some would argue that we have progressed politically and that democracy is blatantly preferable to monarchy, aristocracy, or oligarchy. Others claim that we have an improved standard of living. Some of us do; many do not. Most would point to technology and recite a litany of scientific and technological innovations that have enabled humanity to manipulate its environment in extraordinary ways. But has humanity improved? Are we happier? Pollsters tell us no. I am certain that in an evolutionary sense we are no smarter and no more moral than those we study. I think that Theresa Andriacchi, with her back to the window on Ishpeming's Division Street, is correct and that most often what we call progress is just change. In fact we live in the bloodiest century ever and through science and technology have finally succeeded in creating the device that could

instantaneously destroy all life on the planet. We have expanded our
own population and our resource consumption at such prodigious
rates that there is sure to be little left over. We brush this evidence
aside with a profession of faith that technology will overcome the
worst consequences of our behavior. So if real progress is thus far
a chimera, then what is history for?

History is not about universal truth since causal chronological
narrative does not reflect the way scientists tell us the universe works.
History is not about progress unless by progress we mean consumption of more stuff. And history is not really about knowing the past
since what we can ascertain about the past is extremely circumscribed
by constraints of memory and paucity of evidence. And although
based on fact, history is not about fact. Rather, history provides the
context from which every generation extracts new meanings germane
to their concerns.

History is our myth, our story, our dream of reality, grounded
in the context of the past but created to inform the future. We can
create histories that consider the long view of the consequences of
human behavior, and that strive to include rather than exclude
multiple and diverse perspectives and inculcate empathy for one
another. We will create histories for it is our nature to do so, but will
we create histories that tell a true story? A story about the consequences of human behavior? About human happiness and planetary
survival? About right and wrong, beauty and ugliness, good and evil
and the refined discernment to know the difference? A story for the
present and the future? Not just any story will do.

NOTES

[1]Roger Lewin, *Complexity: Life at the Edge of Chaos* (New York: Collier
Books, 1992), passim.

[2]John Gribbin, *In Search of Schrödinger's Cat: Quantum Physics and Reality* (New York: Bantam Books, 1984), p. 5.

[3]Paul Davies, *About Time: Einstein's Unfinished Revolution* (New York:
Simon & Schuster, 1995), p. 231.

[4]Paul Davies and John Gribbin, *The Matter Myth* (New York: Touchstone Books, 1992), p. 226–27.

[5]T.S. Eliot, "Burnt Norton" from *Four Quartets* (New York: Harcourt, Brace and Company, 1943), p. 3.

[6]William Grimshaw, *History of the United States from Their First Settlement as Colonies to the Period of the Fifth Census in 1830* (Philadelphia: Grigg & Elliott, 1836), p. 223–25.

[7]Henry Adams, *History of the United States during the Second Administration of Thomas Jefferson* (New York: The Library of America, 1986), p. 751.

[8]Oscar Handlin, *America, a History* (New York: Holt, Rinehart and Winston, Inc., 1968), p. v.

[9]L. P. Hartley, *The Go-Between* (London: Hamish Hamilton, 1953), p. 9.

[10]David Carr, *Time, Narrative and History* (Bloomington: Indiana University Press, 1986), p. 177.

⹀ 4 ⹀

Speaking With the Past

Empathy and understanding are two of the better inclinations of our nature, needing only cultivation to become an enduring habit. History is an effective means to stimulate this aptitude. In the historical process of eyeballing the world through the minds of those who lived before us, we sharpen our own sensibilities and can interact with our contemporaries with heightened sensitivity and concern. For if we are products of the past, then knowledge of the past is essential to understand and appreciate each other and live together in a society capable of making decisions that incorporate both a long view and the common welfare.

Blood relationships and familial ties are not prerequisites for bonds with those here before us. I want to tell you about the life of a dear friend with whom I share no discernible lineage. Carlos de Hault DeLassus, who served Spain in the New World for thirty years, died in New Orleans more than one hundred years before I was born. Most of what can be known about him is meticulously stored in a few gray archival boxes at the Missouri Historical Society's Library and Research Center in St. Louis. It is startling that his life should be simmered down to this: sterile boxes, acid-free folders and white tissue interleaving, special lights, and climate control. Nevertheless, more intimacy can be gleaned from these few boxes than some friends exchange in decades of face-to-face conversation. It seems that often we set important things to paper and, because of the labor involved and the desire to keep the page neat and the expression clear, we think before we scrawl. One letter in the DeLassus boxes immediately drew my attention for its detail, its apologetic tone, and the suspicions it created in me that there was much more to the story. Don Carlos wrote it to his son Auguste, probably in 1836.

Dear Son,

As in our conversations I never spoke much of the place where members of your family were born, and as during your journey in France you may have occasion in that country to meet our relatives or some old friends, in order that you should not be a stranger to them, it is well that you remember that your family is from Bouchaine, a fortified city of the French actually in the Department of the North, where it remained until the year 1790. Your grandfather, my father, exercised there the functions of: hereditary mayor; Subdelegate of France; Treasurer of War; Receiver of Taxes; Commissary of Victuals; Receiver of Government Imports; Receiver of the Farmer's Rents; Advisor and Comptroller of their acts; Commissary of the Navy; Knight of the Royal Order of St. Michael; and lastly he was appointed Treasurer of the State of Haynaut, residing there, and then eight other functions were exercised by my brother Dehault Delassus, your uncle. In 1790 and 1791 they emigrated. Your grandfather and your grandmother, your aunt, then a child of fourteen or fifteen years and your uncle Camille, my brother, sailed from Havre for the United States, together with your good uncle Derbigny, who was then a young man attached to our family by a schoolboy friendship with your uncle DeHault, and who married your aunt sometime after. Your uncle DeHault remained in France as long as it was possible, but after the death of the King he was obliged to emigrate to Germany with his wife and their only daughter; and I who was in the service of Spain from the year 1782 found myself on my six month furlough when your grandfather emigrated. I returned to my regiment of the Guarde Wallones in Spain to continue my service, (not as an emigrant for I never was one, since I had entered the service of Spain in 1782 by virtue of the Family Compact between the Kings of France and Spain in effect eight years before the French Revolution). In that time I returned to France one time with the Army, where I remained only about a year. In my first campaigns I was promoted to Lieutenant Colonel because I was one of the first to reach the foot of St. Eline in the Pyrenees at the storming and capture of it, and because of several other fights in that glorious campaign of Spain. In 1794 I was sent by promotion to Madrid attached to the battalion of the Kings Guards. Just before that I received a letter from my father that announced to me that since he had not succeeded in his enterprises in the United States and having spent all the funds he brought with him, and knowing the Governor who was the Baron of Carondelet, his countryman and old boyhood friend, he decided to come down the Ohio River and join him there. He was granted permission together with his family to form the settlement of New Bourbon, where he settled with his family, but very much embarrassed in money matters. I remember, my dear son, what pain those words gave me then. I could not bear it, and though I had arrived at a most prestigious position by my service in the Royal Guarde Wallones, I determined to abandon it in order to join my family in this country. I threw myself on the King's mercy and asked him to do me the favor of transferring as lieutenant colonel to the regiment of Louisiana so as to be useful to my family while continuing my service. This was granted to me immediately, and at my arrival in Louisiana, the Governor, the Baron of Carondelet, congratulated me and appointed me Civil and Military Commandant of New Madrid, where I went with a boat loaded with merchandise which a firm gave me on consignment. I could in this manner accomplish my object for my family. At that time your uncle and aunt Derbigny resided at New Madrid. Your uncle was employed there by the Spanish Government. From then on I was continued in office by all the other Spanish Governors in superior commands of Upper Louisiana. In 1803 I received my appointment as colonel from the King. I remained in St. Louis until Spain had delivered the country to the French who sold it to the United States and I was also responsible for making the transfer to the United States.

Later I again left my family to join my regiment of Louisiana at Pensacola. From there I was sent to Baton Rouge to relieve Governor DeGrand Pre, and I stayed there as Governor until 1810 when the inhabitants revolted. Then feeling disgusted and tired of a service rendered unworthy from neglect by the authorities in Havana and Pensacola upon which I depended to take notice of my concerns, and having no means to resist attack, the fort and everything in a state of abandonment shameful for the Spanish flag, I wrote that my health did not permit me to continue my service, and I stayed with my family. Thus ended thirty years of good service, and I can say, given with zeal, fidelity and sincere attachment to the Spanish nation.

It is then that I married, being entirely free and independent. But my happiness was of short duration. I had the misfortune to lose your mother after five years of our union. Of three children, you are the only one left to me and you are my only consolation with your good wife and your dear children. May we enjoy this happiness peaceably and a long time, and especially may the few days left to me be employed to see you happy and prosperous.

I wanted, my dearest son, to give a simple statement of our origins and the place where the members of your paternal family were born. I allowed myself to be carried into the details of my

private, political, and military careers. At this point I omitted the
details of my actions after my marriage, as you know as well as I,
that it is in the family of my brothers and my sister that we have
always resided and especially in the good and incomparable Derbigny
family.

Colonel Don DeLassus
To Auguste Dehault DeLassus

I remember my own feelings upon first reading this letter, and
the conversation I began with the long-dead DeLassus—a conversation that I have continued intermittently for a decade: You told your
son his own history. But why did you wait so long? I sense that you
knew he would find out much of it from family in France. If you
delayed so long in telling your own son these things, you would be
incensed to know that your private correspondence to Auguste,
intended by you for his eyes only, lasted long after you were gone and
is now in the hands of an inquisitive stranger, who is now putting
your letter in a book for others to see. You would never have willingly
divulged even these details to me, never mind what I pried through
and pieced together subsequently. You were an extremely private man
and you would be angry with me.

"I remained in St. Louis until Spain had delivered the country to the French
who sold it to the United States and I was also responsible for making the
*transfer to the United States." –*Carlos DeLassus in a letter to his son. (Trunk
belonging to Carlos DeLassus, last Spanish governor of upper Louisiana,
ca. 1799, courtesy of the Missouri Historical Society.)

I know, Don Carlos, that your letter to Auguste left much un-
said. You remind me of my own father in this regard. But I understand that you loved Auguste deeply; your letter almost says so but
I suspect that "I love you" were not words that came easily to you.
You were not only private but formal and distant even in your closest
relationships.

DeLassus' agony at his father's bankruptcy betrays an extraordinary sense of family honor, as does his abandonment of a promising military career in order to rescue his parents from their
predicament. The details of his father's status in pre-revolutionary
France indicate how profoundly that bloody spontaneous upheaval
affected the family financially but even more deeply wounded his
sense of family honor. I know now that DeLassus' parents and relatives settled first at Gallipolis on the Ohio River and that they, like
so many others, were duped and swindled by greedy land specula-
tors who preyed on the senior DeLassus' lack of sophistication. I
once drove to Gallipolis to see just where they settled. I cannot
imagine how a refugee band of French nobles accustomed to luxury
and living on rents and sinecures could survive for long in such a
place, where survival required strict economy and hard labor.

Beginning with the foolish scheme in Gallipolis where transplanted nobles injured themselves just trying to fell trees, DeLassus'
father, who went by the title Chevalier Pierre de Luziere, continued
to compound his debts with foolhardy plans for the New Bourbon
Colony. He hoped that it would become a haven for dispossessed
French refugees where he could recreate the life he had known in
northern France, a hopeless dream with tragic consequences for
his son. The awful reality was that the Chevalier borrowed twelve
thousand pesos to finance his doomed plan to settle up to twenty
thousand people in the vicinity of New Bourbon. At first I did not
understand what had happened. Then I pieced it together. Much of
this debt was incurred in 1793 when DeLassus was still in Spain,
unaware of his father's poor judgments and that his own future was
being decided a continent and an ocean away. The Chevalier de-
faulted on his loan and turned to his son in Spain for help, a request
DeLassus could not refuse since it was a claim upon the honor of the
family. Eventually the debt fell into the hands of the Chouteau family

of St. Louis—countrymen, yes, but pragmatic capitalists for certain. DeLassus assumed responsibility for this parental debt and remained mortgaged to the Chouteaus for the rest of his life.

So off you went, Don Carlos, to petition the King for a transfer to Louisiana. Louisiana must have seemed to be the farthest end of the earth from your station at the royal court in Madrid. You probably had to check a map to remind yourself of its precise location. I imagine you felt helpless and forlorn as you voluntarily abandoned a promising career at the center of the empire for anonymity in an unimportant frontier outpost. From your remaining letters, I know that you were physically ill. Is this when the terrible headaches that you mention later first afflicted you? I can hear your sighs and feel your resignation. Sometimes your sense of filial obligation seems honorable but misguided to me, certainly self-destructive but perhaps unavoidable for you. Your assumption of your parents' outrageous debts, which they incurred attempting to maintain their former lifestyle, and your assumption of the obligations of your siblings undermined your peace of mind and haunted your life. Your sense of family honor came from your aristocratic birth, but it was an anachronism in this new world. Yet I do find your sense of loyalty before money, duty above pleasure appealing, perhaps because it is scarce in the world that J inhabit. My family ties are mere tenuous threads by comparison. In contrast with you I lead a selfish life.

Not much remains of the New Bourbon DeLassus knew; just a narrow road up the bluff and a few houses and farmland on the level top. I think that the family's situation was even worse than he expected when he arrived there in 1796. His profligate parents borrowed money from friends and spent it on unnecessary amenities while the youngest brother Camille, who lived near them, suffered the brunt of their insatiable appetites for luxuries, their depression, failing health, and debt. DeLassus did not say so but he must have been deeply dismayed when he first visited them in New Madrid and you must have felt victimized by their aristocratic pretense. How could he not have felt resentment of the Chevalier's consumption of fine French wines, fancy cigars, his silk handkerchiefs, fine hats, multiple pairs of shoes and French soaps, all of which were billed to his son. I suspect he paid no attention to cost. He never had, and in France it was beneath his station to do so. I can imagine that DeLassus' sense of duty was tested; there must have been strained and difficult conversations within the family. His sister Odille and her husband moved downriver to New Orleans, glad to make the break. Faithful Camille remained near his parents, ever the dutiful son.

Your brother Camille is an enigma to me, Don Carlos. I can hear in your words the guilt that haunted you when you thought of him. You knew that your parents had spent his trust fund. Further, you knew the agreement with your parents: In return for staying with them and caring for them in their old age, Camille was to inherit their properties in New Bourbon. But you forced your parents to renounce their obligations to Camille in favor of yourself, in return for which you assumed responsibility for their debts. You had no choice. You did not stand to gain financially. They were all out of funds and the growing pile of debt exceeded the value of their property. All Camille would inherit was debt. I cannot second-guess your decision in this matter. It was wrenching for all of you and made your relationships with each other distant and cool. You were lonely, bereft of that once easy intimacy of family and now in debt on your parents' behalf to all of the prominent merchants in St. Louis and Ste. Genevieve, then small villages where private business was public.

DeLassus never comprehended that in this new world, business is business and friendship is friendship. In this regard he was truly his father's son. After the consummation of the Louisiana Purchase when he was no longer Lieutenant Governor in St. Louis, professed friendships evaporated. Loyalties that he believed to be bonds of friendship dissolved when his power and influence diminished. The Chouteaus, by far the wealthiest and most influential mercantile family in St. Louis and erstwhile friends, now regarded him as a deadbeat. In late 1804, in a rare expression of feeling that I now know as a measure of his own emotions, he wrote to Marie Phillipe Le Duc, a friend in St. Louis:

> *I fear very much as you said that I will be obliged to take further action when I arrive in New Orleans, in order to prove to the public that certain complaints against my predecessors and against me are unjustified; this will be very easy to do, seeing that these people never received anything other than great kindness, and*

that they owe in part or in whole all that they possess to authorities
I mentioned; but in fact they should be mistrusted. I delude myself
in thinking that people know how to make an exception in the case
of men who are just, helpful, kind, and not self-serving, as opposed
to those men who are thoughtless, babbling, jealous, ambitious,
unsociable, who give only an "egg for an ox" wanting only to make
profits and to be more powerful than the parish priest. . . . In the
end those are fake men who can never be happy.

I most heartily concur. Oh, my distant friend, how unhappy you
would be at the end of the twentieth century when nearly everything
in life is transformed into a commodity for sale. You cannot imagine
where the trends that you resisted have carried us. You would be
amazed at how we are bombarded with messages that urge us to buy,
to consume as if this will bring happiness. That which does not have
a sale price is presumed to be of little value. Business now is imper-
sonal and unrelated to friendships. Thus, as I know you would agree,
the finer and more important things in life like kindness, civility,
and unselfishness are devalued. Still I must be careful not to exon-
erate you. You were well intended but not blameless. You participated in your own undoing by your blindness to the rules of the
world around you. Yet your intentions and even the tragedies of your
life make it easy to absolve you. In doing so I can absolve myself, for
what we share, despite separation in time, is a human fallibility that
we must forgive if we are to forgive ourselves and those around us.
Tragedy does stalk all of us, and it is not necessarily a consequence
of our actions.

Both DeLassus' parents died within a few months of each other
in 1806, still clinging to their New Bourbon bluffs. DeLassus was
at his post in Pensacola. He grieved, filled with regret and nearly
overcome by guilt. The focus of his feelings was again Camille, the
brother who bore his sense of familial obligation to their deathbeds.
DeLassus wrote of him that he was the brother who stayed home,
"the only son who stayed near his father to close his eyes." Don Carlos
felt that he should have been the one, that this final act was the
proof of familial fidelity. I left California just a few days before my
mother's death, planning to return the next week. I was too late. My
sister and my oldest brother were there. I too felt guilt, felt that I

missed a final act of obligation, failed to perform the last act of a child for a parent, that I left something unfinished that cannot now be completed.

I think that there were things DeLassus could not bear to put in writing, even to his son. (Don Carlos, did you think it unnecessary for Auguste to know the truth of the Baton Rouge affair, or were you too ashamed to tell him what really happened?) He obfuscated the truth, but I am certain that Auguste knew. There must have been gossip. Seeing those things on a written page would have given them a heightened reality when what he desired most was simply to forget. I know that feeling. There are things about my own life that I cannot bear to put in print, not just because I fear embarrassment but also because written words seem more substantial than memories. Memories exist only in the recesses of mind; written words are tangible and conspicuous. There are things about me that will never be in writing and therefore will leave with me. This also makes me wonder about history. If I had not stumbled on the other evidence, I would have accepted the letter to Auguste and been far off the mark. In this respect the past consists of what the dead left behind, often taking what is most important to their graves. I only know about the Baton Rouge debacle because it was public, with records left that DeLassus did not control. Had it been possible, he would have destroyed them.

So how must you have felt, Don Carlos, when at dawn of September 24 in 1810 you were roughly seized by the American insurgents in Baton Rouge and held under house arrest for several months? You were a prisoner in your home. All those words you wrote to Auguste come to my mind: degraded, tired, sick, ashamed. This was the nadir of your professional and personal life, but it was not the worst of it. In March of 1811 the Spanish Government that you had served so well for so long conducted a formal inquiry into your conduct in Baton Rouge.

They began asking questions in Pensacola and then resumed the cumbersome bureaucratic inquiry in Havana in June of 1812. Wisely, DeLassus chose not to appear in Havana to defend himself. Finally in August of 1814 the tribunal delivered its verdict. It was as bad as it could be. DeLassus was sentenced to death! I was appalled and ashamed for my friend. In retrospect he took the only possible way out. The only way he could have avoided the death sentence was to give his life in a futile gesture in Baton Rouge. I am certain he realized this and tortured himself with the reflection that perhaps that would have been the honorable thing to do. (How many times did you relive the events in Baton Rouge in the fitful hours of the night and in the remembrances of old age? But you chose life.) I do understand why he could not tell Auguste the truth.

DeLassus had experienced a bitter harbinger of Baton Rouge when he was Lieutenant Governor of Upper Lousiana in St. Louis. Unruly and aggressive American frontiersman caused a ruckus in Mine á Breton in early 1804. There they were again in Baton Rouge, disrespectful of all authority and especially monarchy. And there he was, the King's representative. He was appropriately suspicious of their motives and their loyalties. He did not say so but after all his family had suffered as a consequence of the French Revolution and he abhorred all that these men represented: democracy, rejection of hereditary authority, belligerence combined with rapaciousness and an unshakable conviction of their own righteousness. Further, they believed that DeLassus represented an antiquated and debased order that was a casualty of the forces of history. (You, too, must have felt that there were forces loose in the world that were overturning the established order and impossible to control.) I sense that DeLassus viewed this republican and democratic fervor as he might regard a contagious disease. I understand the timidity and fear with which he faced the real revolutionaries in Baton Rouge, especially when he had neither the men, weapons, nor fortifications to properly resist.

What you told Auguste is true, Don Carlos. You were tired, disgusted and ashamed, and abandoned by your King. Spanish authority crumbled. The Monarchy was decrepit. You had only a ruined fort, antiquated and damaged equipment and two dozen men with which to stave off the "tides of history." As a sympathizer and sometime participant in the civil rights struggles and activism of the 1960s, I know that there are irresistible historical forces. You thought that you could compromise with the Americans and therein was your error. You were the visible representative of Spanish authority and therefore the living embodiment and official symbol of the old order that they sought to eliminate. You just fed their democratic frenzy and appetites. These were the sons of the American Revolution and having thrown off one monarchy they were in no mood to profess loyalty to yours.

The terrible truth is that while DeLassus may have resigned from his regiment of Louisiana—this would have been a point of honor with him—he had little choice. For he became the scapegoat for the Baton Rouge affair. And in that "revolt" a small group of insurgent Americans successfully undermined his command and detached the province from Spain. I knew that his explanation was superficial because I realized that he was the Governor when the affair took place, and I had come to know him too well to believe that he just resigned and walked away. I intuitively felt that there was more to the incident than was conveyed in those few terse words to Auguste. I found reference to the records of the trial and purchased them from the Spanish Archives in Madrid. They now sit on my shelf not far from the records of my own grandfather's trial. Both of these men, DeLassus and my grandfather, survived and surmounted public slander, personal humiliation, and culminating tragedy. They were good men. I am fond of both of them.

I know Carlos de Hault DeLassus not only from his letters but also from his portrait, his trunk from Spain, and various household items now at the Missouri Historical Society in St. Louis. I cannot help but conclude that while he would not have regarded St. Louis as his home (for I am certain that he saw himself as a man without a country), that this town did serve as a kind of surrogate because his closest personal relationships, other than his son and with his sister's family, were always here. The portrait depicts an attractive, dignified, and even distinguished man, qualities substantiated in his correspondence. He lived according to ancient codes of honor and dignity and in this regard he became a living anachronism. Just as I cannot escape the place and circumstances of my own birth, neither could DeLassus escape his noble legacy. In his case, however, the culture and values that he represented were out of step with the world he inhabited. Thus he was always ill at ease in a democratic world filled with men on the make with little sense of tradition and still less experience of gentlemanly behavior. He saw the worst of them because he always worked on the frontiers that attracted those individualistic democrats in whom the coarsest qualities were always exaggerated.

I was horrified when I found out the truth of what happened in Baton Rouge. I felt it so deeply, for by then I had come to know DeLassus quite well. I remembered how I felt when a friend sent me the legal files from my own grandfather's trial and subsequent imprisonment and when I found his prison mug shot in the archives of the Bureau of Michigan History in Lansing. I shook, perspiration beaded all over me, my stomach churned, my palms dampened, much like a body's uncontrolled reactions to traumatic shock. *relation to*

My family, too, bears the burdens of the unmentionable. Discussion of my own grandfather's troubles was unthinkable, even though he spent the last decade of his life in our household. We all knew the bare outlines of the tragedy but could not speak of such things to each other. When I look at DeLassus' portrait I see my grandfather, too: a kind, gentle, dignified, and honest man. In the absence of discussion, there can be no reconciliation of the tragedy and the man. But have I somehow misjudged you both, Don Carlos? I fear that you left this same rock upon your son's back. I must tell you about such burdens. *History through personal empathy connection*

It is ironic to me that I have always traveled light and that I, the historian, have assiduously sought to discard memories and all of those physical things that prompt their recall. Until recently, I have always been more comfortable in discarding the past and reminders of it. For me the past has always been loaded with regrets to be ignored, as if all could be expiated by the painful disposal of child-hood toys, photographs, high school annuals, family furniture, and other reminders of relationships. It is simply a protective device, a variation on those that we all devise in an effort to escape what we like least about ourselves. And so not only am I a master at disposal, but, like so many others, I have also been peripatetic and, in my moving from place to place, seeking to avoid the creation of a past that would follow me. It has been a forlorn and doomed attempt to escape the necessity of living within self-defined boundaries, of living some*place*, the requirement that if we are to be human, we each must have a history, an identity.

The wooden chest can't be that old, but it appears to be from the seventeenth century, the uncomfortable relic that stood against the north wall of the dining room in the house on South Pine Street in Ishpeming. The family story, verified by repetition, was that the dark, ornate, brooding chest came from England with the progenitors of my mother's side of our family. Mother always put serving trays and candelabra on the lid. The varnish on the chest was blackened with age, and the carved gargoyles frightened me. A faint smell of mothballs emanated from the side of the room where the chest sat, a smell I still associate with what is old, almost dead. I do not remember the chest being opened before I was fifteen, but perhaps the memory of previous occasions was shrouded by the trunk's importance in that summer of 1964. Startling and emotionally charged events that involve particular objects and places can obliterate memories previously associated with them. Grandfather, who had lived with us for nearly ten years, died that summer in a huge, faraway hospital in Detroit. I, the only child still living at home in the dregs of my parents' slowly faltering marriage, was sheltered from this dying as if at age fifteen I was still too young to be exposed to death, or perhaps my mother, his only daughter, could cope with his dying only through retreat and privacy. She could not permit herself to be exposed, to be seen caring too much. Thus, although grandfather was hospitalized for weeks, there were no visits and hence no good-bye. For me his death crystallized into three events.

At Mother's request on the day of his death, my brother-in-law and I took Grandfather's cat to the veterinarian and had her euthanized before Mother returned home. We buried the cat in the garden where Grandfather grew vegetables, and relieved frustration, as best he could in the chancy Upper Peninsula summers. The death of the cat seemed unnecessary to me, but necessary to my mother who, for all kinds of sad human reasons, felt this death as a personal, inconsolable, unsharable tragedy for which she assumed personal responsibility. Mother could not confront the cat, who had become the unfortunate emotional symbol of death, unbearable loss, and her own guilt.

We met at Lakeview Cemetery. Grandfather's casket rested uneasily in the midst of the oppressive atmosphere of words unspoken and feelings unacknowledged. In five minutes it was finished, few words spoken and nothing admitted. We all retreated. Mother and Father flew home, the rest of us drove, arriving home two days later to tragedy disguised as normalcy, as we had become so expert at doing. We did not speak of missing him, nor did we admit to the pathos of his life, as if somehow we were the great exception, as if we should be immune to troubles and foibles, to tragedy and to grief, to feeling. It was as if by acknowledging grief we would become accomplices in its creation.

The trunk contained all that was left of my grandfather. Mother knew this but I did not. The two of us were alone when at her instigation we lifted the lid and, like pestilence and evil, his life escaped from the box and engulfed me, maybe for the rest of my life. He was the defrocked bishop, the man of shame, unredeemed from his trial, conviction, and imprisonment for embezzlement nearly twenty-five years earlier. Because nothing of importance was spoken in this family, no expiation was possible. Like the rest of us, he just had to live with it. That sort of burden once assumed could not be released, never be put down. If there ever was a time for my mother and me to mourn him and reconcile his life, this was the moment. We did not. The past rested uneasily at our house because it was not welcome. The past cannot be suppressed. I cannot close that trunk.

He saved every sermon he had ever written, and together with his vestments they remained in that trunk. Twenty years of preaching and the trappings of a bishop had been resting there, shouting at us all those years, but we ignored them. Obviously, it was Grandfather who had saved these things. He had had over twenty-five years in which to destroy them. Now, of course, their disposition was Mother's decision. The dining room fireplace was seldom used. My parents worried about its safety, and the condition of the ninety-year-old chimney that slanted through my bedroom directly above. This day no concerns about safety were expressed. It was a clear, sunny morning. Fire has always appeared less powerful, less threatening in the full light of the sun. Yet on that morning a conflagration that illuminated every dark corner would have been most appropriate to me—a raging furnace of flame to purify and cleanse and blot out memory, as we fed the fires with Grandfather's life. Mother handed me the pages without glancing at their contents and I, hesitantly, fed the fire that was dim and unreal in the full sun. Can a fire destroy memory and purify simultaneously? "Mother," I said softly, "shouldn't we save some of this?" "Mother," I said, "I need to read these." Memory lost diminishes what remains; it cannot cleanse. As the dried paper was heaped on the rising flames, the fire rose dangerously into the chimney. The colored vestments, smelling of years of mothball internment, were folded carefully on the bottom of the chest. Why neatly fold garments meant for the fire? Perhaps Grandfather did not intend the burning, perhaps it was only Mother who could not countenance a father's disgrace. In an instant all was curled and brittle, moving as if animate in the midst of the flames, and the heat created irreversible change forever in me. I understood the finality of my actions: that the past could not be called back and that there would always be a part of me now lost and irrecoverable—in T.S. Eliot's word, "unredeemed." And so a part is missing.

How did Auguste feel as you, Don Carlos, were laid to rest in St. Louis Cemetery #1 in New Orleans? Was the past unredeemed for him also? For his sake and yours, I hope you talked before you left.

Despite DeLassus' personal tragedy at Baton Rouge, family troubles, and betrayal by erstwhile friends he did have excellent prospects for happiness in 1811. Finally, in his mid-forties, he married Adelaide, the daughter of Gilbert Leonard whom he knew well in Baton Rouge. He never mentioned it, but I am certain that he delayed marriage and personal happiness because of his peripatetic military career and family obligations. He and Adelaide had three children, as he wrote to Auguste. But by 1817 his wife and two of his children were dead. He does not say how Adelaide died. I know that it was in childbirth. Don Carlos, did you later explain to Auguste why you left your one remaining daughter with your sister-in-law in Baton Rouge when you, in your grief and pain, headed upriver to St. Louis in 1816? Did you tell him about Odille, his little sister, left behind? Did you tell him that she was a twin, the other child dead at birth? Did he know that you feared that you could not raise your daughter? I know that DeLassus sent money for her care and that he expected her to return to him. He wrote frequent letters from St. Louis inquiring after her health; but he was strangely silent when he received the letter in 1817 that she was dead. He did not receive the news, along with a description of her death and burial, until fall. In his anguish he separated himself from your in-laws, and his correspondence with them ceased. Henceforth DeLassus stayed away from Baton Rouge, not wishing, I surmise, to be reminded of all that happened there.

In 1814 when the tribunal in Havana rendered its awful decision DeLassus was about my age, in his late forties no longer a young man. He had served his King as best he could and he had struggled to save his parents from themselves. His parents had died eight years before in nostalgically named New Bourbon just outside of Ste. Genevieve, Missouri, never reconciled to their radically changed status. Now he really was a refugee, a man without a country. He could never return to Spanish territory for he was under a sentence of death. I can only guess at the bitterness which he kept well concealed. Despite his support of monarchy he had run out of monarchs to support. He had to accommodate himself to the aggressive American democrats who had been the tools of his undoing. He had turned Upper Louisiana over to them in March of 1804 and lost Baton Rouge to them in 1810. Now he had to learn to live with them. In all of his remaining letters he never spoke of these things, never even mentioned them to Auguste. But I am certain he discussed them with Pierre Derbigny and his wife, his sister Odille, for he was closest to them and they were aware of what transpired.

It strikes me, Don Carlos, that in your day, time and distance were interrelated in ways that they are not for me. I can travel and remain in instantaneous contact with family and friends. But for you distance was also time. Thus important life events occurred without your knowledge until long after their happening. In your day long-distance communication required a physical movement of people and paper. Nothing could travel at the speed of light through wires or the earth's atmosphere. Did this produce apprehension every time you opened your mail? I cannot imagine not knowing of my mother's death until months after it happened. The phone call came in the middle of the night when the news was just minutes old. At least I had the consolation of knowing that, until that phone call, Mother lived. You might have appreciated that, but I doubt that you would be pleased with the idea of watching or listening to events anywhere in the world reproduced electronically in front of you in what we call "real time." This means you see them as they are happening. Interestingly this influences how the events turn out. People behave differently when they know they have an audience.

DeLassus devoted what remained of his life to Auguste and eventually to his family. While he lived principally in New Orleans to be near them he journeyed up the Mississippi by steamboat for protracted visits with old friends in St. Louis. When he visited St. Louis in 1836, old animosities had faded. He enjoyed conviviality with what remained of your old friends. He never remarried. I am not sure why. My grandfather never told me why he never remarried, either. But I know. He kept a plaster statue of two geese on his desk right where he could see them as he wrote letters each morning. The geese had their long, graceful necks intertwined. Once I asked him why he had the statue. "Because," he replied, "geese mate for life." DeLassus never discussed such subjects but, given his parental fealty, I think that fidelity to his long-deceased wife was a powerful emotion and motivation. But now, in 1836, at age sixty-nine, despite his ongoing struggles to have his land claims confirmed by the courts and the United State Congress, he seemed more content than ever before and his worries no longer preoccupied him. This makes me happy for you, Don Carlos, and hopeful for myself.

This was DeLassus' final trip to St. Louis and he kept a diary. The entry for July 14th is reassuring, for in it he is both content and introspective in ways that he seldom was in earlier years. "I was received by Mrs. Lawless," Don Carlos wrote (in French of course), "with all the graciousness and ease of a lady of the best education and greatest integrity. For a first visit I remained with her nearly an hour, the conversation extending to different subjects and unfortunately a little sad—on the occurrences she had met with in her family and I in mine. In spite of the fact that I tried to change the subject, we always returned to it." Then DeLassus wrote something so wonderfully uncharacteristic that it stays in my mind still. "Sensitive hearts," he wrote, "understand one another too well to remove themselves from their attachments in talking to one another."

Not long ago I was in New Orleans and took time to look for the grave of Carlos de Hault DeLassus, thinking that I would allot several hours to what I was convinced was a goose chase. A friend accompanied me. First we went to a more recent cemetery with burial vaults in neat rows. We checked with the sexton, who told us that if we were able to find the grave at all, it would be in New Orleans' St. Louis Cemetery #1 which held earlier burials. But, we were warned, many of the graves were obliterated to make room for roadway. We searched for a little while among the randomly placed vaults. I heard my friend call out and headed toward her voice. She found your grave, Don Carlos. I admit to picking up a small piece of displaced mortar from it, a piece I now have at home near a photographic copy of an engraving of you. Perhaps you would not have minded. My friend and I returned later and placed votive candles on your tomb. I imagine Auguste standing here before me, bereaved, nearly one hundred fifty years ago.

Because I was born more than one hundred years after your death, I can know you but you cannot know me. Likewise, you help me explore life's meanings and the quality of my own life, but I can never return the favor. You reinforce values that I sometimes find in short supply. You convince me that some things endure from generation to generation, rules of civilized life. You demonstrate that attachments to others are necessary for a fulfilled life. But you also point out the personal cost of adhering to obsolescent ways. Not that I blame you, you understand. It is just that there are consequences. Perhaps they were worth it for you. Maybe I am too malleable, too willing to accommodate my relativistic age where nothing seems unchangeable. We have become accustomed to accelerating rates of change in which nothing is static and little is sacred, and we have accommodated. Yet now when I hear someone comment that we live in changing times, I think of you: your world upended in the French Revolution, your parents born in nobility forced to transplant to the banks of the Mississippi, your own emigration, the gulping of Louisiana and then Baton Rouge and West Florida by the United States, your own accommodation to democracy, the fleeting happiness of your own marriage to Adelaide. I have not even mentioned changing technology. You first came up the Mississippi propelled by oars, poles, and sails. Later you made a much quicker trip by steamboat. What change!

All this perspective and support you give to me, while I am unable to return your favor, not from lack of willingness on my part, you understand, Don Carlos, but from the circumstances of our history.

✑ 5 ✑

Common Ground

The United States of America is a country with defined geographic boundaries, but it is not a nation founded upon the common ethnicity and shared religion that characterize many nations. Rather, we are a nation of citizens descended from every nationality on earth who, at least at the outset, had little in common besides our new place's geography. Lacking a clear definition of nationality, aside from the formality of legal citizenship, the people who live here have always debated the question of what it means to be an American. Our Congress, goaded by the communist paranoia of the Cold War, even established committees on "Un-American Activities," as if being American was so nebulous and abstract that it needed official definition and enforcement.

I, like so many other Americans, have stood in the great hall at Ellis Island and pondered the millions of emigrants who arrived in constant streams through this portal. One member of my immediate family, Anna Karenkevich, first set foot in this nation on that small island in New York Harbor. She was one of those people dislocated by shifting political boundaries after World War II, a Displaced Person. As I stood in this place, I could imagine both her fear and her anticipation. I know it well, for she described it to me often. Anna and millions of others disembarked here to begin the painful process of becoming American. Weary, fearful of an unknown place, each individual was a living testimonial to hope by his or her presence in this great hall of entry. Polyglots in language, customs, and place of origin, full of trepidation at what they had done, yet they were optimistic that this place held potential for a better life. Just by arriving here they had completed the first and most crucial step toward that goal. Now this place demands by its very presence that visitors confront the painful process of becoming American.

87

Standing at Ellis Island is an easy seduction into romanticism about the American experience. A visitor can forget that the process begun here for so many Americans was more benign and certainly more of a choice than the catastrophic violence inflicted upon others who eventually joined in American citizenship. The experiences of Africans who arrived chained together in terror and misery and the systematic slaughter of the people native to this land is a persistent affront to American myths of equality, justice, democracy, and assimilation. While nearly all those people who were "just off the boat" were targets of discrimination, the degradation of former slaves and native people persisted because these people were unassailable contradictions of the myth that everybody had an equal chance in this place. If the image of America as a melting pot ever made sense, marginalization of those people who saw the very idea of a melting pot as a debasing mockery was a necessity. Those whose experiences contradicted the myth suffered disenfranchisement and even denial of humanity justified by that other persistent and pernicious myth, racial superiority. Ironically, only subjugation and racism allowed the nation to perpetuate the myths that Americans wanted so very badly to believe about themselves.

At first glance the Rio Grande is the most disappointing of America's great rivers. For those expecting to see the likes of the mighty Mississippi or the beautiful Missouri, this meandering trickle, a foot deep and a mile wide after it gushes and plummets down the escarpment of its northern plateau, is a diminutive disappointment. Yet from the elevated vantage of an airplane or one of the surrounding mountain peaks, it becomes clear that the Rio Grande sustains life in an arid country. A broad strip of green ribbon bordered with cottonwoods contrasts dramatically with the parched land beyond as the river flows south through New Mexico and then angles to the southeast along the south Texas-Mexico border. In places you can walk across this river even after the mountain snow melt and spring floods. Despite its fractional volume, the Rio Grande's verdant meander is proof of its power, for to either side where the river does not reach is desert. Drop for drop this river carries some of the most precious water on the North American Continent. No wonder that the Rio Grande attracted native peoples thousands of years into the past, a magnetic river oasis in a dry, dry land.

I came to know this world because I lived in it, absorbed it, and because its history and culture were the subjects of my studies. The human culture that huddled in the Rio Grande Valley was magical to me as I coasted down the big hill from Santa Fe to Albuquerque for the first time in 1972, my green Toyota sighing with relief as the loaded trailer pushed for a change. The place names themselves were exotic, foreign to my midwestern palate: Santa Clara, Taos, Isleta, Bernalillo, San Ildefonso, Santa Fe, Chimayo, Truchas, Espanola. I was accustomed to Ishpeming, Humbolt, Champion, Harvey, Iron Mountain. My view of America had an East Coast perspective. The adventure began at Jamestown and moved inexorably west into uninhabited wilderness. I knew better, of course. Indian people had always lived in this valley, and many Hispanic people trace their ancestral arrival in this land to the century before the English scrambled ashore at Jamestown and clung tenuously to the Atlantic Coast and their ocean lifeline to England. This was a different view of America, a view from the west. But seeing, feeling, and touching created an emotional reality absent from textbooks and photographs.

Much of New Mexico's architecture was based on Pueblo building. Traditional adobe construction has no sharp edges, only erotic soft curves, and since it is a concoction of clay, water, and binder, the material appears to have spontaneously generated from the land under it. Adobe architecture rises from the earth, retains the subdued coloration of the desert itself, and when abandoned slowly decomposes into the land from which it was formed, ultimately leaving no evidence of that temporary transformation. There is a symmetry to this construction not only in its shape but also in its benevolent life cycle.

Tony Lucero was an Isleta Indian. He lived at Isleta Pueblo just south of Albuquerque when I was a doctoral candidate at the University of New Mexico. He was born there and expected to die in the same place. This place was his entire world. By the time I met Tony I had lived in New Mexico for several years and what was exotic when I arrived now became familiarly beautiful.

The river, the earth, and life were indivisible in Tony Lucero's world there at Isleta Pueblo, in the river's narrow green strip of life, beneath the cottonwoods, in adobe buildings that came from the same earth that gave Tony life and sustained him and his people. Tony's relationship with the land was vital to Tony. He was as much a product of the river and land as the adobe and the shady cottonwoods, and just as inseparable. Tony could have lived elsewhere, but he would have changed and withered like an uprooted cottonwood in direct sun. He could not be Tony and live anywhere else, any more than Theresa Andriacchi could lock her store in Ishpeming and move to Chicago and still be Theresa. For both of them there is only one place. They are rooted people.

In the summer daytime the Rio Grande river valley swelters. But in Tony Lucero's piece of the valley there is a startling contrast between sun and shade. Under the cottonwoods in the dry heat, perspiration evaporates before it beads on skin and the human body's natural cooling system functions at peak efficiency. Thus the four of us—Tony, my professor from the University of New Mexico, another graduate student, and I—sat on the dusty ground beneath the trees in comfort. We had brought a fresh baked loaf of banana nut bread. Tony retreated to his adobe house and returned with a knife. We cut the bread into crude slices and ate companionably. Our errand was to interview Tony about Isleta tribal narratives. I am certain that we discussed many things that afternoon but I can only remember this one topic: the arrival of the first Spaniards in this portion of the valley in the mid-sixteenth century.

I was fascinated by the image: medieval knights thousands of miles from Europe atop stocky horses muscular enough to bear the weight of rider, armor, and armaments. I recall staring across the desert and visualizing knights in shining armor, baking as if sealed in tin cans in the sizzling heat, moving along the horizon. The image was incongruous, the medieval knights lost and out of place. I cannot imagine what Tony's people thought on that day more than four hundred years ago when the clash of cultures began. The subsequent discussion challenged my formative assumptions about the usefulness of history.

"Tony," the professor said, "tell us what your people did when the first Spaniards were spotted headed north in this valley." Tony gestured toward the Manzano Mountains to the east. "My people got on their horses and ran for the mountains because they were afraid."

I immediately suspected this conversation was to be a clash of cultures writ small. I knew the drift of the discussion and I now know that Tony did too. "But Tony," says my professor, "your people did not have horses yet. Horses came with the Spanish. Before the Spanish arrived your people did not have horses." The silence was embarrassing. I could see no reconciliation of the contradictory exchange. Without a word Tony stood up and headed for the doorway to his house, his shoulders stooped. The three of us stayed quiet. Soon Tony reappeared in the doorway and moved toward us. He carried a well-worn book. He held it out to my professor and said "Here, you can look it up yourself." In my innocence I assumed that he was going to play our game and that he was presenting us with evidence to contradict our contention that his people could not have possessed horses when the Spaniards rode up the valley. But that was not even close to the point. What Tony Lucero handed us was an anthropology textbook. The text proved our point, not his. "What an odd thing to do," I thought. The visit seemed like a failure, an unintended impasse.

Really, I should have been doubly embarrassed when Tony returned with the text and held it out to us. As I reconsidered our visit, it was clear that we had inadvertently insulted his intelligence. Tony was telling us that he was no fool oblivious to the work of scholars like us. He knew as well as we did that scholars insisted that his people did not have horses four hundred years ago. But he had answered the question we had asked. Now I wonder how often he ended similar irreconcilable conversations with that same anthropology text. I suspect that he kept it in his house just for people like us. Despite my personal discomfiture my historian self said that the tribal narrative was incorrect, the story just blatantly wrong. All of the historical and scientific evidence said so.

Narrative explanations that successfully sustained a community and way of life despite the best assimilation efforts of Spain, Mexico, and the United States ought to be judged according to the

methodologies of academic disciplines in a scientific and technological age. What foolishness and pomposity! In my ignorance I
misunderstood so very much. The issue of horses was inconsequential. The question was not the arrival of the horses; it was the validity of traditional narratives and—since to undermine the narrative
is to destroy the culture—hence the viability of an entire culture and
world view.

I learned that judging Tony's world view with my tools was futile, just one more of those ongoing attempts to demolish his culture. But I still could not reconcile this knowledge with my
commitment to history as a discipline and the rules of historical
evidence. I could not overcome the notion that while I could respect
Tony Lucero's narrative, it still contradicted the evidence and was
therefore incorrect. But did the "incorrectness" matter if the story
was successful? Should the story that worked be discarded, a culture
destroyed because it failed my test? How could some people have a
history that passed the test while others did not? I could not reconcile "good history" with useful, sustaining narrative. I am not certain
that I can do it now, although I am less insistent that history produces Truth and I approach my work with a lot more humility than
the day twenty-five years ago when we talked with Tony under the
cottonwood, near his adobe home, all placed there because of the
wide, shallow river that imbued all of the place with life.

Tony Lucero's perspective on the past calls my own into question, and my perspectives invalidate his. I needed to learn to see with
Tony's eyes. That demanded more than an intellectual understanding of why he saw the way that he did. The intellectual part made
it easy to discard Tony's point of view on the basis of objectivity and
historical fact. The Isleta people did not have horses when the Spanish stumbled up the Rio Grande, hence Tony Lucero was wrong. It
missed the point and left me where I began. I needed to accord validity
to Tony's story, to realize that the truth of narrative is not necessarily
to be discovered in its historical consistency, but rather in its
ability to create common identity and shared values and to facilitate
survival.

In time I realized that the validity of narratives must be evalu-
ated, not according to a foreign yardstick, but instead on the basis

of their success in sustaining a culture that provides a system of *Folklore*
coherent beliefs, nurtures a cohesive community, acknowledges the
humanity of all members, and ensures survival of a people. On this
scale Tony's narratives are amazingly successful. After centuries of
external domination and cultural imperialism, Isleta people have
adapted and also persisted.

The conversation with Tony perplexed me for other reasons.
Tony and I had two very different perspectives. What if ten people,
or a hundred, or a thousand were included in the conversation? How
much more difficult would it be to agree on a shared story, a narrative in common? If we identify ourselves as Americans, then we
must share a narrative, a set of common beliefs about what binds us
together and defines the common good. In the absence of such an
agreement we have no reins on an exclusive pursuit of self-interest,
no antidote to personal aggrandizement, and no connections to instill
reciprocal obligations.

Narratives explain the present as a product of the past, implicitly evaluate the past and the present, and by extension anticipate
life in the future. Lack of a shared story not only isolates us from
each other in the present but also severs us from past and future. If
we have no notion of the common good in the present, we surely will
have no connection to those who made the world we inherited and
little concern for the world we will leave behind. This American
tendency toward radical individualism was diagnosed by Alexis de
Tocqueville over a century and a half ago. "Among democratic
nations," he observed, "new families are constantly springing up,
others are constantly falling away, and all that remain change their
condition; the woof of time is every instant broken and the track of
generations effaced. Those who went before are soon forgotten; of
those who will come after, no one has any idea: the interest of man
is confined to those in close propinquity to himself." But de
Tocqueville was also concerned about the consequences of excessive
individualism upon the individual. "Thus not only does democracy
make every man forget his ancestors," he observed, "but it hides his
descendants and separates his contemporaries from him; it throws
him back forever upon himself alone and threatens in the end to
confine him entirely within the solitude of his own heart."[1]

Commemoration of historical events can put present concerns into focus and expose dysfunctional narratives, those that erect barriers between us rather than building common bonds for us. The year 1992 was the five-hundredth anniversary of Christopher Columbus' landfall on San Salvador, and in October of that year I was moderating a panel discussion on the significance of Columbus' voyage to the "New World."

Public historians must not evade controversy. Historical controversy is a hot topic. Books, articles, and news stories investigate "history wars" and "culture wars." Historians worry about censorship and the public denial of their own authority. "Revisionism" is a dirty word. Historical events that attract controversy reveal the invisible barriers and chasms in American society. But these contentious debates, rather than being cruelly divisive, are the essential process through which we can shape new narratives that unite us in common identity and shared beliefs. Controversial topics are controversial precisely because they are markers for what is important in our world.

As I walked down the stairs for the Columbian Quincentennial forum, I anticipated disagreement. The panel included an anthropologist, a historian from a local university, a Native American scholar, and an African exchange student from Ghana. We intentionally selected the panelists to include divergent points of view, multiple perspectives on the past. After my brief introductory remarks, the anthropologist opened with a cogent summary of the consequences of conquest for both the "New World" and Europe. The historian followed with a description of the progress of the conquest after Columbus' first encounter: Cortes in Mexico and Pizzaro in Peru. Then the Native American scholar spoke. She explained that if you view conquest from the perspective of native peoples, it is a questionable blessing indeed. According to some estimates, nearly ninety percent of the native people died as a result of the conquest. Some were slaughtered in battles with Europeans equipped with sophisticated technology, but even for those who did not encounter Europeans directly, death spread in wildfires of measles, smallpox, venereal diseases, and other imported contagions in every corner of both continents. Native people, she concluded, find little cause for celebration on the occasion of the five-hundredth anniversary of Columbus' arrival in the Caribbean. Finally the young man from Ghana spoke. Nine million Africans were captured and brought to this "New World" in chains through a passage of horror in which many died in the dank and filthy holds of slave ships. Those who survived were put to hard labor in the "New World." Their enslavement continued for generations, rationalized by the doctrines of racism. The unfortunate consequences of this forced and inhumane migration of Africans endures in the present. From the perspective of a contemporary African, the Columbian Quincentenary was no cause for celebration.

Yet I knew that for other people, including many in the audience, the Columbus anniversary was a symbolic occasion for celebration. For many, especially those of European ancestry, colonization of the North and South American continents was opportunity. For them Ellis Island and the stirring inscription on the Statue of Liberty were subsequent acts in a drama that began with Columbus's first voyage. "Poor Columbus," I thought, "still at the vortex of controversy." But Columbus was not going to feel the consequences of this debate, and what he did or did not do would not be altered by this discussion. This discussion about the meaning of the past was really about the present, about our narratives, about the kind of nation and people we are now and will be in the future.

After the African student's comments, I invited comments and questions from the audience, expecting divergent opinions that might result in heated debate. A middle-aged woman raised her hand. She stood and addressed her question to the student from Ghana. "Young man," she pointedly asked, "are you telling me that America is a mistake?" He stood up to the microphone. "It depends," he quietly but firmly responded. I did not have such poise or wisdom at his young age. The woman asked the next obvious question: "Upon what does it depend?" "It depends," he said, "upon what happens next." This perceptive answer successfully defused what might have become a polarized and explosive confrontation.

The audience conversation continued for an hour, and it focused on the question posed by the young exchange student. What should happen next? What is the next chapter? How do we make this a good story? A conversation that began with a discussion of events five hundred years in the past was now a conversation about the future. No one in the audience questioned the veracity of anyone else. Disparate points of view were acknowledged and employed as the starting point for dialogue. No one said to the young man from Ghana that Africans engaged in the slave trade in collusion with European slavers; intuitively audience members understood that this was not the question. No one said that Indians warred with each other and often allied themselves with European invaders against traditional enemies. Such comments were beside the point. The real point was to shape a story that would build bridges, heal wounds of division.

How do we construct narratives that acknowledge the perspectives of all who are Americans? Is there a story in which all of these points of view can coexist? How do we accord ownership to all who once lived here, live here now, and will live here in the future? How do we reconnect past, present, and future? The task requires that all of us acknowledge the parallel existence of incongruent narratives that interpret the same events very differently. It demands recognition of multiple perspectives on the past and a shared ownership of the past in which no one perspective prevails. America is after all a work in progress. The meaning of the past, as the young man so succinctly expressed, is contingent upon the present and the future.

This conversation about the effects of the European conquest of the Americas is a metaphor for me because it raised many of the issues with which public historians must be concerned. History is not a museum static and unchanging, nor unassailable fact dispensed to passive audiences. History is about narratives that establish identity, stories that acknowledge differences and seek common ground. It is a conversation about burdens and legacies. The conversation cannot be an exclusive one if it is to be useful, because such exclusivity is a perpetuation of our burdens, an extension of insiders who write the stories and outsiders who are dispossessed victims. If the Native American point of view was not incorporated into the Quincentenary forum, the conversation would have lacked a crucial ingredient.

But incongruent narratives have causes other than race, culture, and ethnicity. The exhibition on the B-29 *Enola Gay* and the explosion of atomic bombs over Hiroshima and Nagasaki at the Smithsonian Institution's Air and Space Museum is a case in point. The exhibition raised issues of patriotism, the American character, the significance of World War II, sacrifices of veterans, ambiguities of technology, and at its core a contest over the kind of nation we will be in the future. Politicians, historians, veterans, curators, and administrators sparred with each other over content and interpretation, and the internal and external disagreements and irreconcilable conflicts led to the cancellation of the planned exhibition and the subsequent substitution of a truncated version that avoided contentious moral issues and muzzled legitimate historical debate. Despite the reduction of the exhibit, the central and most provocative artifact, the *Enola Gay*, was included. Some people argued that because only part of the airplane was exhibited, its impact was diminished. But for me the central artifact is that portion of the fuselage that includes the bomb bay, out of which the atomic age descended upon the planet. Those gaping doors are symbolic enough.

I often travel to Washington, D.C., on business. On one trip, with a few spare hours, I headed over to Air and Space and the *Enola Gay* exhibition. I found the information on the conservation of the aircraft innocuous, even superfluous, a reaction I probably share with most visitors. Then I stood and stared at the aircraft fuselage, stunned by this tangible evidence of the first atomic bombing. I after all grew up in the Cold War surrounded by ominous bomb shelter signs, terrified by my own parents' panic as the Cuban Missile Crisis unfolded. Armageddon was upon us all. Yet I also remembered interviews that I had conducted in Albuquerque with survivors of the Bataan Death March; their horrifying experiences gave me an inkling of the likely bloody costs of a war in the Japanese homeland. But I also recalled my high school reading of John Hersey's *Hiroshima*: frozen shadows, mass incineration, gruesome death. I cannot imagine any greater horror. My most powerful feeling was deep regret that this box was opened at all and anger at those scientists who believe that science is a neutral quest for knowledge.

I paused in a corner of the exhibition area near the fuselage and watched visitors. Two women, obviously strangers to each other, bent down and peered into the bomb bay. From her language and manner, I judged one woman to be an American, probably a tourist. The other woman I presumed to be a Japanese tourist, both from her physical appearance and because she spoke little English. "How do you feel when you look here?" asked the American. This question launched a conversation, communicated through gestures, a few English words in common, and eloquent body language, that continued for at least ten minutes and soon gathered a coterie of interested listeners.

This amazing exchange became a modified reiteration of the Columbian Quincentenary forum as the women sought and found their common ground confronting this artifact that symbolized and conveyed a host of emotions and events. I took great pleasure in the discussion because it encompassed the very conversation that the exhibition's successful opponents worked so hard to exclude. The two women disparaged war, shared remorse at tragedy, and agreed that the legacy of the bomb haunted humanity and threatened our entire species with extinction. They did not denigrate the contributions of veterans, nor did they tally the potential costs of an invasion of Japan. They did not discuss these topics. They searched for a common understanding, a shared story to interpret the bomb that fell down out of this door, and they found one.

Many historians were appalled at the efforts to squash the *Enola Gay* exhibition and viewed mandated changes in its interpretive content as a threat to intellectual freedom and the first step in creeping censorship. Shrill and dire predictions were the hot topics of books, articles, and presentations at professional meetings. In *History Wars'* opening essay, "Anatomy of a Controversy," Edward Linenthal quotes Michael Kammen, then president of the Organization of American Historians. Kammen called attention to a "vindictive partnership that prompts elected officials to punish (or threaten to punish) their foes by withholding public funds. . . . Historians become controversial when they do not perpetuate myths, when they do not transmit the received and conventional wisdom, when they challenge the comforting presence of a stabilized past."[2] *History Wars,* edited by Edward Linenthal and Tom Englehardt, includes "Culture War, History Front," an essay written by Mike Wallace. Wallace writes that "in the event of future *Enola Gays*, professional bodies should launch their own investigations. If such inquiries find that an institution has operated in compliance with generally accepted standards, and been subjected to unwarranted harassment, then the entire community should speak out vigorously on its behalf. . . . If all else fails, and we are faced with more shuttered galleries, we may have to consider borrowing methods other dissidents have found useful."[3]

While the warning flags were necessary cautions and calls to arms useful, they were an overreaction. They presume that the political nonsense "inside the beltway" is an indicator of a national loss of common sense. (I do not think so.) This response also reveals the insecurities of many historians. This is a hard time for some professional historians. Many Americans now seek to make sense of their own pasts oblivious to the assertions of exclusive authority made by the professionals. While I think that it is vital that we oppose censorship of exhibitions, I am convinced that there are conversations that we need to have among ourselves. Those conversations ought to focus on the issue of authority and the explicit bases upon which the legitimacy of historical interpretation may be judged.

As I listen to the screeches of indignation from professional historians, I think of the two women staring into the gaping bomb bay of the *Enola Gay*. I can hear them talking. I am enheartened.

Artifacts are evocative when visitors possess enough information to connect the object to the concerns of their own lives. The Statue of Liberty, the White House, the battleship *Missouri*, Ford's Theater, and smaller objects such as an original diary of the Lewis and Clark Expedition are evocative. The *Enola Gay* is also an evocative artifact. Most living Americans grew up in the dismal and frightening shadows of the atomic bombings at Hiroshima and Nagasaki. Most living Americans remember the terrifying nuclear competition of the Cold War. We remember the clock that still calculates the chances of a nuclear holocaust in a stark chronological countdown. Thus the *Enola Gay* does not require extensive interpretation. The outcome of the historical and political debates did not have an impact on the experience of the two women near the gleaming fuselage of this aircraft that symbolized the worst fears of generations of Americans, and perhaps of the earth's entire human population. Objects such as this one are profound stimuli for historical conversations that no politician, veteran, or historian can prevent or control. Visitors are capable of interpreting it for themselves. Their own lives provide the context that assigns meanings.

But sometimes in public history, participants lack context and therefore cannot engage in conversation. A group of African-American St. Louisans recently got together with staff of the Missouri Historical Society. This group is assisting us in the interpretation that will be presented in an exhibition entitled *Seeking St. Louis*. At this particular session they were looking at a painting called *The Last Slave Sale*. In the painting the slaves are standing on the top steps of the Old Court House, which is still there on Fourth Street in downtown St. Louis. The auctioneer is ready, and a number of white people have gathered in the street below the steps. We asked the audience to write down their reactions to the painting. They were ambivalent. Then the curator provided contextual details. "The man who painted this," she said, "was an ex-soldier, a Confederate who, after the Civil War, bitterly concluded that he had fought on the side of injustice. He spent the balance of his life painting scenes like this one depicting his view of the abomination of slavery. There is," she continued, "a civic tradition in St. Louis that on that day, the white audience refused to participate, effectively canceling the sale. This was not a slave sale," she concluded, "but rather a public protest against the sale of slaves in St. Louis."

The man seated next to me leaned toward me. "If you exhibit the painting," he urged, "you must tell the story." I agree. Public historians provide context in which pertinent meanings can be deciphered. The meaning of this painting changes dramatically when people know the context. Then this painting is transformed from one more appalling reminder of the bitter experience of slavery into a symbol of resistance to injustice. Ironically the event depicted in the painting cannot be historically verified; there is no hard historical evidence that this protest against slave auctions actually occurred. But perhaps it does not matter. Perhaps the most important fact is that St. Louisans want to believe the story. The persistence of the story, in itself evidence of resistance to slavery and injustice, reveals the better side of our natures. Interpretations of the past that fail the test of historical evidence still have real consequences. I am reminded of Tony Lucero and the horses.

In other instances visitors bring different levels of context and hence varying perspectives to the conversation. A cart, painted with bright red and green enamel, is for the moment in large-object storage. The vertically mounted grinding stone may be the only factory-made part in its construction. The rest of it seems makeshift. There is a gasoline or kerosene can strategically attached over the sharpening stone so that water can drip on the stone through a crude handcrafted spigot protruding from the can's bottom rim. Handles with castoff bicycle handgrip covers allowed the operator to push the entire apparatus cantilevered like a wheelbarrow on two well-worn carriage wheels. When the contraption was parked, the owner sat on a wooden bar between the handles and turned the stone by pushing his feet up and down on two pedals. The attached umbrella can be opened to protect the operator from sun or rain. Anyone with a little mechanical inclination can tell that this quaint machine was designed as a portable device for sharpening blades, but without firsthand knowledge it is not possible to ascertain much more. There is a sign attached to the cart: *Hand and Power Lawnmowers–Knives–Scissors–Tools Sharpened–3931 Schiller Place–Ph. 481-7952.*

The cart is one of my favorite objects. I am attracted to it because of the story it symbolizes and because it dramatically demonstrates the distinction between antiques and historically significant objects. As I take small groups through the storage areas, we pause and look at this strange device. No one wants the cart in the front hall or living room. It has little antique market value. But often I see wistful smiles and even an occasional tear of nostalgic recognition as people look at the device. "That's Tony's Scissors Cart." Tony Gagliarducci immigrated from Italy to St. Louis in the early 1920s to join other members of his family who were already settled in the city. He worked in his brother's restaurant until 1924, when he began his sharpening business, pushing his 250-pound "scissors cart" up and down the streets of his city. The red and green colors reflected his pride in his Italian ancestry. For sixty years Gagliarducci pushed his cart and rang his bell in search of blunted instruments—from hardware stores, beauty parlors, barber and butcher shops, and private households—which he returned with finely honed edges. In the fall of 1988, Gagliarducci and his family donated the cart to the Missouri Historical Society. Tony Gagliarducci has since died.

For those who remember Tony and his cart, the connection is emotional and immediate. I can detect it in faces, wisp of tears, and words. This artifact takes them to another place and time. They recall life in the old neighborhood. They see people and places now gone, and they mourn the people, the places, and their former selves while reveling in the memories. They contemplate and evaluate change. But for others, Tony's cart carries no such meanings. Yet once they have the context, they do evaluate change—the decline of neighborhood life, increased crime rates, the disappearance of businesses like Tony's conducted face to face with friends and neighbors. And they all recognize that Tony and his cart were an integral stitch in

"This artifact takes them to another place and time. . . Tony and his cart were an integral stitch in the neighborhood tapestry." (Tony Gagliarducci's cart. Larry George, Southside Journal, 1983, courtesy of the Missouri Historical Society.)

the neighborhood tapestry. Not all agree on how to interpret the interval of change between Tony's neighborhood and the places where people now live. The cart's meanings are ambiguous. What is progress? Are new neighborhoods improvements over the old? Is life better or worse? Tony and the cart are symbols of important issues if relevant questions are asked, if the cart is set in appropriate contexts.

We facilitate the discovery of common ground. Multiple perspectives on enduring issues are our business, and the potential importance of our work extends beyond forums, exhibitions, and the other venues and methods we use to engage the public in dialogue. The enduring issues that often rest uneasily on the civic table are clouded by an inability of some people to acknowledge that when perspectives differ no one is necessarily wrong or even stretching the truth. If it is the task of the public historian to provide context in which differing points of view can be explored, diversity acknowledged, empathy inculcated, dialogue facilitated, and common ground defined, then we must be seated at that table when important issues are discussed and consensus pursued. If we abstain, we ignore the implications of the past and we undermine our legitimate claim to society's support. The process of seeking common ground is also the process of composing good narratives in which all can find themselves represented. Only through this process can the civic enterprise proceed and communities flourish.

Scholars from diverse disciplines, journalists, politicians, and others have contributed to a recent, copious, and growing literature on civic disengagement. Some examine the decline in membership in community organizations like service clubs and bowling leagues. Others point to ever lower turnouts of voters. Author Todd Gitlin describes the splintering of America in *The Twilight of Common Dreams: Why America Is Wracked by Culture Wars*. "Still," Gitlin claims, "we will not see what lies on the other side of the politics of identity unless, unflinchingly, without illusions, we look, look again, and are willing to go on looking. For too long, too many Americans have busied themselves digging trenches to fortify their cultural borders, lining their trenches with insulation. Enough bunkers! Enough of the perfection of differences! We ought to be building bridges."[4]

The problem is more invasive than just a tribalization of Americans into identity groups divided by cultural battle lines. In *The Cynical Society: The Culture of Politics and Politics of Culture in American Life*, Jeffrey Goldfarb explores the origins of debilitating mutual distrust that fortifies divisions. "Cynicism in our world is a form of legitimation through disbelief," Goldfarb asserts. "There exists an odd but by now common practice. Leaders use rhetorics which neither they nor their constituents believe, but which both leaders and followers nonetheless use to justify their actions."[5]

We are adept and well practiced at recognizing difference and unfortunately expert at acknowledging what we do not share. Several years ago the Missouri Historical Society sponsored a forum on the court-ordered voluntary school desegregation program that was mandated to ameliorate the resegregation of the region's schools caused by white flight from the City of St. Louis. The forum attracted black and white lawyers, parents, teachers, administrators, and students, from urban and suburban schools. Initially people in the audience were suspicious and distrustful; they expected dissension and hostility. And indeed that was the tenor as the conversation began. But the mood shifted as common ground began to emerge. What we shared, and what compelled all of us to show up at all, was a common concern for children, a conviction that all children deserved equal access to educational opportunity. Once this common concern, amid the recognition of severe difference, was acknowledged, the conversation shifted from acrimonious debate over busing to a discussion of how to provide the best opportunities for high-quality education for all children.

However, the process of seeking common ground as the basis for action can be extremely rancorous. A few years ago St. Louis Mayor Freeman Bosley recognized Forest Park as both a symbol of civic importance and a victim of urban neglect. Forest Park, established in 1876 on St. Louis's western boundary with more than 1,100 acres, is a special piece of urban real estate. It is one of few places in the region where all citizens loosen the boundaries of race, politics, age, work, and education and mingle on a basis of relative equality. It is a good place, amenable to informal association and conducive to dispelling mistrust. But the park was shabby, crumbling in spots, desperately in need of some care and renovation. Mayor Bosley, the city's first African American in that office, appointed a committee to gather public opinion and formulate a plan for the park's renovation. I was a member of the executive committee of the Forest Park Master Plan Committee. More than two years later, after more than two hundred meetings involving thousands of citizens, we had developed a plan. We did not have consensus, but we did have enough agreement to proceed. To accomplish even this we struggled with the nexus of Forest Park's past, present expectations for the park, and future hopes and fears.

I cannot estimate the number of permutations and combinations of citizen perspectives on the park. Racism seemed to prevail; political boundaries reinforced racial divisions. Some African Americans displayed an attitude that "now it is our park." Environmental advocates wanted cars out of the park, further construction prohibited, and at the environmentalist fringes some people espoused a fuzzy notion that the park ought to be wilderness. For these earnest people with overriding concerns for the human impact on the global environment, the park plan was a battleground in which compromise was anathema. Some city residents questioned the right of county residents to even participate in the process, inadvertently reflecting the costly decision made over one hundred years ago to politically split the city from the county. Each interest group, and there were dozens, distrusted all the others and, convinced of a lack of honesty on everyone else's part, suspected one another's motives. Although a plan with substantial agreement emerged, distrust, suspicions, name calling, and sly sabotage threatened to scuttle the effort on repeated occasions. The common ground was elusive.

The process was drawn out, cumbersome, frustrating, and often seemed about to fail. But it did work. It would have been faster and simpler to gather a small group of like-minded people and devise a plan for the park. But such a plan would have failed even if it was identical to the one adopted. The product of an exclusive process will not be publicly palatable no matter how impressive its merits. Process matters, and in the future public process will have to account for multiple perspectives. Public policy can only evolve from a common story, which is to say some agreement on what kind of park, or community, we want. The story must evolve from past experience, and it must be inclusive. The development of public policy cannot afford to exclude points of view, nor can the process of narrative construction.

While I am involved in many civic endeavors, I find that one of the most rewarding is my involvement with Citizens for Modern Transit, a citizen-based coalition that advocates expansion of light rail within the St. Louis Metropolitan Region. My initial interest came from my conviction that automobiles were choking us with pollutants and congestion. Gradually I recognized that there is more to it: that mass transit is an issue of race and class, of land use, population density, infrastructure cost, taxation, urban design, and the development of livable places for people. Every one of these is an enduring historical issue, and citizens' perspectives on each are conditioned by the past, by present definitions of the "good life," and by anticipation of the future consequences of contemporary decisions.

I was president of Citizens for Modern Transit for three years. My continued involvement in light rail and mass transit advocacy is drawn from my concern for the decline in American civic and community life and the insidious threat to democracy that is its consequence. We need better places, and we must forge common agreement on their attributes.

Several years ago I gave a keynote address to a national conference on mass transit. Part of my assignment was to explain to the conference participants why an eccentric historian was involved in this kind of advocacy. I tried to provide them with historical perspective on issues related to mass transit and community life. I told them that while some people would argue that light rail is a solution to the ills of sprawling metropolitan regions and a means of reduction in airborne pollutants, we ought to remember that streetcars, trolleys, interurbans, and commuter trains were the initial impetus for sprawl.

The technology is neutral; how we use it reflects our values. We can use light rail and other technologies to either exacerbate or ameliorate this prodigal waste of resources, relationships, and heritage, and the escalating mortgage on the planet that threatens to be our legacy to the unborn. Whether or not light rail can reverse decades of urban abandonment depends on how it is used and whether it is matched with changes in tax laws and zoning policies.

When I look at the desolate and abandoned places in my city, I know that something has been irretrievably lost. It is not just the bricks on the pallets near the demolition sites that are lost. (Those bricks become the garages and patios in the exurban meccas where cars rule and exacerbate our alienation from each other.) A priceless legacy from the past is discarded with every demolition. Relationships are sundered and forgotten. We lose community and we lose roots. The communities we have abandoned are irreplaceable resources as surely as the fossil fuels consumed in the process of abandonment and replacement. We surrender reminders of connections to those who have gone before us, and we are increasingly confined to life in a bare and chilly present, disconnected from the past and heedless of the future. What will we leave our grandchildren to replace what we have demolished?

History is not a museum, and it does have implications. So now I have left my protective pedestal of historical objectivity and become an advocate with an agenda. Yes, I have, and that is the whole point. Those of us who are history's practitioners have much to set on the civic table, within our institutions and as individuals. All of us, and all human beings, have different perspectives on the meaning of life, the pursuit of happiness, and the character of good places, on justice, liberty, and equality. Yet for all these differences, we seek to build a civilized life and a just society, and that depends on finding common ground, for there we discover we have shared aspirations that can only be pursued in concert. We acknowledge, even celebrate, diversity but in concentrating on our common ground we find an American identity without which we merely inhabit the same space on the planet. Our work is to facilitate the recognition of multiple perspectives, of the diversity that is our birthright, but then to embrace our common humanity and shared destinies as the only basis for united action.

NOTES

[1] Alexis de Toqueville, *Democracy in America, vol. II* (New York: Random House, Inc., 1990), p. 99.

[2] Edward Linenthal, "Anatomy of a Controversy" in *History Wars*, Edward Linenthal and Tom Englehardt, eds. (New York: Metropolitan Books, Henry Holt and Company, 1996), p. 60.

[3] Mike Wallace, "Culture War, History Front" in *History Wars*, Edward Linenthal and Tom Englehardt, eds. (New York: Metropolitan Books, Henry Holt and Company, 1996), p. 197.

[4] Todd Gitlin, *The Twilight of Common Dreams: Why America Is Wracked by Culture Wars* (New York: Henry Holt and Company, Inc., 1995), p. 237.

[5] Jeffrey Goldfarb, *The Cynical Society: The Culture of Politics and Politics of Culture in American Life* (Chicago: The University of Chicago Press, 1991), p. 1.

⌖6⌖

Values at the Core

History is the conversation through which we construct narratives incorporating multiple perspectives to explain the past, evaluate the present, and project the future. But are all perspectives equally valid and hence worthy of incorporation into the narrative? What about perspectives that erupt with bigotry and hatred or advocate degradation of women or undermine the scientific evidence on human despoliation of our planet? Aren't there voices that ignore the fundamentals of human decency and minimize or deny the higher spiritual needs of humans? What of the viewpoints that would justify greed, cruelty, injustice, selfishness, intolerance? These perspectives demand condemnation, not uncritical acceptance. They must be included in the narrative but only so that they can be examined and exposed. And what about perspectives embedded in our culture, such as an implicit confidence in the power of science and technology to ameliorate the worst consequences of human behavior? This kind of attitude toward environmental dangers and damage can lull us into inaction and ease our responsibilities—and inflict long-term disasters on the quality and even the endurance of human life on earth. Such perspectives must be made explicit, then critically examined and cautiously weighed.

Before I moved to St. Louis in 1988, I had not lived in a large American city with nineteenth-century industrial roots. Albuquerque, where I had lived for seven years in the 1970s, was a modest city then, a post-World War II boom town fueled by a temperate climate and the defense spending escalating with Cold War fears. Racism simmered, despoiling relationships between the Anglos and the disparate Hispanic and native peoples. But racism in New Mexico did not seem as endemic to me, perhaps because of my own naiveté. I had no preparation for the pervasive, pernicious racism of St. Louis where politics, school funding, planning, zoning, housing, arts and entertainment, economics, and infrastructure decisions are all infested with suspicion and lurking anger. St. Louis is not atypical. But I have come to think that it is a better place than some comparable cities because of a general acknowledgment of the economic and social cost exacted by endemic racism and a growing community resolve to remedy racism's worst effects. It is not that St. Louis is a more caring place, but rather that community leaders recognize that the societal costs of racist behavior are paid, not just by its obvious victims, but by everyone.

This place has at least two parallel histories. Not long ago I attended a small meeting of African-American community leaders and some well-intentioned regional business executives. My role was to bridge the chasm of misunderstanding. At that meeting we began the process of reconciling the past. What began as a conversation about economic opportunity led inexorably to an extensive dialogue about why African Americans and whites had such incongruous perspectives on the region's past. It was starkly apparent that, although we live in the same place and face the same problems and opportunities, we do live in separate worlds and our perspectives are determined by very different pasts. When white business leaders think of this place's past, the St. Louis' 1904 World's Fair looms into mind. African-American leaders are aware of the fair, but its meanings are different for them. African Americans know that one of the fair's objectives was to reinforce white attitudes of racial superiority, not only toward African Americans but toward all people of color. While white St. Louisans remember the fair as the most prominent event in their place's early-twentieth-century past, African Americans think of the East St. Louis race riots of 1917, an event most whites have obliviously neglected.

Miles Davis grew up in East St. Louis and learned his music there and also over on the west side of the Mississippi River. Miles Davis knew of:

> . . . black workers replacing white workers in the packing houses. So, the white workers got mad and went on a rampage killing all them black people. That same year black men were fighting in World War I to help the United States save

the world for democracy. They sent us to war to fight and die for them over there; killed us like nothing over here. And it's still like that today. . . . Anyway, maybe some of remembering that is in my personality and comes out in the way I look at most white people. Not all, because there are some great white people. But the way they killed all them black people back them—just shot them down like they were out shooting pigs or stray dogs. Shot them in their houses, shot babies and women. Burned down houses with people in them and hung some black men from lampposts. Anyway, black people there who survived used to talk about it. When I was coming up in East St. Louis, black people I knew never forgot what sick white people had done to them back in 1917.[1]

I am a great fan of Miles Davis' haunting jazz. This music is a glimpse of our soul. When I want to understand more about my city, I listen to these beautiful sounds. Not only do white St. Louisans *not* celebrate the achievements of this marvelously creative and internationally acclaimed musician, most of us do not even know that he is one of us. We ignore this beautiful part of who we are. Based on race, we amputate some of the best of ourselves. Of course, to acknowledge that Miles Davis is one of us is to bridge a deep river boundary and jettison attitudes that are enduring historical burdens. The burden will remain to infest the future unless all of us here recognize that to be a St. Louisan, to be an American, is to be part African American. We cannot be whole and healthy and deny this centerpiece of our American legacy. But to do this we will have to incorporate what happened in East St. Louis in 1917 and acknowledge the daily insults and injustices that are also a part of our legacy. This is the African-American past, a parallel history.

In 1997 an increase in sales tax funding for mass transit, specifically for light rail expansion, was on the ballot in the city and county of St. Louis. Even this worthy proposal was polluted with racism. Residents of some predominantly white neighborhoods opposed the tax increase because they felt that light rail would bring "undesirables" to their neighborhoods. At the time I was the president of Citizens for Modern Transit, a primary advocate for passage of the tax increase. I recorded radio commercials, participated in call-in radio programs, wrote "commentary" pieces for newspapers urging approval, and was frequently quoted in St. Louis' only daily, the *Post-Dispatch*. I received racist hate mail. The language was vicious, irrational, and disgusting. I would, if I could, dismiss these people as "nuts" but there are too many of them.

Most of us are disgusted by what happened in East St. Louis in 1917, and most of us despise the content of that mail I received. We condemn such destructive behavior, and so do responsible historians. But on what basis? Can we dismiss such behavior on the basis of personal likes and dislikes? Is our horror at the actions of Adolph Hitler caused by our not "liking" his slaughter of millions of people? I think not. Whether we are explicit about underlying values or not, we condemn such behavior with reference to deeply held convictions of right and wrong.

Some actions and the perspectives upon which they are based have disastrous consequences for humanity; even long ago events continue to extract a price from present generations. Understanding cause and effect is central to the historical process. History, with the advantage of hindsight, is a process of examining consequences. Yet why bother with consequences unless judgments follow? Judgments, which allow us to change ourselves, redefine our relationships, improve future prospects through understanding, empathy, and ultimately forgiveness and reconciliation, are implicit in the historical process.

Who decides which perspectives and what actions are worthy of emulation? I am moving onto difficult ground. The only way to evaluate perspectives that are good or evil or ambiguous and discriminate among them is through application of a standard measurement. By whatever name the standards are known, they imply values, ethics, and principles that are not relative. Absolute values are unpopular these days; past pronouncements of absolutes, like doctrines that upheld slavery, racism, subjugation of women, or prodigal consumption of resources, have frequently justified inhumane and destructive behavior. But a denial that we can know anything for certain, including the difference between right and wrong, is precisely the source of the pervasive malaise of this "postmodern age." We cannot dodge the issue by insisting that history is just "facts" and that the historian is impartial. It is time to be explicit about values and in doing so provide the antidote to postmodern relativism.

Values have always been implied in the work of practitioners in every discipline. Historical interpretation expresses and exposes the values held by the interpreter. Historians, like everyone else, view the past through the prisms of their own experiences, even if that prism is one of disciplinary objectivity, as in my initial skepticism of Tony Lucero's horse narrative. Although a point of view in a historical work is rarely explicit, I have never encountered a historical work without one. The varying interpretations of the significance of the Lewis and Clark Expedition or the causes of the American Revolution immediately come to mind. Most historians balk at arguing for the universality of the values that underpin our work. But acknowledgment of values does make history useful, for it is the basis upon which we recognize the implications of the past, make sense of human experience, and project a better future.

And we cannot dismiss universal values with accusations of "presentism," which is the imposition of contemporary standards in judgment of the past. This is not what I mean by values. I do not imply that we ought to judge Thomas Jefferson's enslavement of Africans by the standards of today or have Christopher Columbus stand at the bar of historical judgment for the consequences of the European conquest, settlement, and exploitation of the new world. History is not a search for heroes and villains nor assignment of credit and blame. I cannot judge the actions of past humans who acted in the contexts of their own times, but from the perspective of the present I must acknowledge that human enslavement and the conquest of the Americas both had pernicious consequences; and I must advise that the cultural values that justified them be rooted out. I know what neither Jefferson nor Columbus ever knew: I know what happened next. We must learn that human beliefs and actions have consequences, both intended and unintended. We must learn to consider and evaluate all consequences based on broad principles drawn from past experience, the only guide we have. Our retreat into relativism and even cynicism is a comprehensible reaction to events of the twentieth century. But for the sake of ourselves and for the well being of those who will follow, it is time to get over it. If we cannot, we imperil humanity. History does have implications, and ignorance of both history and its implications is foolhardy.

The twentieth century was launched with an aura of eager hope. The great world's fairs of the late nineteenth and early twentieth century are accurate barometers of optimism. These grand show-pieces exuded optimism in stark contrast with today's lurking fear that the world is out of control, the future unpredictable, and that the individual can do little to correct it. In my own city of St. Louis people still look wistfully and nostalgically backward to the Louisiana Purchase Exposition of 1904. While the event was undeniably grand, with electric lights, alabaster buildings, crystal fountains, and millions of ecstatically pleased visitors, what is most appealing to our contemporaries is the confidence, albeit racist, ethnocentric, and jingoistic, of the glorious spectacle. Like other fairs of the period, the 1904 World's Fair was postulated on the existence of a rational world that could be improved and even perfected through science and technology and the "blessings of civilization" by means of western-style institutions either imposed or voluntarily adopted. However, the optimism with which the century began was undermined by gloomy cynicism by the end of the century. Two bloody World Wars, wrenching economic depression in the western democracies, the Holocaust, the atomic bomb, and the Cold War fractured our earlier hope and confidence, and the assumption that direction and meaning can be discovered in the past was pessimistically challenged.

The consequence has been the ascendancy of individualism, intemperate materialism, and self-gratification at the expense of all else. In *Thinking With History: Explorations in the Passage to Modernism*, Carl Schorske explains that "two World Wars dealt a series of blows to the confidence that Western liberal culture, especially American culture, had placed in history as the scene of progress, of collective, rational self-realization. With the loss of faith in progress, history was also weakened as a mode of understanding the various domains of human culture from the arts to the economy. The ties to the past were weakened. Although the complex process of breaking from tradition in the arts and other branches of elite culture reaches back into the nineteenth century, it was accelerated by the crisis of progress."[2] In *History without a Subject: The Postmodern*

Condition, David Ashley chronicles the conversion of history into images disconnected from the past and thus into a commodity with little meaning, its only worth determined in the marketplace.[3] I think of Ashley's thesis as I sit in theme restaurants or see television commercials that wrap products in a representation of the past with a view of a long-gone generic American main street, or even when I listen to the arguments for "cultural tourism" in which the worth of history and culture is debased to its value as a marketable commodity, the presumption being that only with a market can there be value. In *The Twilight of Common Dreams: Why America is Wracked by Culture Wars,* Todd Gitlin associates the dilemma with the idea of "America as a force for individual freedom, and that of the left as a force for equality." These ideas, he argues, "arose from the same stock, these beliefs in progress and redemption: rival claimants to the heritage of freedom, equality, and the rest of the promises of the modern world. During their battered—and battering—histories they have provided pictures of the whole, offered meanings for sacrifice, laid out compass points for a turning world, promised that human beings could take hold of their own destinies and, together, transcend blood and accident and economic station and become more than themselves, more, even, than their local communities, members of something encompassing and enduring."[4] So here we are, sundered from our past, detached from the future, isolated from each other, and bereft of optimism, confidence, and even hope. Postmodernism rests uneasily on the wreck of history.

As we abandoned the past as a source of direction we embraced science and technology, and now for many these twins are the new faith, the new source of values. Once the cultural confidence of the 1904 Louisiana Purchase Exposition was undermined all that persisted was the period's conviction that science and technology would feed the poor, heal the sick, produce unimaginable marvels, and result in happier, more prosperous people. Scientific faith is embedded in our culture, our economy, and our expectations for the future, even though we may not be conscious of its presence. Faith in science prompts many of us to expect that miracle cures will ultimately solve those problems of our own making such as overpopulation, environmental degradation, inadequate food supplies and dependence upon finite fossil fuels. While science may indeed alleviate some problems, we can expect, based on past performance, that it will generate as many difficulties as it solves. In order to effect fundamental change, we must modify our own behavior. But we cling tenaciously to science and technology as the one arena where we remain uncritically confident that progress is possible.

Thomas Lynch is an undertaker but he is also an author and poet. In the midst of my own writing I take time to read and reflect. A friend and colleague gave me a copy of Lynch's book, *The Undertaking: Life Studies From the Dismal Trade*, which, given the title, I set aside on the night stand. But it is more than light fare. This man whose business is care of the dead does his work because of his profound reverence for life and because of his anxiety about what we have done to our souls and our ability to make ethical judgments. We are confused about science and technology. Technology can "tell us How It Works but not What It Means," Lynch observes. He points to our embarrassment at making judgments between what is right and what is wrong. "In the name of diversity," he writes, "any idea is regarded as worthy as any other; any nonsense is entitled to a forum, a full hearing and equal time. Reality is customized to fit the person or the situation. There is *your* reality and *my* reality, truth as *they* see it, but what is real and true for us all eludes us."[5] What Lynch describes in eloquent terms is the timid essence of postmodernism and the cult of confidence in the experts to fix our dilemmas. When values become relative, there are no values, and we are left with no guideposts that allow us to seek the common good in concert with each other. So we leave it to scientists to seek truth.

Physicist Stephen Hawking is a brilliant physicist with a marvelous facility for explaining complexities to non-experts. I have relied extensively upon his lucid explanations of complicated topics at the theoretical boundaries of contemporary physics. But his exclusive faith that all the mysteries of the universe will be explained by science frightens me because finally in Hawking's logic man does become the measure of all things, existing in a universe bereft of meanings beyond those human beings assign. In this world the only absolutes, the only truths, are those expressed in scientific theory. I know that there is more to existence, that humans require values that are neither relative nor open to scientific scrutiny. But in *A Brief History of Time: From the Big Bang to Black Holes*, Hawking concludes that "so long as the universe had a beginning we could suppose that it had a creator. But if the Universe is really self-contained, having no boundary or edge, it would have neither beginning or end: it would simple be. What place, then, for a creator?"[6] In conclusion he equivocates on the matter of the existence of the deity. He exposes his belief that ultimately scientists will discover a "theory of everything," the unified theory, the philosopher's stone of our age, that will be broadly comprehensible to humans, not just specialists. "Then," he says, "we shall all, philosophers, scientists, and just ordinary people, be able to take part in the discussion of the question of why it is that we and the universe exist. If we find the answer to that, it would be the ultimate triumph of human reason—for then we would know the mind of God."[7] Physicist Paul Davies goes even further in *God and the New Physics*. "I began," he writes, "by making the claim that science offers a surer path than religion in the search of God. It is my deep conviction that only by understanding the world in all its many aspects—reductionist and holist, mathematical and poetical, through forces, fields, and particles as well as through good and evil—that we will come to understand ourselves and the meaning behind the universe, our home."[8]

Several years ago I spoke to a group of university graduate students and faculty in Kansas. My comments assessed the limits of science and argued that solutions depended upon people, that in order to solve the issues of our day such as environmental degradation or family and community disintegration we must adopt value systems that compel us to change our behavior. Several faculty anthropologists took vocal issue both with my lack of faith in science and my insistence upon values and ethics, rather than scientific theory, as the basis for modified behavior. The problem of science is that while it may provide explanations and solutions, science cannot determine what is good for us, what is right and wrong, beautiful or ugly, and how to tell the difference. This scientific faith has permitted many humans to opt out and refuse to accept the consequences of their own behavior. I have listened to executives of biotechnology firms insist that problems of overpopulation and inadequate food supply can be solved with genetically engineered foods. The message is that we ought not worry about such things. Watch any evening's diet of television advertising, and you will be urged multiple times to have faith in science, technology, and the free market to improve the health of humanity, repair damage to the planet, produce unlimited foodstuffs, make us all happy, and guarantee an infinite supply of resources from a finite planet to sustain us. The message is outrageously irresponsible. It disenfranchises those who listen because it tells them that all is well and that their behavior is not relevant. In some respects the message implies rewards for irresponsible behavior. Cleaning up the consequences of poor stewardship of our own bodies, of each other, and of the places we inhabit stimulates demand for ever newer products and makes the economy hum. I am left wondering just who is in charge. Ironically all responsible scientists who study the planet and the life it sustains tell us that if we do not change our behavior soon we face life-threatening planetary crisis.

Whenever we are tempted to believe that science joined with technology will fix what we break, we need to remember the *Enola Gay*'s gaping bomb-bay doors. We should recall the unprecedented carnage of the twentieth century's wars made possible by technologically sophisticated weaponry, the unparalleled efficiency of the "final solution," the disaster at Chernobyl, the spread of drug-resistant strains of bacteria. And I think of the pile of radioactive waste from atom bomb-making in St. Louis and the day I stood in an old St. Louis factory on a forlorn site now contaminated with asbestos and PCBs. Postmodernism is in part a consequence of the failure of science and technology to live up to promises of a better world while simultaneously enabling humans to determine the fate of life on the earth. We now have the power to kill all life slowly, or blow it up in a series of great blasts. But that is not all. We harbor grave misgivings at our newfound ability to manipulate nature: to mechanically suspend people between life and death, harvest organs from the dead, stimulate the production of cow's milk, genetically alter plants to be resistant to disease and chemical, and clone sheep in a frightening parlor trick. Stephen Hawking and other scientists may rejoin that science just seeks to know and that the use to which the knowledge is put is a separate issue. I think that scientists live on this planet, too, and as members of the species have a stake in its future and hence must assist in the evaluation of their own work. Yet I also think that the natural inquisitiveness of our species is irrepressible, so it is up to the rest of us to apply rigorous evaluation to the technologies that science makes possible. If we are fully informed, we can make judgments about the wisdom of specific technologies and how, or if, we will make use of them.

Most of us have misgivings about the atomic bomb, and many of us wish that it could be crammed back in the box and the lid sealed. But just as insidious, although less dramatic, are seemingly innocuous technologies that we uncritically accept. Just now my phone rang. I was in mid-sentence but I stopped writing immediately to respond to its insistence. I sometimes wonder if our grandparents and great-grandparents would have so readily accepted the notion that every house ought to have a telephone if they had known every time this newfangled machine rang they would stop whatever they were doing—eating dinner with families, reading a book, making love, kneading bread, sleeping, or just gazing out the window; that nothing was so important that it would not be interrupted without notice by a jangling, persistent bell. Now we carry our cellular telephones with us. Now the expectation is that we will always "stay in touch." I read of Internet junkies who require treatment for their addictions to this global mall where anything goes. Information and wisdom are confused. And what of the neighborly conversations that took place in backyards as people hung out the wash? Or the hot evenings spent on front porches with eyes on the street instead of in artificial, air-conditioned comfort? And then of course television absorbs dozens of hours each week in passivity, consuming time that was once spent reading, visiting, playing card games or baseball, or some other socializing. There is, of course, the leisure time argument: Technology frees us from drudgery. But what does it free us to do? Watch television in isolation? Maintain households where it takes two working spouses just to make ends meet? There is no evidence that technology has truly liberated us. I am not a Luddite. My house is air-conditioned. I drive a car. If I need bypass surgery, I will be grateful for it. But why don't we get to choose how we will apply technology?

In order to do so, we will have to agree on the underlying value system upon which such choices must be based.

I was sitting in a seminar room at Washington University in St. Louis. A dozen bright architecture graduate students were around the table. I was to speak to them about community, an idea that presumably is important for those people who will be designing where we work, live, play, and shop in the future. I made an egregious error. I assumed that a community has to exist *somewhere*. So I talked about good places, the ones that encourage informal relationships, nurture mutual trust, and create a sense of common enterprise. One student raised his hand. "You use an obsolete definition of community," he said. "My community is not a place! It does not matter where I live. The people I live near are not my neighbors." "Just who are your neighbors?" I asked. "My neighbors," he responded, "are those people that I choose to associate with. I visit in my car. I send them faxes. I exchange e-mail. I call them on the telephone. I fly on weekends, and I meet them whenever I want to." He had no community of place. He saw no need for involvement with those who shared his place. "What happens when you and the people you live near have to vote on issues of common interest, like a school funding issue?" I lamely asked. I wondered, without asking, what sort of buildings he will design if relationships based on proximity are of no consequence. This young man's relationships depend on technology, not proximity. We need to discuss this new world. We should not just let it happen by default.

Without shared values and principles as a basis, we will not modify our actions. I am convinced that the most important general truths available to us are to be found in what we can know of the experiences of humanity and the conclusions that can be drawn from those eons of human experimentation. Others agree. Ecologist Murray Bookchin argues for historian Marc Bloch's "principle of hope." Bookchin sees "sweeping common problems that have besieged humanity over the ages," and he affirms the idea of historical progress.[9] He urges us to believe in the possibility of progress, and he argues against cultural relativism and pessimism. The point to the past will be lost and humanity imperiled if in our relativistic timidity we refuse to draw conclusions from the past and if we per-

sist in the belief that the tens of thousands of years of human life on
the crust of this planet have no guideposts to offer us. Neither human
nature nor the fundamental rules have changed substantially. We
have not come to the end of history; in fact, we are as much in need
of the wisdom it offers as we ever were. We control our own destinies
as individuals and social creatures by the hundreds of significant
and insignificant incremental decisions that we make each day. But
first we must decide to exchange cynicism for hope, and relativism
for the conviction that there are transcendent truths in our world if
we will but make the effort to seek them out. Change is possible, and
we are responsible.

As I spend more time in the Upper Peninsula of Michigan, the
place itself emerges in unanticipated ways. I am now imagining this
place in an updated contemporary version. Now I am connecting my
memory of that old place, still rooted in my childhood here, with
new experience in the same place. Ghosts are still here; I will not
release them, for they give continuity to my imagination and mark
my own trail through time. I have rummaged through places and
photographs imbued with personal meanings constructed more than
thirty years ago. I have lingered in cemeteries, stood on the graves
of loved ones, frantically driven over the so-familiar landscape. I have
agonized over what is gone, confronted my own aging in the gray
hairs, wrinkles, and sagging flesh of friends and relatives I have not
seen in decades. Now, finally, I have connected the past of this place
to its present. I can see underneath the change that initially startled
me with its dramatic measurement of the passage of my own life.
Now familiarity emerges and gives me reassurance, confirming my
own past and the outlines of my own memory. I hear and perhaps
have re-acquired some of that soft, lilting accent reflective of the
French, Cornish, Finnish, and Irish blend of these people, my people.
I practice the distinctive cadences, inflections, and tones. Once more
I am comfortable with the language of my youth, including my own
nickname that I left behind here.

Here we use the word "camp." In other places it might be a
cabin, a cottage, a chalet, a second home, but here anything but
camp is pretentious. Camp is a retreat once implying rustic log cabin,
well water, and outhouses, usually on a lake or a river. Now it may

be a house with running water and electricity, perhaps even pretentious and ostentatious, but it is still a camp. When I first arrived, I
said cabin. A friend reminded me that the word cabin is loaded
because here it conveys a sense that the user is not of this place and
is attempting to impress. When I used the word "cabin" even when
I modified it by explaining that I meant camp, my listener thought,
"So just who does he think he is? Not one of us, that's for sure."
Quiet intolerance of pretension is a fundamental characteristic of
this place. Now I remember.

My cousin Rhena does not live here although she spent entire
summers at her family's camp on Lake Michigamme when we were
growing up. A family row of camps was on one subsidiary arm of the
lake. Most of the camps were built of notched logs, sparse rustic
frame construction. The walls were really just modesty screens that
hid us from view but did little else except slow the wind and shed
water. Aunts, uncles, and cousins came from different places for a
summer-long family reunion. We gathered for enormous picnic
breakfasts on the beaches and randomly explored the islands. The
camps were separated by water and even miles of double-rut roads,
but all of them were in a sense satellites of my grandparents' ample
log camp, the site of family gatherings during the summer.

Many of my fondest memories center here. Much of the place
was "developed" by my father after my grandparents' death, a logical step to maximize the value of the land now owned by my father
and his siblings. Now the place is more like a special subdivision
than a retreat in the woods. (It is woods here, not forest or country.
It is another important resistance to pretension, like "camp.") Because this place was so special to me, its "development" was a poignant point of personal loss, especially since I have visited so seldom
since my final departure nearly thirty years ago. My cousin still spends
a week each summer at her family's camp with her husband and
daughters. Her daughters are nearly all grown now, and I expect
that in future years either she will not come back here or she and
her husband will come alone.

I went looking for her on a Friday afternoon. I asked my sister
to go with me. Although Anne lives in the area, she does not want
to visit this place. Perhaps her attachment was even deeper than mine

and consequently the change has been even more painful and her particular ghosts less benign. I stop at Rhena's camp. Her husband tells me that she is up the road visiting with our aunt. I go in search. The roads are all new so I have to detour to the shore to look at familiar landmarks to know where I am. After a wrong turn and a quick backtrack, I find her. We sit at my aunt's camp and visit for a few polite minutes. My cousin and I walk out, and she says that she will drop her van off at her camp and asks if we could go someplace in my car and talk. I follow her back. "Where is your favorite nearby place?" I ask as she gets into my car. She considers the question and then says, "Would you like to go to grandmother's camp?" "All right," I say with trepidation. Confronting the decay of memory places is hard for me. Grandmother's camp was sold, I know, but never reoccupied. I suspect that the purchaser bought the land as a speculation. We park and walk the few hundred yards to the abandoned

"Grandmother and Grandfather died in 1966 and the camp has been vacant since. But it stands defiantly upright—decrepit, decayed, minus doors and windows." (Grandmother's camp on Lake Superior. Photo by Sue Frisk, 1998.)

place. I think Rhena picked this place because she knew that we both needed to remember in order to reconnect with each other. She was so right.

Really I am surprised that anything remains of the place. Grandmother and Grandfather died in 1966 and the camp has been vacant since. But it stands defiantly upright—decrepit, decayed, minus doors and windows. I am glad I came. Rotted logs on the shaded, sunless side will tumble soon, and the structure will collapse. Yet in this decaying structure memories are confirmed because this place is their attachment to something independent of my mind. If it were not for this place, part of me would be a dream. It is not the only structure that is my confirmation; it is the place itself. The land rises to the campsite from the lake through swampy lowland where Forget-Me-Nots planted by my grandmother still bloom. There are rocky, low cliffs on one side of the point and a small beach on the other where in a special Upper Peninsula ritual Grandfather and I would take nude early-morning swims, with Ivory soap because it floated. This was a sudden and frigid wake up, substitute for a warm transitional bath or shower.

Rhena and I walk around the camp exterior, chattering incessantly about our own memories, confirming, expanding, clarifying. Perhaps the chattering also begs the question of whether either of us really wants to go inside. This place is a bond between the two of us and it connects us to dozens of others living and dead who are our extended family. Our memories are not gold-plated. We discuss the alcoholic free-for-alls that inevitably happened here, pitting family factions against each other. I wonder why, since these painful battles erupted at nearly every family gathering, the family still showed up for frequent re-enactments. I think that no one wanted the arguments and pledged each time that they would not let it happen again. Yet the alcohol flowed and the inevitable was repeated. "Rhena," I say, "do you want to go in?" "Yes," she softly replies.

There is not much left. Everything useful has been removed. Grandfather died in January, Grandmother in August. I was sad at their deaths but I did not know then how much had been lost and how much was buried with them. They were the family glue, the attractive force that brought us together, and their camp was the center. I did not think about it at the time that not only were they gone but that this place lost its function when they died. Carefully we climb the stairs, sidestepping debris and noting the telltale sawdust left by carpenter ants who competed with rot to claim credit for the ultimate demolition of what remained. "We were not allowed in here," Rhena said as we peered into the small room to the left of the top step. Grandmother and Grandfather's bedroom.

We left quietly. Once outside we talked about our own relationship, still solid despite long separation and distance. We walked back to the car, arms around each other's waists, telling each other how much we love each other. This was a miracle. Remembering confirms our attachments to each other. I think of Lincoln's Gettysburg phrase: "mystic chord of memory." Memory places such as this remind us of attachments to others, living and dead. We cannot live without these places, for when they are gone we live a dream with no confirmation, no validation in the world around us. Change is an immutable law. But if change is too rapid in the world around us, we are bewildered, imprisoned in the present, disconnected from those around us and making do with relationships that are fragile, unmoored, and unconfirmed. Relationships are not nurtured in undefined space and unreal cyberspace; they are created and nurtured in real, familiar places. I wonder how the architecture graduate student will feel in thirty years. I doubt that the camp will still stand when I return. The place will still be there, and perhaps some confirmation will be possible, but I am glad I came this time and that I came with Rhena. Forlornly I wish that we could all gather here one more time to heal, forgive, and reconcile. But it is far too late.

As my weeks pass in the Upper Peninsula, I spend less time in the past because I have connected it to the present where I live. I am the control experiment for my own work. Can reconnection and remembrance of one's own past heal? Yes, they do. Are memory places vital to the process? Absolutely! I spend less time in memory places, or maybe just less time thinking about them when I pass through them. They are here. I can go to them for confirmation whenever I need to. I feel a growing sense of tranquillity in this place. It is a personal reconciliation, not with another person but with my own past. My ease comes from a growing self-understanding precipitated by the linkages to different ages of myself that this place provides. This is a deep human imperative, to understand from whence we came and to connect the twists and turns of our lives in a coherent narrative. Without this, our own sense of ourselves is truncated, a book with missing chapters, random pages ripped out. But with this imperative, we can construct the narrative that encompasses the 1904 World's Fair and the East St. Louis race riots, thus acknowledging the racial corrosion that afflicts my city and only then facilitating racial reconciliation. I speculate that it is this sort of amnesia, this fractured identity that afflicts our entire nation in its ongoing paroxysm of change in which relationships, neighborhoods, and communities are transitory. Perhaps our nation needs a version of my own personal reconciliation. Memory is a universal value that establishes our humanity and creates identity both for individuals, communities, and nations. Those of us who work in public history are its unwavering and unequivocal advocates. We understand the consequences of disjunctive narrative and of the rates of change in which memory is overwhelmed and its referents obliterated. For us, memory is a core value.

But now I am drawn to places that were peripheral to my childhood. We did not visit Marquette often when I was a child, although it was only a dozen miles away. My town, Ishpeming, was then self-contained, a walking town in which necessities of life were available and concentrated within two blocks of the intersection of Main Street and Cleveland Avenue. On infrequent trips to Marquette we would take time to drive along the Lake Superior shore. In my childhood it was an ore boat hunt. The prize was to see one of the familiar boats at either the Upper or Lower Harbor docks. The boats (never ships on the Great Lakes) are sometimes a thousand feet long with superstructure on each end separated by the removable hatches into which the iron ore extracted a few miles to the west was poured down long chutes that were lowered down to the hatches, spilling ore as they tipped. I still seek the ore boats, but now I crave Lake Superior. It was present in my childhood map of the place. Now I cannot imagine the place without its frigid, clear, beautiful blue-green waters. It now emerges as I drive, and I recognize the lake as the determining characteristic of this place as much as the Mississippi and Missouri Rivers' confluence dominate my mental map of St. Louis.

It is not that my knowledge of this lake is encyclopedic; I have never even traveled around it, although I want to and I may before this magical summer of discovery is over. I do know that the lake is hundreds of miles long and wide and that it contains ten percent of all fresh water on our planet. But that is about the extent of my official geographic knowledge. Mine is a more intimate, emotional, and radiant knowledge. This lake is inside of me, the exact center of my emotional map of the world. I do not know who I would be without it. This water is my definition of splendor, beauty, tranquillity, violence, chill, ice, winter, spring, life and death. This water cascades through my mind incessantly as though over craggy rocks, with me everywhere, in faraway places, dreams and waking. It is what makes this place and me different from all others. Sometimes when the ghosts of night awake, I seek its water as a palliative for my jangled

"This place moves me away from my life into a transcendent world where I lose track of time, . . . a place of connection to everything in this world . . ." (Lake Superior. Photo by Sue Frisk, 1998.)

spirit. Now I recognize these things and I will never be gone from the lake so long again, even though I carry it with me.

This is not one lake. I sit on granite outcroppings over the water, listening to the water sucked in and then expelled in a gush from crevices somewhere below. Elsewhere I walk on high bluffs where many people have carelessly slipped and lost their lives. I look down on the water but it is never diminutive; it is too large and too powerful to be dwarfed by craggy cliffs and my transfixed gaze. And I walk miles of sand beaches, digging my feet in as the soft brown sand compresses with my steps. Branches and driftwood lie in a tangled line many yards up on the beach beyond the water's edge. They rest where they were thrown at the high mark of the waves that thunder across the beach in the storms of November when this now tranquil lake turns violent and savvy sailors hastily head for shore. But now the lake has gentle, rolling waves and I slowly descend into its chill—feet, legs, thighs, hips, stomach, chest, and finally shoulders. The chill feels different on each part of my body. Finally I swim, but not for long as the cold sinks into my core. I seek the sun's delicious warmth on the beach. There are not a lot of people here. Swimming in these waters is an achievement. It is not for everyone. At either end of the long beach, reddish cliffs create an impenetrable blockade, hundreds of feet high, variegated reds and browns. Just below the waterline along the beach there is a band of small multicolored rocks, shimmering colors, sprinkled with agates, painful on feet but beckoning. Each stone is a jewel, polished by the clear water. At night, even in the faintest light, the lake shimmers, white caps sparkle, and the surface is still striated with wind currents that sometimes just graze the surface and at other times stir up froth, especially as rollers heave up to the breakwaters or the rocks.

I tell you my emotions, not what I see. This place moves me away from my life into a transcendent world where I lose track of time, depart temporarily from reason to a place of connection to everything in this world, overcome by a profound and consuming sense of belonging. The isolation and loneliness of being human is subdued, and for a moment my mind expands to encompass all of existence and I am conjoined with the universe. I know that I am a microcosm of all that I see, hear, feel, smell, taste. I float in the lake.

For just a moment I am the rocks, the water flows in me, the sky is within reach, the northern lights' green glow bursting up are me. There are no boundaries. Everything is everything else. There is no other. My mind whirls. This is infinitely better than a sweet dream.

In our rational, objective, hurry-up world we have little time for transcendent experiences and we discount their value. Yet we view them as the experiences that make life worth living. We spend millions of dollars traveling the globe seeking such uplift and exhilaration and inner peace. We seek escape in music, poetry, religion, dance, art, sports, nature, oceans, mountains, love, isolation, crowds, and in the solace of quiet places. We have no complete explanations, yet we crave transcendence. This is fundamental to humanity and without it we are diminished in capacity and potential, removed from sources of inspiration and the wellsprings of creativity, deprived of tranquillity. In these experiences the human spirit soars, insights gleam, and wisdom abounds. And we all seek and require the respite and relief that these experiences provide. Good places, good communities offer people opportunities for inspiration, crucibles for creativity, and realization of potential. The necessity of such places must inform all that we do. This we can know from the past.

Trees grow fast in this climate, and their presence belies the abused land, pitted with caving ground, cut over many times, crisscrossed with barbed-wire fences that cordon dangerous ground. I know the land that fronts on Lake Superior. From a plane I can see modern efforts to reclaim land from the ravages of open-pit mining operations that made huge, deep gashes and gargantuan piles of waste tailings. Reclamation amounts to making a gigantic dish out of the pits and planting the concave surface with grasses. Eventually the trees will grow, but reclamation is just a cover up. Near this place the pits still grow deeper and wider at the Empire and Tilden mines. The piles dug out of the earth are now mountains visible from miles away, where there never were mountains. As I drive from the west toward Ishpeming, I can see the new peaks. Replacing the old head frames as mine markers, they have become the pre-eminent symbols of this place's extractive economy.

I read an essay on the economic future of this region. In "Crucial Crossroads: The Economy At Century's End," Harry Guenther, director of the Northern Michigan University's Bureau of Business and Economic Research, prognosticates about the future and offers advice. "Opportunities exist," he writes, "for more rapid economic development of the Upper Peninsula which result from a set of unique conditions and events. They will not come our way again. Seizing these opportunities can significantly change the pace and structure of economic growth in the region. . . . Developing such a strategy requires a growth culture, a less risk-adverse community leadership, and a clearer understanding and identification of the intellectual resources of the community and the region's real competitive strengths."[10] This unequivocal gospel of progress—from my own alma mater in Marquette—bothers me because it espouses a vision that if implemented will be just as destructive as the values now symbolized by the waste piles and pitted surface. It is not a new future; it is the same old past projected into the future. And this message is not unique to this place; it is the tattered refrain that still sways over most of our nation because we cannot imagine a new verse or meter.

Every community in our nation needs to think more broadly about the future than simply focusing on economic development. There are limits to economic growth unless you buy into the scientific and technological gospel. This myopic thinking may be good for business but it is bad for people. We need to accept a new way of planning the future. We must embrace as another core value a broad principle of sustainability that encompasses a balance of all those elements vital to human happiness. There are multiple components to this concept: environmental quality, good schools, jobs, health, safety, a sense of cultural continuity, a built environment that encourages interaction, and a broadly shared consensus on the principles that inform public decision-making. This is the kind of growth capable of rising above individual aspiration and of pursuing the common good, a community where it is possible in concerted action for each person to participate in a civic enterprise that elevates the whole. Sustainability thus defined is not just a principle of environmentally sound economic development but also a vision of the future in which people and communities are nurtured, supported, and safeguarded.

The Upper Peninsula is being "discovered." It is not just the relatively pristine environment and wilderness; it is also the kind of community that this place sustains. It is even the language. In this place people speak with a thoroughly distinct accent. There is even a name for it: "yooper talk." Combined with distinct food and folkways, "yooper" defines a particular culture. No kidding, I have become accustomed to not double-checking the locks on my car doors, and I do not lock my apartment. It is not an affectation. It is merely unnecessary and so no one bothers. This is not just because of the scarcity of crime; it is more a symbol of trust and an indicator of community. Tourists cannot tour the particular culture of this place without eroding it and massive or even incremental economic development will displace those who are here now and will eradicate the regional culture. Doors will have to be locked as change accelerates. Not only is it increasingly a tourist destination but it is also a refuge for increasing numbers of people seeking escape in summer from the cities to the south. Life here is changing, culture here is becoming a commodity as it is elsewhere. Natives who have stayed here because of the quality of life that the place offers are now priced out of the real estate market.

There is a new place up on U.S. 41 on Ishpeming's outskirts, "Da Yooper's Tourist Trap." A parody of what makes this place special, it features drunken hunters, bathroom humor, gross exaggeration, tourist trinkets, and elaborate but vulgar jokes constructed in three dimensions. People here have very mixed feelings about the place. I am both embarrassed and uneasy about this attempt to commodify and market a culture. I fear that it is an indicator of cultural debasement, a view of culture as exaggerated self-parody. "Da Yooper's Tourist Trap" advocates no reverence or even appreciation for what generations of people in this place have built and treasured. This place embraces the lowest common denominator so as to catch the most tourist dollars. Given the business these entrepreneurs are in, I think they know exactly what they are doing. But do they know how much it contributes to the demolition of what ought to be lovingly and carefully conserved? Soon those who live here will conclude that if this portrayal of themselves is accurate then it is not worth saving. It is ourselves that we have put up for sale.

My sister Anne, her husband David, and I decided to go to the Marquette County Fair in mid-August. I speculated that here I might find exhibitions of local culture: food, crafts, perhaps even dance and folklore. But the central feature, besides the generic midway, was a truck race through a track of gooey mud and over a series of jumps into mud pits. The fastest and soupiest mud-spattered trucks and drivers win. I hoped for traditional Finnish rag rugs, spicy Italian cudighi sandwiches, but not much of the Upper Peninsula was at this fair. I think that it is one more barometer of the homogenization of even this distinctive culture and may be also reflective of a diminution of local pride. Most of the audience was very young; they came for the truck racing or brought children for the midway rides. It was not a community event.

The Upper Peninsula cannot have a future in which people's real needs are put first unless the people of the U.P. construct a new narrative, a reordering of the past to establish new priorities. So history is at the core of the future. It requires the process that I have described, an inclusive discussion about legacies and burdens and the values that will be used to distinguish them. Sustainability in its broadest sense is a core principle that must be used to identify legacies so that the culture and environment of this place will be a shared legacy that must be a vital component of the future. Economic development will be included, but in a manner compatible with the other ingredients of a sustainable community in which people-oriented needs come first.

I have proposed four core values as organizing principles in the community-focused work of public history organizations and public historians. They are not exclusive; rather, each core value implicitly encompasses a multitude of vital principles. But the point remains that these values at the core are critical tools for evaluation of perspectives on the past. These four values—memory, transcendence, sustainability, and mutual obligations—have, I believe, permeated my discussion, but their crucial position invites a summary.

Mutual Obligation. A community is a place but it is more: It is a mindset that exists in the people who comprise it. It is an attitude that acknowledges people's connections with each other, a sense of responsibility for one another and accountability to one another, that have always been the basis of civic enterprise and of civilization itself. Through investment in the common good, individuals in a community transcend immediate self-interest and act for the good of the whole.

Sustainability. From this sense of mutual obligation emerges an acknowledgment that the living generation does not have a right to use everything up and that the future too has a claim on the planet and a right to a reasonable quality of life. This commitment to sustainability is an issue of equity within generations and between generations. We are not owners with unlimited rights but trustees with only usufruct rights. In 1987 the World Commission on Environment and Development issued *Our Common Future* which defined sustainable development succinctly and elegantly: "Development that meets the needs of the present without compromising the ability of future generations to meet their needs."[11]

We will not behave in ways that create and sustain good communities unless we acknowledge responsibility for the long-term common good. Thus the two principles of sustainability and mutual obligation are inextricably intertwined. So we need to construct narratives in which we acknowledge each other's perspectives, learn to value common purpose, and replace a claimed ownership of our places with a recognition of trusteeship. We will not delegate such important work to experts, and we will not abdicate our own responsibilities to a foolhardy faith in science and technology.

Transcendence. Our new stories will accord primacy to the spiritual and emotional requirements of our species and we will acknowledge these demands as the wellsprings of inspiration and creativity that are responsible for many of our most laudable achievements.

Memory. Public history practitioners must ensure that change does not overwhelm continuity. Through remembering we construct identity for ourselves and our communities. Through re-remembering we construct new narratives that underscore mutual obligations, insist upon broad principles of sustainability, require the creation and preservation of those places and experiences that inspire and provide spiritual sustenance, and recognize the importance of memory itself.

I hear the raucous cackling of loons in the Lake Superior twilight. I sit transfixed by ancient echoes across luminous waters on the edges of granite rocks. I look out over streaks of colors reflecting wind changes and depth variation, areas of calm alternating with sequences of foaming breakers. This is how I know that I am human. This is how I know that I am alive. This is how I am bonded to you and to time past, present, and future.

NOTES

[1]Miles Davis, with Quincy Troupe, *Miles: the Autobiography* (New York: Touchstone Press, 1990), p. 15.

[2]Carl Schorske, *Thinking With History: Explorations in the Passage to Modernism* (Princeton, N. J.: Princeton Univesity Press, 1998), p. 227–28.

[3]David Ashley, *History Without a Subject: The Postmodern Condition* (Boulder, CO: Westview Press, 1997), passim.

[4]Gitlin, *The Twilight of Common Dreams*, p. 3, 4.

[5]Thomas Lynch, *The Undertaking: Life Studies From the Dismal Trade* (New York: W. W. Norton and Company, 1997), p. 158–59.

[6]Stephen W. Hawking, *A Brief History of Time* (New York: Bantam Books,1988), p. 140–41.

[7]*ibid.*, p. 175.

[8]Paul Davies, *God and the New Physics* (New York: Simon & Schuster, 1983), p. 229.

[9]Murray Bookchin, *The Philosophy of Social Ecology: Essays on Dialectical Naturalism* (Montreal: Black Rose Books, 1996), p. 177.

[10]Harry Guenther, "Crucial Crossroads: The Economy At Century's End" in *A Sense of Place: Michigan's Upper Peninsula*, Russell M. Magnaghi and Michael Marsden, eds. (Marquette: Northern Michigan University Press, 1997), p. 99.

[11]A. M. Mannion and S. R. Bowlby, eds., *Environmental Issues in the 1990s* (West Sussex, England: John Wiley & Sons Ltd., 1992), p. 24.

⤳ 7 ⤳

Intersections*

Persistent issues examined through a prism of core values are the framework for the practice of public history. Concerns about ecological degradation, nurturing of good communities, attachment to place, the intrinsic necessity of memory for our species, vitality of human relationships, ambiguous impacts of technology, and the capacity of this earth to sustain our children and bequeath to them the requisites of a decent life are all intimately interconnected. In my community work in St. Louis I am struck by the ways in which disparate well-intended interest groups operate as if their particular area of concern is disconnected from any other. Thus people who advocate on behalf of mass transit seem oblivious to the intersections between transportation policy and the quality of urban environment and economic development. Others, concerned with social justice, do not recognize that land-use policies that subsidize "sprawl" encourage erosion of the urban tax base, concentration of poverty, and racial segregation, and leave those who can least afford to pay for it with the burden of a crumbling city.

This is a problem in all American communities, even my remote hometown of Ishpeming. Think about your town for a moment. In most communities the businesses that supply life's necessities are now on the outskirts, no longer prominent fixtures on Main Street. Usually residential real estate values are higher for property near the highway and the new shopping strips and malls than those older homes near the old downtown. Most people who can afford the more expensive homes on the outskirts have left the older, closer-in neighborhoods. You might observe that distances between home,

---

*An earlier and much different version of Chapter 7 "Intersections" was written for *Public History and the Environment*, Philip V. Scarpino and Martin Melosi, eds., to be published by Krieger in 1999.

shopping, school, and work are greater in the more recent developments than they are in the areas built before World War II. The differences between the new and old town are a consequence of the spread of automobile ownership, governmental subsidization of road construction, marketing trends in real estate development, and increasing affluence. Increases in taxation, decline of downtowns, and automobile dependency have interconnected causes.

I am by nature and by profession a storyteller. The business of public history is to facilitate the composition of good narratives based on the consensus that emerges from inclusive discussion sorted through core values that expose destructive perspectives. When I consider how to discuss the intersections of perspectives with values, and the relationships between environmental concerns, memory, community, and the future, I think of narrative as the best way to illustrate my points. So here is a story about enduring issues, perspectives, core values, and intersections.

Along the slow rise of the Missouri River on the run from St. Louis to Kansas City, Amtrak's "Missouri Mule" hits seventy-nine miles per hour. Small towns once dependent upon railroads whiz past, no longer train stops and now dependent upon cars and highways for access to the rest of the world. The Missouri River runs

"The train is a good place . . . people mingle, chatting, recapitulating the day's events. The camaraderie is apparent. Strangers become friends and share stories." (Woodcut, Ohio and Mississippi Broad Gauge, Isaac Wyman, General Western Agent, from Sketchbook of St. Louis, Missouri Historical Society, St. Louis)

alongside to the north. Once the river bore the country's trade but
business shifted to the rails and then the river's work was further
diminished by trucks and cars, and now it carries only a trickle of
its former flood of commerce. Older railroad grades are still visible,
arcing bulwarks between our tracks and the river, abandoned for
higher ground in a scramble to get above unpredictable spring flood-
waters. On this trip two exquisitely restored vintage passenger cars,
a dome car and an observation car, are coupled to the end. The
refurbished cars are luxurious. Wood paneling, brass hardware,
upholstered chairs, end tables with flowers in vases, an attentive waiter
with chocolate chip cookies and apple juice compensate for the erratic
unbalancing swaying of old suspension systems. Both the geographic
and manmade features visible from the right-of-way reveal a tangled
series of past events that involved years of interaction between people,
the river, and the land. The past is implicit in the very structure of
the present.

I don't know my fellow passengers very well. Sue, a middle-aged
woman, sits near me. Now living in suburban St. Louis, she was raised,
one of sixteen children, on a southern Illinois farm. Her parents
still live there. I encourage her with questions. She talks about them
back then.

"When Mom was pregnant, she would take solitary walks in the
woods, and Dad worried. 'Go find your mother,' he would say. 'No,'
Sue told him, 'she is doing what she needs to do.'

"Mom had two miscarriages," Sue continues. "She took the three-
month-old fetuses, one and then later another, and buried them,
and a part of herself, in the ground. Later Dad wanted to plow and
plant this part of the land. Mom reminded him, and Dad let the plot
alone. Dad is a good farmer," she says. "He judges soil fertility by eye
and feel, his corn is always the tallest, and he and Mom still go for
walks in the woods. And now near the end of his life he will not give
up farming." Sue muses now, wondering why, with decent health
and a good income, her parents do not travel like other people for
whom life's final horizons loom close. But Sue knows why, and she
wants her husband to spend time on the farm so he will understand.
As she finishes her story, I can feel my emotions rise and I hope my
feelings are not visible on my face, for Sue is trying to be matter-of-
fact about this.

I quietly speculate about generational change. I recall Bill McKay's beautiful cattle ranch in Montana, where occasionally I visited for the weekend. The ranch nestled close up against the Beartooth Mountains to the north of Yellowstone National Park. On a sun-drenched Sunday morning Bill woke me early and we climbed into his open jeep for a ranch tour. While I was awed by the foothill landscape, the smell of the mountains, and the blue-green color of the grass enhanced with morning dew, I was more entranced with his words and his animated face. Age wrinkles made his face even more expressive than it might have been with the smooth skin of youth. Or perhaps, his wrinkles are love lines of attachment for his place in the world. He talked, I listened as we bounded and bounced over the land in the war surplus jeep. Upon reflection I realized that Bill's unceasing descriptive monologue as we drove was not really about the landscape we traversed although those were the words he used. In describing the landscape in such eloquent loving terms he was describing himself, what it was that he held most dear. Just as Sue's parents cannot leave their farm, Theresa cannot leave her store, and I am loathe to be without Lake Superior, Bill can never leave this place because there is no boundary between the land and Bill himself. They have merged into one, indivisible. When he is gone, he longs to return. He is attached by remembrances of a lifetime, by the sheer beauty of his place, by the intimacy developed through hard work on the ranch, quiet moments of reverie in mountain shadows. As he worked his land, the land was working on him. When I see him in the distance standing in the mountain pasture, I see a singularity. Bill is responsible for what he loves. He can do no harm. His attachments for his place incorporate a most profound environmental ethic.

My neighbor John is on the train. We sit at the small table and watch Missouri landscape roll gently by. John lives in an old house built about the same time as my own. We are discussing roof maintenance, bathroom remodeling, and wood stripping—comparing notes on the tribulations and joys of century-old houses. "You know, I feel like a custodian. I don't feel that Grace and I really own the house." I nod, knowing exactly what he feels. "The house," he says, "has been there for a long time, and I expect that it will be there long after Grace and I are gone. We have even discussed moving to a condominium in one of the old gracious apartment buildings in the neighborhood, but Grace says she cannot live without the porch. No apartments we have seen have anything like our porch. We sit there on a warm summer evening, and with the ceiling fan whirling away it is really comfortable."

"John," I say, "we bought our house because we loved the porch." I don't mention it in our conversation, but I am thinking about the Sunday trek I made to Bellefontaine Cemetery hunting for the graves of Thomas and Hildegard McKittrick, the couple who built our house in 1897. Bellefontaine is an expansive nineteenth-century cemetery park, a place of peace and carefully landscaped beauty where the living and the dead interact. There are no flat headstones for the convenience of lawnmowers in this place: here architects designed mausoleums of red granite, obelisks of stone, elaborate tombstones with carved angels and elegant epitaphs in curving tree-shaded lanes— a city of the dead. I looked for Mr. McKittrick with the help of the sexton. "Before or after 1900?" he asked and then pulled out the three-by-five card with the block and lot number.

An infant son is interred next to Thomas. (His wife Hildegard died later and was not buried in St. Louis.) I surmise he died in one of the second floor bedrooms in our house, perhaps the little one next to what must have been Hildegard McKittrick's bedroom. McKittrick's wake was held at his sister's, in the house two doors west of ours.

The Pettus lot is just a cemetery block east. Eugene and Marguerite Pettus lived in our house for fifty-two years after the McKittricks. I remember the label in the third floor cedar closet: "Mr. Pettus's suits." I think of the drawer in the attic still labeled "Thomas McKittrick's junk drawer." I write in my office on the second floor of our house in the room I am certain was first Thomas McKittrick's and then Eugene Pettus's bedroom. Their floor-to-ceiling clothes closets are three feet to my left as I write. Last week I found in the fireplace mantle woodwork a coupon, yellow and dirty. "Good for one glass of Booth's Ginger Ale," it read. "Just one glass will make you a constant patron. Hand this check and dispenser's check to cashier. 611 Locust Street." I wondered what was at Sixth and Locust in, say, 1900. I could find out easily enough and even ride downtown to the site in just a few minutes . . . but the McKittricks and probably the Pettuses would not recognize it.

I find solace in knowing my place, who lived there, who built it, and guessing at their motives. My reasons are hard to explain; they are feelings more than reasons. I like a sense of continuity. My place is a tangible reminder of my own trusteeship because the place came before me and will likely survive me. Since I cannot take it with me, I know that I do not really own it. The monthly mortgage checks are really lease payments. I crave such things, and other people I talk to about this acknowledge their own attachments to house, neighborhood, photographs, or the familiar shapes of a place. We seek reassurance that we are not imprisoned in a disembodied present, not severed from those connections so necessary for our well-being, and that our decisions matter because they have long-term consequences. Our places shape us in profound and subtle ways. Attachments to them create trusteeship of places, like my feelings about my house, like Bill McKay's affinity with his ranch. In our professional work we divide the two for convenience. We call Bill's need to care for his land an environmental ethic, and we call care of old houses historic preservation. But both rise from the same essential human instinct: attachment to place.

As the Missouri Mule winds around another curve, I mention this to a fellow passenger named Pattie. Pattie, thirty-six, is the mother of three young girls. She is also the mayor of one of St. Louis's still affluent nineteenth-century rail line suburbs. Her tenure has been rewarding but not easy; she survived a very unpleasant recall election. We talk about democracy in late-twentieth-century America. Gradually our conversation turns to the importance of place. We discuss St. Louis' grand nineteenth-century City Hall with its imposing architecture, magnificent rotunda, and its placement in relationship to the civic opera house, the classical central library, and the Soldiers Memorial building initially constructed to honor veterans of the "Great War." We contrast this with newer suburbs and their strip-mall city halls. Pattie suggests that the difference has something to do with a diminishment of civic life: less focus on the importance of "us" as a community and more on the "me" individualism and self-gratification. I have spoken casually with this woman on several occasions, but never until now seriously enough to sense the passion, dedication, and commitment to community building that clearly animates her.

Our discussion turns to neighborhood planning. We talk about the merits and the defects of suburban cul-de-sacs and streets on grid patterns, the ways the structuring of space influences human relationships, and the extent to which modern street layouts often reflect the same sense of planning as sewer systems or natural gas distribution networks. We agree that these street systems adapt the same engineering and design principles to the collecting and distribution of automobiles from garage door and driveway to street to arterial to highway. Whole communities are built to maximize the efficiency of automobile movement as if this pattern reflects human needs as well. "Perhaps," she says, "poor design and planning have something to do with decreasing levels of civic involvement. Only forty-nine percent of Americans who are eligible to vote even register." I think about this. The previous day I had given a talk to a Rotary Club whose ranks have dwindled by half since I last spoke to them just two years before. I asked the President of the club to explain the membership loss. "People are just too busy and they do not seem to have the same dedication to this community," he responded.

Pattie and I both lean over the table towards each other as the intensity of our conversation rises. We discuss the characteristics of spaces that facilitate informal relationships between people, the bonds of civil society. I tell Pattie about the unpublished memoir sent to me by Ruth Anderson, a woman who grew up in St. Louis in the twenties and thirties, and her wonderful chapter on alleys.

Ruth Anderson introduces the chapter with "Oma (grandmother), who considered the alley an extension of her house, and regularly scrubbed our section of the alley." She continues with descriptions of the milkman's predawn deliveries, twice-weekly garbage pickups, and of Tony, the fruit and vegetable man; Mr. Pappas who sold dishcloths, towels, needles, pins, thread, corset laces, knives, scissors, pots, and pans; Mike, the Polar Wave ice man; Joe the flower man and Myrtle his horse; the man who bought "rags, old iron"; the man who mended umbrellas; the man who sharpened knives and scissors; and the coal man. She writes:

... the women grabbed their purses, dishpans, and baskets to gather in the alley to haggle and bargain. ... This was also the time for news and gossip.

"Did you hear the McGillicuddys had another boy?"

"Ach, and they so bad wanted a girl. What does that make already, six?"

"I just heard that Clara and Fritz are going to Germany soon to visit his father, who's very sick, dying maybe." I listened avidly when they spoke in German because I knew then that the bit of news under discussion was off limits for kids. Now and then I'd catch a familiar word like verrückt, but that only made me more curious.[1]

This was not a trivial conversation nor was the alley a trivial place. Through such conversations trust develops, bonds are forged, attachments to people and place created. This snippet of conversation is a nascent narrative and because it builds community and concern for place, it is a good narrative.

Neither of us is foolish enough to believe that we can recreate the past, but that is beside the point anyway. I ask Pattie whether she agrees that technology is inherently isolating. "My daughters think that we are crazy because we refuse to air condition our house," she replies. "But it's fine for them to know that when it is hot, people sweat. It creates a palpable sense of the passage of seasons, and people survived here long before air conditioning was invented. I remember when people first bought air conditioners," she continues. "You could immediately tell who had them. At first only a few people were inside with their doors closed in the evenings and on weekends instead of sitting on porches and steps, walking along the street, informally gathering in the public outside space where it was coolest. After a few years nobody was outside anymore." We are not going to do away with air conditioners either, but we will have to find ways to compensate for the isolation that air conditioning encourages.

Then we discuss books: Dan Kemmis's wonderful *The Good City and the Good Life: Renewing the Sense of Community*; James Howard Kunstler's *The Geography of Nowhere: The Rise and Decline of America's Man-Made Landscape*; and Ray Oldenburg's insightful *The Great Good Place: Cafes, Coffee Shops, Community Centers, Beauty Parlors, General Stores, Bars, Hangouts and How They Get You Through the Day*. Although they have very different perspectives, the three authors agree that quality of space has an important impact on civic life, informal associations between people, and human happiness. Oldenburg makes the connection between place and relationships especially vivid:

> In using *nearby* facilities, in visiting them afoot and regularly, the residents of an area effectively create a casual social environment and reap its benefits. The pedestrian mode of transportation invites human contact that automobile transportation precludes. People get to know their merchants and their neighbors; from the many, the compatible few are able to discover one another. Neighborhoods, like small towns have never been "big happy families." Rather, the key to their amenities is that they facilitate the discovery and easy association of people destined to become special to one another. . . . From among the many, a contingent of casual friends emerges. For some there will be the great gift—a deep and abiding friendship in the form of one who also lives close by and is *available*. For all, there is a control valve. One can have as much engagement and involvement with the neighborhood as one wishes. Those who prefer none may have it just that way.[2]

I consider my summer apartment in Marquette. It is in a large complex of apartments, nearly all of them unfurnished and available for long-term lease, but mine is furnished and can be leased on a week-to-week basis. Although there are well-tended islands of grass, asphalt visually dominates. People do not mingle outside much because there are no places where they can do it. Despite the lack of places for informal social engagement, this complex caters to the retired. I note older couples and singles, especially women, coming and going. Some are ill. I see some elderly men who hobble around the concrete perimeter on daily outings, several with walkers and the telltale signs of strokes. I am but a temporary resident in search of efficiency. But these people really live here. They have no maintenance worries, and they do not have to shovel snow or cut grass. Occasionally I see what I presume to be adult children picking up elderly residents for outings, doctor appointments, shopping, visits. But I surmise that this is a lonely place because it is a hard place to develop relationships. I cannot imagine that people love this place. Just where and how would they compose narratives of attachment, and just what is there to love about this place? The buildings and the acres of asphalt could be anywhere. When I leave, I will put this place in my mental bin of forgettable places I have lived. For many residents it is unfortunately the last place they will live before nursing homes or death.

The train arrives in Jefferson City, Missouri's capital. This is our destination today; we are not going all the way to Kansas City on the "Mule." Instead, we eighty representatives of Citizens for Modern Transit are here to meet our legislators and tell them once again about the importance of mass transit. I am the chair of this citizens advocacy group, and I am involved in light rail and transit advocacy because I know what dramatic consequences transportation decisions have had in our region. My goal during my tenure as chair of this very effective organization is to broaden community understanding of the relationships among transportation decisions, land use policy, infrastructure costs, clean air, rates of resource consumption, urban abandonment, suburban sprawl, historic preservation, and most importantly livable neighborhoods. In *The Next American Metropolis: Ecology, Community and the American Dream*, Peter Calthorpe puts it this way:

 Today the public world is shrunken and fractured. Parks, schools, libraries, post offices, town halls, and civic centers are dispersed, underutilized, and underfunded. Yet these civic elements determine the quality of our shared world and express the value we assign to community. The traditional Commons, which once centered our communities with convivial gathering and meeting places, is increasingly displaced by an exaggerated private domain: shopping malls, private clubs, and gated communities. Our basic public space, the street, is given over to the car and its accommodation, while our private world becomes more and more isolated behind garage doors and walled compounds. Our public space lacks identity and is largely anonymous, while our private space strains toward a narcissistic autonomy. Our communities are zoned black and white, private or public, my space or nobody's.[3]

My city, St. Louis, is unfortunately an extreme example that proves the point. Between 1950 and 1990 the population of the St. Louis region grew slowly by only 35 percent, but during that same forty-year period the acreage of developed land increased by 355 percent. Dismally, the city of St. Louis lost more than half of its population and nearly half of the inner suburbs were also losing population.[4]

Predictably, St. Louis ranks high on indices of urban sprawl, poor environmental quality, and extreme racial and economic disparity.[5] This is what I have come to call the great sorting out, and it afflicts most of our nation to varying degrees. Fed by racism, lubricated by automobiles and highways, and encouraged by unimaginative developers and planners, we have hyper-segregated ourselves by income in developments with homogenous real estate values. In many communities like St. Louis with an African-American population disproportionately poor, this results in de facto racial segregation as well. An African-American friend made a pungent observation in the midst of a conversation about the causes of urban sprawl in St. Louis. Fed up with obfuscation, she looked around at the predominantly white group and said, "Nonsense: this happened because people like you left the city to get away from people like me."

There are two sides to this process: Abandonment is one and the other is dispersal. We disperse into the fringes, where absolutely automobile-dependent subdivisions go up instantly, each one comprised of stick-built houses in the same price range and on lots that range from a half acre to three acres. Houses are zoned for single family, set back uniformly from the street, without alleys, generally without usable front porches, homogeneous, strung along curvilinear streets that end in cul-de-sacs, often without sidewalks. Driveways and garage doors are prominent. Each of these new developments generates demands for new roads, bridges, schools, libraries, sewers, water mains, government services, police and fire protection. These necessary amenities are only fractionally paid for by the developer and property owners and largely become a part of the tax bill shared by the whole region. Obviously enormous quantities of finite resources are consumed in both the house construction and in the building of the infrastructure to sustain them.

Meanwhile farmlands, wetlands, and other lands are consumed at prodigious rates.

These edge cities are further segregated by function. Zoning ordinances separate residential development from retail, commercial, and industrial places. Many of the communities are devoid of civic spaces: There are no grand civic malls and in some instances government offices are unobtrusively located in strip shopping developments. Schools are very large, and size combined with location requires most students to ride buses. There are few neighborhood parks although there are regional parks that also require travel by automobile. Indeed, every trip requires the insertion of a key into an ignition and the consumption of scarce fuel accompanied by emission of pollutants from combustion. Most often people who work in restaurants, stores, hospitals, and other service businesses cannot afford to live near the people they serve. Ironically, even the police and fire personnel upon whom people depend for their very lives often must live elsewhere. Civic life is diminished and people are isolated.

I am again reminded of Ishpeming. The student body of the public high school that I attended is now half the size it was when I was a student. Granted, we boomers stretched its capacity. After I graduated, a new consolidated high school was built outside of town. Since the population has not increased, I surmise that the consequence for the remaining population is not lower taxes but tax increases instead. The new high school is not in proximity to anything; everyone rides the bus. So now the new high school is not the same community fixture as was the old one in its prominent downtown location across from the community hospital. Sprawl is a hot big-city topic but dispersal of population and decline of community institutions is a small-town affliction, too.

Architecture, the very design and arrangement and materials, in these places is impoverished because builders and buyers do not insist that anything be built to last. I contrast that architecture with my own century-old home in the city of St. Louis. Now, after one hundred years, the copper valleys on the slate roof need replacement. The slate itself is still in good shape. I appreciate the mindset of Thomas McKittrick who built the house knowing that it would endure. He constructed, perhaps consciously, a message from the past, a message of aesthetics and values and of confidence in a future beyond his lifetime. It is a mixture of hubris and humility, a desire on the one hand to build something enduring as a monument to his achievement, but on the other an implicit acknowledgment that his house would last long after his body and bones rested in Bellefontaine Cemetery. McKittrick also acknowledged societal obligations in his undertaking, an understanding that buildings built by a man with the means to do so must be built to endure. This was how things were to be done.

These new barren and impoverished developments in towns big and small have more serious complications than their transient nature. The ties of community in these places are tenuous because these places are without stories that bind, experiences that build trust, an understanding of common interest upon which civic life and democracy depend. These places lack narrative. Communities are built with narrative, built upon shared memory, a sense of the common good as opposed to individual interests, a commitment to the distinctive qualities of a place. Narrative implies a recognition of a shared past, a sense of history, a mutual understanding that your place is assuredly not interchangeable with countless other places. But the structure of these exurban developments is not conducive to the informal association between residents that fosters community and hence community does not emerge. People encased in automobiles fan out from their subdivisions to shop in a far-away mall, attend church or temple and visit friends, and they rarely mingle with those whose houses are nearby. In most cases the prior history of the place where their houses are has been obliterated with the new development, and no one is left to tell the tales. Further, their physical arrangement insures that community cannot develop. The nature of the new place is not suitable for the creation of new stories, of narratives that give meaning to the place, shared identities to the people, and common purpose to civic life.

The rootlessness of contemporary life is reinforced in these places with uniform residential real estate values. If income goes up, if the family grows, or if a larger and more expensive house is desired, the family moves out to another place that boasts higher real estate values. Likewise if income decreases or other family circumstances change, people must move out of the place to find what they need. Because most people view residences as merely temporary, they do not build to last and they have powerful incentives to avoid deep attachments. Such places are not environmentally sustainable and they undermine civic life and democracy, because they have no history, no bonds of common interest, no shared stories, no sense of identity. They have no shared past and despite the best efforts of some residents they really have no shared future.

As I drive through small towns all over America, I see the very life sucked out of downtowns with an attempted reincarnation in the guise of fast food joints and chain discount stores adjacent to the nearest highway. Some of these establishments even adopt architectural and decorative history themes to make an artificial past where no real past exists. The highway strip in Ishpeming sponsors Heritage Days while the real heritage—downtown—is abandoned. I see older residential areas disintegrating as people even in small towns opt for new houses constructed on suburban models built on the outskirts. I see locally owned businesses decimated as people are seduced by the low prices and huge selections in the square boxed, asphalt-surrounded, automobile-convenient chain stores on the highway. Meanwhile what was the town square shrivels, locally owned stores wither, and what was once civic space where people informally associated is abandoned. The brownstone building on the corner with retail shops at sidewalk level and offices or residences above is vacant, the last movie theater on Main Street closes, and the people go to the miracle market just off the interstate and the multiplex cinema ten miles away. This is no way to build community and nurture civic life. This is no way to strengthen ties that bind and buttress democracy.

St. Louis is a city of brick. High-quality clay was deposited by the Mississippi and Missouri Rivers as they meandered through the valley over eons, slowly precipitating their burdens of fine earth over wide swaths of land. Pressed and baked in rectangular bricks, this earth became the building blocks of the nineteenth-century city. Now, the city is being un-built. Now I drive through nineteenth-century streets, and I see again and again neat pallets of brick. The pallets are not at construction sites, but instead they are piled next to demo-lition projects. The bricks are salvage. They will become the deco-rative fireplaces and backyard patios in a suburban development, while the compact neighborhoods those bricks had built, neighbor-hoods that contained housing for multiple income levels and permit-ted mixed residential, retail, and commercial development erupt in piles of dust and debris. I am appalled by what is happening here. Neighborhoods where people walk to stores, church, school, and parks and share an informal life on streets and sidewalks are pockmarked with vacant lots, garbage, and rubble, often characterized by vio-lence as they are abandoned to those who cannot escape.

However, the destruction is not just physical oblivion. It is an even more ominous kind of oblivion. It is a desecration of the ter-rible sort that would have occurred if Sue's father had plowed up the ground where his wife buried her unborn children. What is happen-ing in cities and towns all over this land is a forgetting, a truncation of narratives that attached people to each other and to their places and gave them a sense of lives lived before their own and lives that will be lived later. This is the real destruction, for in this process something singular, intangible, and irreplaceable is gone, never to be recovered except in commemorated form at "ghost reunions."

Gregory Freeman of the St. Louis *Post-Dispatch* described two of these notable but forlorn gatherings in one of his columns.[6] In both instances, former residents of these former neighborhoods—one decimated by an interstate highway that plowed through it and the other demolished to make way for a hospital parking lot—felt a sense of loss, not just of the buildings, the space, the "old days," but an irreplaceable loss of community. "Neighborhood was very impor-tant to us in those days," said Delores Abernathy Dickens. African Americans lived in this area as did those with Polish, Italian, and German backgrounds. "We all got along," said Dickens, who is black. "This was before the schools were integrated but we all played to-gether. We went to our schools and they went to their schools, but we all got along." The neighborhood was mixed both by income and race. "But we were safe," Delores noted. "You didn't have to have locks and burglar alarms and things like you do now. If you went away, somebody would keep an eye out for you, and if they went somewhere, you'd do the same for them."

Gladys Cofield, a resident of the second neighborhood, observed that "we just thought there'd be a few people at first, and then it just grew and grew." More than a hundred people signed up to see former neighbors. Like Dickens, Cofield says that her neighbors were all very close. "Today, I don't know who my neighbors are except those who live in the next couple of houses," she said. "In those days, we knew everyone on the block and we cared for everyone on the block." Ties to this place and its people were so close, Cofield says that next to her parents dying, "my greatest fear was that one day we would all grow up and not be as close. Of course that happened," she said. "But it will be nice to bring everyone back together again—if only for a few hours."

Places are produced in that wonderful interaction of people, place, narrative, and time. When the people desert these places, narratives are forgotten, ties break, and the place is unmade. What is un-remembered in abandonment cannot be re-remembered in transient automobile suburbs with too few places for shared experience and story making. The extreme is amnesia, and it means that those afflicted do not know who they are anymore. They are disoriented, isolated, and robbed of the ability to recognize emotional attachments to others. The sufferers do not have a coherent story anymore. Un-remembering is the enemy of good places and of public history.

Some narratives are even more expansive than those that establish individual identities. Some ripple beyond into the neighborhood and immediate community. Late-nineteenth- and early-twentieth-century St. Louis civic narratives are symbolized in public architecture. Dearly held ideals are reflected in public hospitals, grand parks, public fountains and public art, an extensive public library system, the memorial built to honor veterans of the First World War, a civic auditorium, the network of public bathhouses, courthouses, boulevards. These impressive public works embody the idea of the public welfare, the common good, and the certainty that the civic enterprise transcends the individual. Such edifices were meant to uplift, entertain, inspire, and civilize. Rarely are such places built now. Our single-minded focus on the individual and the bottom line preclude such extravagant expenditures that do not directly benefit the individual nor produce profits.

Recently I participated in a city-sponsored charette to identify reuses for St. Louis' Municipal Auditorium, a building that is the tangible affirmation of so many civic memories. But the planning premise, that any new use needed to be "economically viable," was wrong. As I probed with questions, it became apparent that this meant that whatever use was made of the building it had to be self-supporting. The building was never intended to be self-supporting. This is its death knell, and the best that can be hoped for is that the building will be mothballed until better sense prevails. The Municipal Auditorium was built to serve a vital civic purpose, not an economic one, and those civic purposes were determined to be worth the expenditure of public funds. While I value the building, I think that the attitudinal shift since the building was first opened is a bigger loss than the demolition of the building would be. We need to rethink what builds civic life and what inculcates the mutual obligations that are essential for our common welfare. Not only is this building endangered but so are thousands like it everywhere. And this mass demolition will only be a symbol for what has become of us and of those commitments to each other upon which our democracy and civilization depend. We cannot commodify everything without endangering ourselves.

Yet, even if the people and their personal and civic narratives could be transplanted to a new place where new stories could be made, the damage is still horrendous. For abandonment is not only a physical and human disaster; it is also an environmental debacle. These places were built at enormous cost of resources and energy. Houses, civic structures, retail and commercial buildings, and public facilities such as schools and libraries are carted off to landfills. Infrastructure such as sewers, streets, sidewalks, water mains, utilities, street lights, and gas lines capable of sustaining a much larger population are now dramatically underutilized but must be maintained for those who remain. Yet the tax base shrinks. So we destroy the buildings, abandon the infrastructure, and replicate it all on the fringes. In doing this we lay a heavy mortgage upon this planet, a debt to be paid in the future and by tomorrow's children. This is reckless and shortsighted. It reeks of the selfish "I," of the isolated "me," and it incarcerates us in a chilly here and now, absent of connections to past and future and, deplorably, even to each other.

Destruction of places, environmental degradation, poor aesthetics and design, uncritical use of technology, increasing taxation, rigid zoning, population dispersal, segregation by race and class, concentration of poverty, homogenization of culture, human isolation, the decline of civic life—all these elements are interrelated. At the core these unfortunate consequences are both causes and effects of the disappearance of sustaining and embracing narratives. And narrative is at the very core of public history.

All public history organizations collect and preserve narratives. Our collections—the artifacts, documents, maps, paintings, photographs, prints and engravings, the archeological evidence, films, oral histories and audio tapes, books, and buildings—are only symbols and connections. Symbols because they represent values, aesthetics, thoughts, actions, and culture of those who were once alive and who built our places. Connections because they are tangible evidence that others once lived in our places. The narratives symbolized by our collections relieve us from permanent confinement in a momentary present, and they allow us to transmit knowledge from all generations, thus permitting experience and information to accumulate and disseminate rather than disappear with death. We are the living link in a continuum of our species that began in an indeterminate past and extends through an unknowable future.

Narratives are based in selections of fact, but meanings are subjective and are given legitimacy through broad acceptance. Michael Delp writes in *The Coast of Nowhere*: "My father loved wildness. He loved the fact that you could stand only so long in the current of the river until your feet started to drop out from under you. And he often said, over his shoulder when we were fishing together, that you could take something out of your imagination you didn't like, just like you would out of your pocket and let it go in the river and it would never come back."[7]

What we make of the symbols we collect is an interpretation, a mental map, a facsimile of our world that is regularly updated. What we do is a core characteristic of our species. We do not tell everything as we compose our narratives. Much of what happened in the past is forever lost, buried with ancestors, forgotten, destroyed, or discarded. Further, a narrative, a history if you want, that told everything would have little meaning. Our readers, listeners, or visitors would insist that we identify what is most important and that we point out causal relationships, construct a narrative, ascribe meaning, tell a story with a beginning, a middle, and an end. Narratives, histories, are for the living, not for the dead. They explain the world to us in meaningful ways. They are updated and revised to include present circumstances and are expressive of future aspirations. We are advocates for usable narratives. We know that narratives connect people and place. We know that in our work we make choices about which narratives to preserve and tell. We also know that we live in a time when civic narratives are devalued, that we are more detached from our places and from each other, that we are trying to build communities where places for the construction of narratives are scarce.

What sorts of narratives should we advocate? We must strive to facilitate creations of narratives like Sue's that connect her parents and their place in an intimate relationship; like St. Louis' dream for the Municipal Auditorium; and Ruth Anderson's that connected her to neighbors and neighborhood; and Bill McKay's attachment to his land, and the sense of trusteeship that John and I attach to our old houses. Not just any narrative will suffice. The stories we promote must speak to enduring concerns in their present manifestations. What is a good place? What obligations do we owe to those with whom we share a place? What inspires the best of which we are capable? What do we owe to those not yet born who will occupy our place after us? New narratives must respond to these questions. Good narratives encompass all of the interconnected and intersected concerns that define good places for people. They address the importance of relationships and the quality of natural and built environments. They stress continuity, embrace spirituality, and acknowledge that we are but trustees of each other and our places.

The "Mule" picks us up for the return trip in early evening. The night is luminescent and chilly. The train is a good place. Dozens of people mingle, chatting, recapitulating the day's events. The camaraderie is apparent. Strangers become friends and share stories. I think of Sue's story, John's house, Grace's porch, Pattie's experience as mayor, and of Thomas McKittrick's house, now my house—a day of narratives shared in a place conducive to their telling. The last train car has an observation platform outside the rear door. I walk out. The train's rush through the night leaves a pocket of eerily still air on the platform. I stare into the night astounded at a revelation of reverse perspective. As I look at where the train was, I see tracks, ties, trees, roadbed and sky coming together and then disappearing in the distance. Here, on this platform, I look into the past. I see where we have been. If I was in the engineer's cab in the front of the train I would peer into the future. Future and past conjoin right here on this train at this instant. This I think is an apt analogy for history. Past and future are separated by only an infinitesimal present. The dividing line is tiny. The difference is a matter of perspective.

NOTES

[1]Ruth Anderson, unpublished MS (St. Louis: Collections of the Missouri Historical Society, 1998).

[2]Ray Oldenburg, *The Great Good Place: Cafes, Coffee Shops, Community Centers, Beauty Parlors, General Stores, Bars, Hangouts and How They Get You Through the Day* (New York: Paragon House, 1989), p. 288–89.

[3]Peter Calthorpe, *The New American Metropolis: Ecology, Communities, and the American Dream* (New York: Princeton Architectural Press, 1993), p. 23.

[4]*Transportation Redefined* (St. Louis: East-West Gateway Coordinating Council, 1995), p. 17.

[5]*Where We Stand* (St. Louis: East-West Gateway Coordinating Council, 1996), p. 55–57.

[6] Greg Freeman, "Scattered Neighbors Find Solace in Reunions," *St. Louis Post-Dispatch*, September 6, 1998.

[7] Michael Delp, *The Coast of Nowhere: Meditations on Rivers, Lakes and Streams* (Detroit: Wayne State University Press, 1997), p. 105.

∽ 8 ∾

Friends and Colleagues

The practice of public history is collegial, collaborative, and interdisciplinary, and definitions of significance are community-derived. Therefore practitioners must embrace collegiality, seek collaboration, recognize the limitations of their own disciplines, understand strengths and insights characteristic of other academic disciplines, and be actively engaged in their communities. A comparison of traditional academic job descriptions for historians with our own work suggests that public historians may not be historians at all. Instead, we find anthropologists, linguists, archeologists, architectural historians, sociologists, specialists in literature and poetry, criminologists, political scientists, or professionals in any academic discipline that explains or examines human behavior or perception. Public historians even come from outside the traditional arts and sciences including schools of conservation, education, design, and fine arts. A person who uses sophisticated scientific techniques in a conservation laboratory to examine the composition and the construction techniques of an artifact, the editor of historical publications, the development director who prepares a case for funding, and the computer expert who oversees the collection management database are practicing public history. Trustees who represent the community, set policy, give support, and provide oversight as well as the volunteer who teaches in a historical museum are practitioners of public history.

In many public history organizations members of the public are now practicing public history as they examine their own pasts and debate the meanings of objects and narratives. Public historians do not own history. History is owned by those whose past is described in the narrative because that story, their own version of it, resides in their memories and establishes their identities. If public involvement is not integral in the process of public history, the conclusions are meaningless. This step is the only way to release the power of history to heal, but it requires new relationships between history practitioners and the community who are to become collaborators, full participants in the historical process. Maybe this is the most difficult transition for us since here we must share authority with people outside the institution's walls.

An inclusive relationship in the community is not a head count but a process through which we actively seek to incorporate all of the community in the conversation of enduring issues. If we do not, the conversation is incomplete, and we will repeat the old mistake of telling exclusive stories accepted by those who tell them but marginalizing others. While total inclusion is an ideal and not an attainable goal, active efforts will result in a narrative that encompasses more perspectives and consequently represents more people and a greater consensus about the meaning of the past and the possibilities for the future.

My three graduate school years at the University of New Mexico were an extraordinary experience. I was entranced with this real "land of enchantment" and enjoyed the luxury of long days in Zimmerman Library. It seemed like hard work at the time but now in retrospect I see it as an opportunity given to few. The books stacked in front of me on long wooden library tables were treasures, and the ambiance of the reading room was conducive to concentration. The older portion of the library was built in pueblo style with subdued earthtone colors, hewn vigas and herringbone pattern latias overhead that interacted in beautiful, unpredictable ways with soft light from the high windows, a shadowed environment that varied hour by hour. But the graduate school process with the painstaking efforts required and finally the harrowing experience of comprehensive exams, oral interrogation, and the production of an acceptable dissertation convinced me that history was a profession, and that unless one went through this intense process capped with fearsome rights of passage, one could not legitimately claim to be a historian. A historian's job was to conduct archival research, analyze the information retrieved, interpret its meaning, and disseminate the results in scholarly papers, articles in professional journals topped off with an occasional book. And oh yes, time spent in the classroom. It was an appealing life. Finally after surviving the doctoral ordeal I was an initiate qualified to define historical significance, interpret the past, and publish for my colleagues. At that time the supply of history professors far exceeded the demand. So I became that pariah, a public historian. Thankfully public history has become more acceptable to academic historians in the years since. Occasionally I still think that the professorial life might be an attractive retreat for me, a good way to wind down a career.

Between 1976 and 1988 when I moved to St. Louis, I worked in three public history jobs. I was drifting. My academic training had inculcated in me a conviction that history was only for those who were properly initiated, and I could not reconcile that with the necessity of compromise and the mechanics of presenting history to an audience outside of academe. If this was not so, why had I endured the rigors demanded of a doctoral candidate? One answer, most unsatisfactory, was that public historians were the trained translators of the complex work done by academic colleagues. That meant public history was just "watered down" history for the public and that academic historians were at the apex of a hierarchy in our profession where the real work of making sense of the past was done. It also meant that authority over the past was exclusive. This view was adopted and promoted by the National Endowment for the Humanities. Grant guidelines that stipulated criteria for funding of museums and historical organizations required that academic historians develop or at least review and approve public history interpretations. Definitions of a qualified historian were narrow; although there were exceptions, a historian was someone with a doctorate in history who worked in a college or university, and the more publications on the historian's vita the more qualified the person. Some public historians began to resent the almost predictable recipe for exhibits funded by NEH. In retrospect I think that while the academic involvement was good, it was heavy handed and inflexible. It reinforced the two-tiered chasm between public and academic historians and presumed that the differences between scholarly publications and public exhibitions were minor, while in fact they are very different media that employ distinct skills in selection of subject matter, interpretation, and production. The interchange between public and academic was invaluable but the balance was wrong.

For just over two years I was Curator of History at the city-funded Museum of Albuquerque; then I went due north to Billings, Montana, as Director of the Western Heritage Center, a small regional history museum funded in part and governed by Yellowstone County. Finally in 1979 I moved to Helena as the Director of the Montana Historical Society, a state-funded, full-service historical organization. I stayed for nine years. Because I still had not reconciled my academic training with my employment in public history organizations, I lacked any framework for my work. During those years I felt that my academic training was of limited value, that my work lacked any compelling motivation. For me this was a period of gaining experience and gathering ideas that eventually brought forth the ideas I now espouse. But at the time I felt that public history was "history light." I accepted that it has entertainment value, a role in "cultural tourism," but not much else. I did not broaden my definition of who was really qualified to practice history. While I questioned the value of my own academic training I still insisted, at least to myself, that it was the prerequisite to the legitimate practice of history. Really I questioned whether history had any value. As I viewed it at the time, study of the past was marginal to the world's real concerns.

Since the Montana Historical Society was state-funded, we competed for funding with all other state government functions in the biennial legislative sessions. For most of my tenure I was fortunate to work with a very sympathetic governor who once studied history at the University of Minnesota Graduate School. But the recurring legislative ordeal made the minimal importance of history inescapable to me. I should have consoled myself with the peculiar penchant for American states to view history as a governmental function. Our nation was founded on a rationale that rejected a European past and replaced it with a new and optimistic "enlightenment philosophy" buttressed by experience in a "new world." So especially on the frontier where "civilization" was recreated, it was important to give legitimacy to the enterprise. Legitimacy meant history, and these new territories and states created historical societies to commemorate the achievements of those who persevered and reinvented civilization and democratic institutions in the wilderness. This process attracted the attention of historian Frederick Jackson Turner, who made it the foundation of his "Frontier Thesis." By the time I got to Montana the pioneer generation was long gone and the need to preserve memories of their achievements was not compelling for historians or legislators. Certainly historiography itself changed; Turner's ideas were the focus of an ongoing "debunking." The traditional rationale for state funding for history no longer prevailed.

While we successfully secured increased funding through the legislative process and while most legislators were concerned and as supportive as the state's financial situation allowed, I had to make awkward justifications for our requests. In private conversations and in committee meetings the hard questions were asked. "Look, state resources are limited. We've got overcrowded prisons, problems with funding formulas for public education, and increasing welfare burdens. I like what you do but it is a low priority." Our funding requests competed with prisons and other state institutions, roads, welfare, social services, education, and more. Directors of state institutions packed committee hearing rooms with people who were institutionalized with every conceivable physical and emotional disability. Educators presented compelling emotional arguments for better preparation of students from kindergarten through high school and into higher education and graduate school. Highway engineers spoke of substandard roads where dozens of drivers and passengers were killed. Law enforcement officials presented evidence justifying increased staffing to stem rising rates of crime. During this same period the Anaconda Copper Company finally pulled out of Butte, precipitating high unemployment in that part of the state, while the agrarian and ranching economy of the eastern two-thirds of the state was plunged into the farm crisis threatening not only economic livelihood but a way of life as well. There were infinite unmet critical needs and finite resources, and it seemed even to me that funding for the historical society was a low priority. Sometimes I even felt a bit hypocritical in making my pitch for increased state funding. Although I did my job well, my graduate school conviction of the import of history was undermined in the real world of competition for public and private funding. How could I with a clear conscience plead for more money for history while knowing well the problems of fellow citizens whose basic daily needs were unmet? I thought a lot about this. Clichés about learning not to repeat the mistakes of the past, or "you can't know where you are going unless you know where you've been," seemed very trite and yards short of sufficient justification. I kept my skepticism to myself. It would not do for the director of the historical society to have doubts about the relative worth of the institution's work. Maybe I chose the wrong profession and should have gone to law school after all.

I admire anyone who achieves a long career in a state-funded history organization; my tolerance for the natural workings of government was at an end after nine years. Government checks and balances do not end with separation of judicial, executive, and legislative functions. The bureaucracy itself is riddled with checks and balances that make daily business cumbersome. Montana, with a small population and a proportionately small state government, was more streamlined than most state governments. Nevertheless I came to know that the best that could be achieved was to solve any problem for two years, because the state legislature met only biennially. The same issues would come up session after session although the cast of characters changed. For the new legislative leadership, the questions were new and required reconsideration, while for me they were old and repetitive. Survival in this milieu requires more patience than I could muster. Likewise the bureaucracy looked rational on paper; it was reasonably clear who had responsibility and authority for decision making, but it did not work that way in practice. The system was not as neat and concise as the organizational charts implied. Decision making was difficult and procedures cumbersome. In one instance we needed to contract with an artist to produce a painting of the Lewis and Clark Expedition for a historical exhibition. Those responsible for purchasing insisted that we had to request bids and select the lowest qualified bidder. Exceptions to such absurdities were hard to come by since no one wanted to be responsible for waiving procedures.

Despite such frustrations I gradually evolved a more self-satis-
fying definition of my work in public history although it was not
complete when I left for St. Louis, and admittedly is still a work in
progress. I often thought of Bill McKay's Montana ranch and his
inseparability from his place but I did not connect it to history. Nor
did I connect pressures on the continuance of this way of life as a
threat to individuals and communities or as frightening harbingers
of the future. Nor did I recognize that abandonment of rail lines
that linked small towns or school consolidation that eliminated
schools that were often focal points of community cohesion were the
business of public history. I saw the wrenching consequences of
accelerating change and the anguish of many people who suffered
them and I was concerned, but I did not connect all that to my work.
I still harbored vestiges of my graduate school training in which
history was the business of experts, its proper focus big things. I did
not connect the big forces influencing America's economy and society
to what was right in front of me. While I knew about national forces
that produced the farm crisis and threatened a way of life, it did not
seem to connect with the way I then defined the role of history. I saw
the victims in the halls of the state capitol and while I knew that
history could explain how this happened, I also knew that explanations were not what these people needed. I still thought that the role
of history was to deliver up explanations. I did not understand that
my repugnance at the consequences of some change and my work
of history were interrelated. In order to connect I needed not only
to accept that past decisions had consequences, but I would also
have to accept the premise that historians must make judgments.
Furthermore I would need to understand that those people standing
in the capitol halls with their signs of protest had to be involved with
others in that process in order for their efforts to succeed.

I recall Tennessee Governor Lamar Alexander's "Tennessee
Homecoming" campaign in the 1980s. Governor Alexander used
his state's history as a basis for its future. He invited everyone to
"come home" to a good place, a state defined by its past and created
by its history. I know the campaign, an economic development tool
to attract businesses and tourists, was designed by tourism experts
and marketing gurus. But it was more than that and I was intrigued.

In Tennessee, history seemed important in the present, crucial to the future.

Slowly I was beginning to see values from the past that could be extrapolated. But Tennessee is a long way from Montana, and I was still a distance from making connections to my work in public history. I held tightly to my sense of historical objectivity.

New arrivals to Montana are most attracted by the spectacular landscape in the western portion of the state. The mountains, certainly beautiful, have gaudy splendor and impress easily. Crystal streams, verdant high valleys, and snow-covered peaks demand attention. But eastern Montana like all of the great plains needs to work into our minds. The subtle beauty requires an appreciation of that "top of the world" sense that everything curves away and down at the horizon. These plains can be disorienting because landmarks, like the land itself, are so understated—no high peaks, no plunging valleys. There are gently rolling rises, barely discernible, an occasional tree, a rare rock formation, but these signs are neither especially apparent nor remarkable until the land becomes really familiar. Self-perceptions are conditioned by the landscape our eyes can encompass from one spot. When human eyes see to an unimpeded horizon in every direction, humans must acknowledge their own smallness. It took me years to learn to read this land and develop a comfortable appreciation for its message.

I accepted an invitation to speak to the annual banquet of the "Circle Chamber of Commerce and Agriculture" because a good friend issued the invitation. Circle, Montana, in McCone County, is far out on the eastern plains of Montana, not close to anywhere and a day's drive from where I lived in Helena. Once in Circle I checked into a white clapboard hotel near the railroad tracks, the only hotel in town, a husband-and-wife operation that had no other guests that evening; there were no tourist stops here and no interstates even close. A large crowd attended the banquet, but as guest speaker I was invited to go through the ample buffet line first. This was a meat-and-potatoes town and the buffet offered plenty of both. Everyone in attendance knew everyone else well, and an easy camaraderie prevailed. Once the group settled down, finished eating and visiting, it was my turn. My friend Orville made the introductions, and I spoke. The audience was friendly, appreciative of my long drive and my words. The president gave me a tanned sheepskin emblematic not only of the region's economy but also of a way of life. I went back to the hotel and went to bed. I needed to be on the road early since I had a commitment back in Helena late the next afternoon. But that is not the story.

The real story, the one that has stuck in my memory vividly, happened very early the next morning. I got up in the dark, showered, packed my clothes, and grabbed my thermos bottle. You had to pick coffee spots carefully out there; some towns had alkali water that made coffee unpalatable to the uninitiated. Since my expenses were being paid by the Circle Chamber of Commerce and Agriculture, I expected to depart without seeing the proprietors. But all the lights were on in the entryway, and I heard voices mixed with hushed noises. I rounded the corner and saw the couple who owned the place at the counter. "Here's some rolls," the woman said. I was dumbfounded. I realized why she was so persistent in quizzing me about my time of departure. These were not store-bought pastries but fresh-baked cinnamon rolls. Finally in my early morning fog and amazement, I managed to say "Thank you." "Could I fill your thermos with coffee?" she offered. "Yes," I stammered. I was embarrassed by their unexpected hospitality and at a loss for appropriate gratitude. I left with a good stock of rolls individually wrapped in napkins and a quart of fresh coffee. This was not a bed and breakfast, no promises of fresh orange juice and gourmet eggs and biscuits. These were good people doing what came naturally. Circle is an isolated community where people have an acute sense of neighborliness and regard their obligations to each other seriously. They thought there were only two kinds of people: old friends and new friends. No one was anonymous. I was an outsider but I did not receive any special treatment. They extended to me the same niceties that were their routine. I had not been treated this way since I lived in Ishpeming.

When I look back on my trip to Circle, I can draw many meanings from it. But at the time I did not. I did not perceive that the discrepancies between the way of life in Albuquerque or Helena and the relationships in Circle were consequences of history, the result of different rates of change, different values, and distinct narratives. I still did not connect past and present in a meaningful way. But I was assembling the pieces.

While I had not yet even connected history to contemporary community issues and so did not understand its potential power, I was redefining my definition of a historian. In fact, I did write and deliver a paper on collegial and collaborative history. As I reconsidered who was qualified to practice public history, I also began to redefine the historical process. When I reflected on my experience in public history and compared it with my academic years, I found dramatic contrasts. During my tenure in Montana we did major exhibition work. In that nine-year period we replaced all the permanent exhibits, so I had plenty of opportunity to both watch and think about the exhibition development process. We really struggled. The requirement that a historical exhibition must have a bona fide historian unequivocally in charge made the process a jarring one because it disenfranchised other key staff and did not make best use of curators, archivists, and other personnnel. Yet the projects were inherently dependent upon the participation of all of these people. Although I was still trapped by the notion that a scholar had to be in charge, I was beginning to see the liabilities of this kind of process. Finally I realized that the problem was my definition of a historian. Once I realized that all of these people were public historians with equal capacity to contribute to a successful outcome, a truly collaborative process was feasible. While a collaboration must have a manager who watches timetables and oversees budgets and resolves disagreements, this process does elicit contributions from all participants, provides them with ownership of the product and the process itself, and results in better exhibitions.

When I came to St. Louis, my colleagues and I reformulated these principles on an even broader scale. Gradually we have made collaboration a hallmark of all we do and incorporated the community into our collaborative process. Not only is this a better process, but our more precise definition of history itself obliges us to such an expansive collaboration. If history is a process of inclusive discussion, then in order to engage in history, collaboration is mandatory, not optional. This now seems so vital to us that we will add commitment to the collaborative process to our institutional roster of core values.

So we have redefined the qualifications section of the historian's job description, and we have added collaboration to the list to required skills. But another question is about historical significance. I recall struggles to decide what to include in our major exhibition in Montana entitled "Montana Homeland." In some respects we abdicated the obligation by delegating the entire responsibility for interpretation to a lead historian. The impeccable logic of it appealed to me: If we were doing a historical exhibition, then a historian had to decide the content. So the historian in charge made the choices, in consultation with other historians and with reference to collections available to support the interpretation. The result had two primary problems. First, the interpretation, with no explicit value system to support the choices, was haphazard with regard to what really mattered to Montanans. It had become a product of informed personal choice. Second, we had assumed that in ten thousand square feet the exhibit had to be "comprehensive." Even in a relatively new, sparsely populated state, a comprehensive exhibit was not possible, but that was the protective rock under which we hid. I am no longer sure what "comprehensive" means; but as an interpretive goal it reminds me of the encyclopedic nineteenth-century histories. They are encyclopedic only by comparison, and they imply that history is an undifferentiated mound of information without interpretation and without a ranking of relative importance, the trivial and the momentous uncritically intermingled. Our exhibit process really did dodge what was important to the people we existed to serve. When we did succeed in featuring an enduring issue of contemporary concern, we were merely lucky. The process was not designed to produce that result.

As I reflect on my experience in Montana, I am not certain that we could have focused our centerpiece exhibition on enduring concerns. Because the Montana Historical Society received funding from the state legislature and because the members of the Board of Trustees were gubernatorial appointees, there was low tolerance for controversy, although we never tested the limits. Other factors would have fettered attempts to focus our work on enduring issues and concerns. The Board itself was not constructed to reflect the community that the historical society was charged to serve. While it was a good board, its relative homogeneity disallowed diverse perspectives on the state's past. For example, when the issue of how the Lewis and Clark Expedition was to be portrayed, no one on the board could enunciate a perspective other than that of a traditional white male of the hegemonic class and culture. Thus had the board desired to dictate a one-sided interpretation, a single perspective on the issue, it would have gone unchallenged. Finally, we had not even discussed the idea of history as an inclusive conversation of multiple perspectives on enduring concerns. All of us operated with an older definition of history as immutable fact, and many discussions of the newer definition would have been necessary before we could talk about enduring issues or multiple perspectives. Modifying the popular definition of history is an arduous and time-consuming process, and I was certainly not prepared at the time to engage in such a dialogue with either my staff or my board.

It is important to note the board's vital role as guarantor of the organizational mission and the historical process. Consequently board membership cannot be left to chance or the unpredictable vagaries of political process. Yet control of board composition in a governmentally affiliated institution is tenuous at best and depends upon the depth of understanding of those who appoint the board. Internal consensus that the organization's role is the stimulation of public discussion of enduring issues is essential, but convincing public officials and trustees that controversy and debate is positive evidence that the institution is involving people in pertinent discussions is a formidable challenge.

The obstacles to board diversity are many and daunting. Once I was frustrated with an appointment to the Board of Trustees of the Montana Historical Society that I knew the governor was determined to make. I had no particular objection to the individual but the appointment added nothing to the balance of the board. I made the mistake of cornering the governor, who was a friend as well, at a cocktail party and voicing my concerns. I should have known better. This governor understood the issues but the appointment was subject to political pressures. He properly chastised me. "Archibald," he explained, "whenever I make appointments I end up with a bunch of disappointed, sometimes angry people and one ingrate. Furthermore," he continued, "if you want to make the appointments, you run for governor." He was right of course. I was single-minded in my concerns while he had to consider factors that were foreign to me. This was the only time I saw him bristle, and I knew to abandon the subject.

I also knew that for many reasons I no longer wanted to work for a governmental agency. Among my frustrations was a growing sense that the historical process that I wanted to facilitate was, though not necessarily impossible in government, painstakingly difficult. I have profound respect for those who persevere in this work. I know the intrinsic difficulties with the legislative process, the bureaucratic structures in which responsibility and authority are divided, and the issues of appropriate governance.

Montana was the place where I gathered ideas and evidence, but I did not combine them in a coherent approach to history in the public interest until later. The question of the value of history to society persisted until I resolved the issue of historical significance. Just how should we decide which topics to include and which to exclude in exhibitions, publications, theater, curriculum, and in every other form of dissemination? How should we decide what to collect, what to eliminate from our collections, what to conserve, process, and catalog? Traditionally we have built our priorities on an academic model. Because academic historians define significance in their own areas of expertise, we have assumed that the same model is appropriate for public history. Thus public history organizations have lodged these responsibilities with appropriate curators, conservators, educators, and archivists. And these people do their best in an institutional vacuum where these crucial decisions are subject to the preferences of internal experts with little outside guidance. This was the central issue for me. I could not justify the expenditure of public or philanthropic dollars on these well-intended activities that were often disconnected from the concerns of those citizens who paid the bill. Not that what we did was not interesting, sometimes provocative, often informative, quaint, nostalgic, but not necessarily pertinent to the real world. This is what made me ill at ease in requesting increased funding for history in competition with desperate real needs for precious dollars.

While the Missouri Historical Society does get support from the St. Louis Metropolitan Zoo-Museum Tax District funded by the taxpayers in St. Louis City and St. Louis County, we are a private, not-for-profit institution, not a state or county agency. A significant part of our revenue comes from private and corporate contributions, bequests, grants, and other non-governmental sources. Hence, we are still in competition for philanthropic dollars, and to justify our place in the competition our activities must be closely—even vitally—connected to the needs and concerns of our public.

When I arrived in St. Louis, much of what the Missouri Historical Society did was driven by traditional definitions of significance because we had not yet developed an alternative. For example, we did a marvelous exhibition entitled *Saint Louis in the Gilded Age*, funded in part by a generous grant from the National Endowment

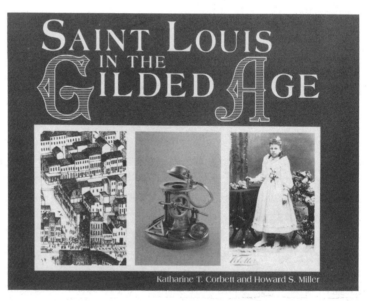

"The practice of public history is collegial, collaborative, and interdisciplinary . . . as in this exhibit which included the work of at least 40 people in a dozen different fields." (Cover from exhibition catalog, "Saint Louis in the Gilded Age." Missouri Historical Society Press, Missouri Historical Society, St. Louis)

for the Humanities. Using the traditional model, a lead historian developed the interpretation with help from outside consultants; she also wrote the exhibit book, which was really an important contribution to the understanding of the period. This eloquent, artifact-rich, and quite beautiful exhibition examined late-nineteenth-century St. Louis through an academic model of race, class, and gender. By many measures the exhibition was a success. The National Endowment was pleased, scholars gave it good reviews, and visitors enjoyed the rich collections presented in a well-designed exhibition. But our surveys indicated that most visitors missed the point. The exhibition's message of race, class, and gender as determinants during the gilded age in our city did not connect. I do not think that it was because the exhibition's message was obtuse, but rather because the interpretation was not within the context of the experiences that visitors brought to the exhibition. Although race, class, and gender impinge on the lives of many people, these concepts are not the primary lenses that most people use to focus their lives. Race, class, and gender simply do not rank high on lists of daily concerns. Perhaps we did not make the contemporary connections clear enough, but whatever it was that *Saint Louis in the Gilded Age* lacked, we needed to reconsider the process used for development of exhibitions.

Public history organizations must develop formal and informal networks of relationships based on mutual trust with their communities to ensure a continuous honest communication. This is not audience research. It is an equal exchange with community representatives. Certainly this requires that exhibits, collecting initiatives, research initiatives, and all of the programming be developed with community dialogue, which can only take place in an atmosphere of trust and with a commitment to honor conclusions. Participants understand from the outset that they are not simply providing information to be accepted or rejected by the staff "experts," but that every question will be answered and every suggestion thoroughly considered. Staff are conscientious about following up every inquiry and suggestion before the next meeting. This is an effective method for including multiple perspectives and embedding enduring community concerns in the interpretation. Now we realize that the discussions that take place in the meetings are themselves critical components. Here we not only educate ourselves and plan interpretation, but we also incorporate the community. We implicitly acknowledge the validity of differing points of view on the past, we discuss the values that apply, and we diminish the barriers between community and institution. We have used similar processes in research projects, program initiatives, and publication projects. We will broaden our application of collaborative process and refine our technique as we gain experience. I have witnessed the interaction with various groups in discussions about the interpretation in our new core exhibit. We are relinquishing authority, and the community is assuming ownership of the results.

However, community history is not a free-for-all. We have tight agendas and timetables, and the roles of staff and community representatives are distinct. Although meetings are conducted by a person from outside the institution, the agendas are prepared by staff. At the core exhibit meetings we prepare a preliminary script, or outline, for the exhibit section. Artifacts are brought to the meeting room: objects, art, film and audio recordings, documents, photographs. Staff members present draft designs for the exhibition and the meanings and interpretations preliminarily assigned to the artifact assemblages. Community representatives offer their own perspectives on the artifacts and the plans and suggest significant topics that are missing. Questions are asked from all sides. It is a fascinating exchange in which our ideas are tested, refined, and improved. But we learn too about viewpoints and issues and subtexts that are not apparent to us, about collections in the community that are pertinent to the topics, but most importantly we are privileged to participate in a discussion of enduring issues in our community. There are additional benefits. We break down barriers between ourselves and the community. We make new institutional and personal friends, enriching our own lives but also recruiting new members, inspiring community advocates, and creating a pool of potential volunteers for the institution. Participants develop a new understanding of the historical process and see that their perspectives are valid. This very discussion is an initial step in defining common ground and the elements of a new narrative for our place, a microcosm of the broader community dialogue we exist to facilitate. Attendance at these meetings is high, and all the participants express the desire to continue. People are empowered because they see their stories in a larger context and know that their history and memories matter.

Staff members balance the perspectives against the historical evidence and core values and ensure that conversations reflect enduring community concerns. They are increasingly adept at evaluating concerns and injecting core values into the conversation and the products. This process of evaluation on the basis of core values and enduring concerns is less formal than when we began our experiment in institutional change because now we have an institutionalized understanding of the implications and an institution-wide ownership of the framework. At the outset we created committees to evaluate and establish priorities on a matrix of enduring issues and core values. We now talk about strategies for improving our community collaboration and engagement, instinctively adhering to the framework we established. We have fewer conversations about definitions and more discussions about implications and applications. These elements now inform every discussion about historical interpretation that takes place within our institution.

As I left a recent meeting with my colleagues, I reflected on the experience. The conversation was animated, the historical content stimulating, and the commitment by all of us to history as a process crucial to the definition of common ground gratifying. It was an unparalleled discussion, intellectually sophisticated but with a point. I was struck that after all these years of seeking and experimenting, I now know what history is for. I also realized how very fortunate I am to be associated with such extraordinary people: people dedicated to community and absolutely convinced that the community's future depends on shared narrative that can be created through the historical process.

If we are to understand the enduring issues in our community, we cannot be distant and detached. In fact, community knowledge is as vital to our work as subject expertise. How can we do community history focused on enduring community concerns without active engagement in the affairs of the contemporary community? Because there are few graduate programs that prepare students for such work, we have prepared ourselves. Thus many of my colleagues are actively engaged in community-based organizations of all types. In other instances, we have recruited people to the staff who are community experts, and we have provided subsidized subject area training for them. Public history work must place equal emphasis upon subject area training and sophisticated understanding of community. Add it to the job qualifications: "The successful candidate will possess a demonstrated record of community involvement and provide evidence of a thorough knowledge of contemporary community concerns and dynamics of community change."

There are other techniques for making a historical organization or history museum into a center of community. Sensitivity to multiple perspectives is the beginning, for people must believe that their points of view will be respected and that happens only in a neutral place. And dialogue about perspectives on enduring concerns happens most freely on neutral ground. As a neutral venue the Missouri Historical Society is now a gathering place for many community organizations, a place where they discover common ground and formulate agendas that address enduring concerns—the Smart Growth Alliance, Citizens for Modern Transit, Citizens for City Charter Reform, neighborhood improvement groups, special-interest history organizations, and many others. Our service as a community center changes perceptions of the institution, enhances our visibility, and expands membership opportunities. While we have maintained our traditional base of members, we have attracted a whole new category of people who actively work to make our community a better place. In the past these people did not see a history organization as germane to their concerns. Now they do. In addition our associations with other community groups has revealed overlapping interests and has led to both single and ongoing collaborative projects that have extended the reach of all of the organizations involved to the whole community's benefit.

Not only are we neutral ground for community discussion and the development of community collaborations, but we get actively involved, for we are committed to the application of the historical process to real community issues. Most of the community conversations about important issues include one or more staff people from the Missouri Historical Society. We have changed perceptions of the character of history and its community value, and so our participation in the community is solicited.

Our community activities are not extracurricular but intrinsic to our mission. Broad community contacts help us become familiar with multiple perspectives, prepare us to discuss common ground, and are often the initial step in important collaborative relationships. The institution cannot establish priorities based on enduring community issues without defining those issues and understanding varying perspectives on those concerns.

The concept of enduring issues is, on the one hand, subjective, but on the other not esoterically complicated. Think about your community, however you may define it. Imagine a representative group of twenty-five people seated around a large table. Distribute paper and pencils to everybody. Ask everyone to write down the ten most important issues confronting the community. While your participants will describe issues differently, all twenty-five will substantially agree on what the issues are. I have done this not only in St. Louis but in other communities of various sizes all over our country. Some of the issues will be particular to that community while others reflect local variations of national concerns. For instance: education reform, crime and safety, environmental quality, infrastructure, taxation, community leadership, family life, and neighborhood quality. Although people will agree on the most pressing issues, predictably they will not agree on a course of action, revealing diverse perspectives based on their own life experiences. Frequently several concerns can be combined into a larger issue. For example, we lumped a large number of concerns under the issue of sustainability, expansively defined to encompass environmental quality and community health. As we have gained experience with this concept, we recognized that enduring concerns are not institutional restrictions but rather guidelines to direct our conversations about institutional priorities. And as our community contacts expand, our understanding of community concerns is more precise. What we have really accomplished is an institutionalization of a new way of thinking about the historical process and our relationships with our community.

This ongoing process of institutional change dramatically affected our internal relationships and planning processes. Larger museums and historical societies are divided into bureaucratic functional units that compete for recognition of priorities and funding requests. Planning is done on a departmental basis, and departmental plans are given priorities by administration and board according to a written institutional plan. We tried this and were disappointed with the results. In effect all prioritization ends up in the director's office because it is the only office in the institution whose business it is to hold an institutional perspective. Within our framework of collaboration, enduring issues, and core values, most of us hold an institution-wide, community-focused perspective on the institution's work. Hence planning is an ongoing institutional collaborative process that establishes priorities based on how well those activities best address enduring issues, involve community collaboration and discussion from multiple perspectives, and allow us to advocate for the necessity of broadly shared community core values. My responsibilities as president are to participate, monitor adherence to the institutional mission, and ensure the application of core values to multiple perspectives on enduring issues. The administration establishes an estimate of available funds, but our discussions of priorities begin with community issues and needs and only then proceed to internal allocation of funds. Within our framework the priorities are established by colleagues who are responsible for implementation, and implementation nearly always requires interdepartmental teams. Both our internal processes and planning are collaborative. We understand that a good process best insures good results.

Existing collections do not become instantly obsolete as a result of this framework; however, there are changes in the symbolic values of objects, documents, even historic structures. I recently watched a video tape of a sheep shearing, carding, spinning, and weaving demonstration. Adult volunteers demonstrated techniques for children who were then encouraged to participate. Museums and historical organizations sponsor thousands of similar demonstrations each year, sometimes using first-person interpretation. But if this is to be more than a demonstration of quaint obsolete technology, new questions must be posed. How do we produce cloth now, and what were the transitions in the textile industry that made hand-operated looms obsolete? What happened when work was moved from the household to factory? What forces produced these changes? How were people affected when they became factory workers instead of artisans? Is this unequivocal progress, or are some things gained and others lost? What do you think about the impact of technology on your own life—automobiles, television, medicine, kitchen devices, computers, telephones? How does it influence your relationships and the way you spend your time? How has it changed your family, your community, the way we do business? Can technology solve all humanity's problems? Who controls technological change? And finally of course the inevitable conclusion that decisions have consequences, that we have responsibilities. Otherwise, history is nostalgia, educational in a general sense, but remote and disconnected from the world we live in now. Abdication of responsibility is not possible since that too is a choice with consequences for the future. The list of possible discussions is endless but the goal is to connect the object or activity to things that matter to people now. We do not need to suffocate all the fun and enjoyment out of history, but we need to recognize that it has a point.

I am thinking of the Chatillon-DeMenil Mansion, a historic house in St. Louis, on a bluff overlooking the Mississippi River and also situated uneasily on an urban interstate highway. Nearly any town of any significant size has at least one such historic house. Most of them, with some prominent exceptions, have low visitation and financial difficulties. Most belonged to some local notable and often began as a historic preservation effort. Many have very limited staff, some no paid staff at all, and are dependent for their survival upon the efforts of dedicated volunteers. Construction of this house began in 1848, and only fifteen years later the structure was remodeled beyond recognition. Was the past any more stable than the present? What was once a country house far outside the city's boundary was now a southern mansion built to the specifications of Nicholas DeMenil, one-time slave holder and southern sympathizer. In the waves of post-Civil War emigration the country house became a city house surrounded by urban neighborhoods and breweries. All of these transformations occurred within twenty-five years of the first stone being set in the foundation. Now, 150 years after the "mansion's" beginning, the neighborhood is seedy and bedraggled, its economic base disintegrated, its residential population decimated by suburban migration. If the original residents returned, they would only recognize a few chunks of the house and of course the Mississippi River below. Yet the house's history is a dissertation on enduring issues. What we see here now is the result of change created by enduring forces in our nation's history—emigration, industrialization, technological change, white flight, suburbanization, federal transportation policy, decreasing urban population density, altered neighborhood and community character, and the federal prohibition law. Changes that affected our region and some that altered the entire nation reach right here to this house and its history. Now the house and the neighborhood that was later constructed around it are obsolete, the human and natural resources that were invested in making this place wasted. So what has happened here is also a sad environmental story. This house is a marvelous opportunity to discuss change and its consequences and to make judgments about gains and losses, right and wrong. And it is a place to discuss contemporary choices about the kinds of places we want to live, the relationships we want to nurture, and the values we hold in common.

But the whole opportunity is missed. Even though the house and the place have undergone tremendous change, the interpretation of the house is restricted to the short period of time in which it was the residence of the DeMenils. Since few original interior furnishings remain, the inside is a museum of decorative arts strung through period room settings. The house's history does not matter much. In one sense it is a mythical past for people seeking refuge in a past that was stable and simple, and where change, if it occurred at all, was slow. The interpretation of this house is typical of many such houses scattered across our country.

One of the pleasures of my Montana years was to travel around that marvelous, many-splendored state to places like Circle. Most small towns in Montana boasted of their historical museums. It was the first place they took visitors. Sometimes their displays and records were located in a structure of local historical significance but often they were in a newer building built with donated labor and materials. Initially, although I kept my opinions quiet, I judged these museums "non-professional." The Historian in me was speaking again.

I was applying the same test that Tony Lucero at Isleta Pueblo had failed years before. I understood that these community museums were different, but I concluded that the difference was in their lack of professionalism. I was wrong: These small beloved museums were functionally different.

What they present is not history in the conventional academic sense; rather, they are some of the building blocks of community. What they offer is a sense of identity, an affirmation of individuality, and evidence of continuity. These places are memory markers for the community, and little context is needed. People walk in with their own memories and artifacts, and in the museum's objects and in the conversations that happen there, remembrance is tangibly confirmed. The numeric explosion of such places is not evidence of a revived interest in old-fashioned history but is instead evidence of community resistance to homogenizing forces. Many of these places are no longer centers for anything and may no longer even have their own government representation. But we can remember. No locally owned stores remain, no neighborhood school or community square, but we can recall them. I think that these places are important. They are civic spaces where bonds of community are reinforced, places for discussion of important things. They are not professional, and they are not appropriate models for our work but in them the right discussions often happen.

The changes I advocate are not words on papers, and they are not the same old business. They are wrenching, time consuming but worth the effort. All staff, but especially professional staff and executives and governing boards, must think differently, act differently, and change the business they are in. Roles change, and those who cannot accept this radical remaking will leave the institution. These changes must begin at the top because they are too far-reaching to implement any other way, but they will not be brought about by memo. Implementation requires consistent and persistent internal discussions to create a shared understanding of implications, to initiate the collaborative process that is central to the transition, to substitute a discussion of community needs for concern with institutional needs. Eventually the community-focused environment must be internalized by everyone who is responsible, in any way, for implementation. It becomes a way of thinking and acting, not a document in a desk drawer or in a showcase at the annual members' meeting.

Transference of institutional ownership to the community is the most arduous change because it demands that staff and board share authority for direction of the institution. Researchers and curators no longer arbitrarily determine what is significant nor do they unilaterally assign meanings. Instead they must become community facilitators. Presidents and directors become facilitators, too, and guardians of process rather than final arbiters. Trustees must tolerate multiple perspectives and diverse voices and accept the risk of cacophony. We must cease to measure the institution's success on consoling internal benchmarks and learn less comfortable quantitative and qualitative indicators of general community health. We must take on a host of new friends and colleagues: the people and the community we exist to serve.

~9~

Everybody's Business

Business practices are remote from my existential experiences with Lake Superior, loons, and the northern lights. Yet in an oblique relationship they are inter-connected. The value of our transcendent experiences is hard to transfer to a P&L statement, but we in the institutions that must help provide those community-building experiences rely on good business practices in order to continue our mission. Without them we are destitute and ineffective.

I left Carleton College during my sophomore year because I needed to be near family, friends, and my place in Marquette. I went to work in what was then St. Mary's Hospital, where my duties included transporting bodies to the morgue. Then I enrolled at Northern Michigan University in Marquette. I had no idea what I wanted to do. While at Carleton I had grazed widely through the academic smorgasbord: English, astronomy, paleontology, mathematics, and geology. At Northern I pursued practical disciplines that most directly prepared me for employment, gobbling big doses of economics, business, and accounting. The underlying fundamental axioms of these subjects make them self-defined as objective and quantifiable disciplines, especially economics and accounting. Students are taught that if they do the manipulations correctly they get tidy, verifiable answers. These subjects ignored the big questions and at the outset I thought they were noncontroversial, value-neutral, and, unlike the arts and humanities, immune to endless debates over interpretation. At that time I needed the reassurance of predictability.

But I continued to be a nocturnal hospital orderly, where I found little of the predictable but much of the conundrum of life. I saw death in many guises—through an anonymous tangle of tubes and foul bandages, in pinched faces and diseased flesh and sharpened bones—yet I remained fully connected to life. One midnight as I pushed my gurney down a darkened hall, I saw that the elderly patient in Room 203 was at last in a deep coma. He was a handsome old man, with thick silver hair and frail, elegant hands, presumably without relatives or even friends, for his final stay in this hospital had brought no visitors or even messages. I stopped at the door of his room; I heard nothing but his soft, faltering breathing, and my own somewhat unsteady heartbeat. I felt his pulse, faint, slow, fading. I drew a chair up to the side of his bed and held his hand. Through his pulse I could feel death approaching. It was no macabre instinct that kept me there through the pre-dawn hours, but rather a feeling of awe and a kind of communion, the fulfillment of an obligation granted to every living generation not to be fought off or denied but accepted as a condition of life. The other staff tried to dislodge me, reminding me about other duties more in line with my job description. But the business of dying seemed more appropriate, more compelling on this particular night.

My nature seems to be to question assumptions, and it was not long before I began to question even the assumptions of value-neutral disciplines such as economics. I was forming my initial insights that *values* were buried in business, marketing, and accounting. I remember an exchange with my professor in a microeconomics class. "Economics," he said, "is based on the predictability of human behavior." "What is he saying?" I thought to myself. I asked him to give me an example of what he meant. "Suppose," he said, "that you tell me that your favorite soft drink is Coke. With that information I can predict that when you go to a soft drink dispenser, you will put your money in the slot and push the Coke button." I debated the point with him. If the question is what soft drink is my favorite, I will answer Coke, but that does not mean that every time I put coins in the vending machine, I will push the Coke button. Sometimes I am in the mood for a root beer, an orange soda, or even ginger ale. Maybe there is a way to statistically predict my behavior, but the professor did not make that case. I left the exchange feeling that economics had let me down. I had sought certainty, but now I had to acknowledge that despite trappings of objectivity, economics and business were as value-laden as the humanities. Their practitioners just did not admit it. After this discussion of economics and human behavior I never again viewed business as "just business." I knew that it was as open to varied interpretations as any other discipline. Charts, graphs, financial statements, economic theory, and business techniques are subjective despite their straightforward form. My subsequent experience confirmed my tentative suspicions.

Economics is packed with values, for economic subjugation produces people who have no ownership in society and no stake in the future, people who, lacking both education and employment, cannot follow the rules because the rules do not work for them and make no sense to their lives. We are perilously close in this nation to the creation of an underclass and its perpetuation from one generation to the next. The very possibility of an underclass due to economic defeat is unjust, inhumane, and a threat to our democracy.

Economic disparity, with its lasting impact of restricted educational and employment opportunity, is often rationalized by the precepts of racism. When I came to the Missouri Historical Society in 1988, I was astounded by the pervasive racism in St. Louis. Racism is attitudinal, emotional, carefully taught and learned, and then brewed with class distinctions to concoct an explosive mixture that must be approached as such. Corporate executives and African-American leaders in St. Louis agree on the threat posed by the status quo. In meetings of a variety of organizations that I attend, I have observed a growing consensus that we all have a stake in an aggressive expansion of economic opportunity to include those who are dispossessed, not necessarily because of the injustice of wasted lives but rather as a consequence of an expanded definition of enlightened self-interest and effective business practice.

On my visits to dozens of other historical organizations and museums in our nation each year I inevitably hear the word "diversity" and see the proliferation of "politically correct" topics covered in exhibitions, publications, and other programming. It is as if by using the words and nodding in recognition of a problem, we have somehow solved it. Now even the word "diversity" is faded and shabby to me. It is an innocuous word, a "warm fuzzy" euphemism but not necessarily a true solution to a real problem. To say that we are "diverse" is nearly meaningless: No two of us are alike. We are all different. We vary by age, height, weight, gender, culture, experience, race, genetics, and in a plethora of other ways. In the public history field, we engage in programming that appeals to diverse audiences and then assume we have done our jobs. We do exhibitions that incorporate minority history. We publish articles about women. We present programs on civil rights, ethnicity, and race. But I often hear the lament that "we have done a great job of diverse programming in our institution, yet minority participation remains low." Many of us have learned the inaccuracy of the popular cliché, "If we do it, they will come." Further, our pronouns inadvertently reveal a big part of the problem, with the implication of a dichotomy, a chasm between "we" and "they."

There are exceptions, of course, and obviously racially or culturally specific public history organizations and historic sites have different experiences. But we need to modify our use of the innocuous "diversity" word and acknowledge our real concern: our need and desire to stimulate greater involvement of people of color in our institutions, as our audience and supporters but also to assist in the search for solutions to the larger endemic social problems. Practically, if the problem in our communities is lack of economic opportunity, particularly for people of color, how can we really contribute to solutions by presenting programming for "diverse audiences"? It is patronizing and demeaning to offer exercises in diversity to people who need jobs, business contracts, and other economic opportunities, and the most outstanding history program will not likely be successful if our target audience is people whose overwhelming concerns are finding jobs and paying for food, housing, health care, children's schooling. I think that we often respond by implying that as historians and history organizations we just do history. Jobs and contracts are not our business; creating economic opportunity is someone else's responsibility. We need to accept the fact that we are also corporate citizens, and our symbolic influence belies our relatively meager economic resources.

If the primary problem of our region is the unconscionable expansion of an African-American underclass, then our institution has been an integral part of the problem. We had only one professional African-American staff member, and although we were fiscally responsible, we did not monitor how and where we spent our dollars. We mouthed the usual excuses. "We would like to hire more people of color but there are just no qualified applicants." "We have an obligation to taxpayers and donors to spend our dollars where we get the best product for the best price." "We cannot pay a premium for goods and services; that would violate our fiduciary obligations." I said these things. I was complicit. I assumed naively and incorrectly that the way we conducted our business affairs was value-neutral. And yet twenty years earlier I had sat in business classes and questioned assumptions.

One of the reasons for my oblivious neglect of this issue was my Montana experience, where my institution was a state agency with very little control over specific spending decisions, its policies governing expenditures established by other state agencies. The Missouri Historical Society was not subject to the same controls. But no matter where we are, in this nation how we decide to spend dollars is never neutral. And unfortunately dollars are the most important measure of intent and worth in our culture. Who gets the dollars is the most powerful sign of who and what matters here. I knew this. I grew up here. How could I forget? People who have a disproportionately meager share of dollars see this as a denial, both tangible and symbolic, of their self-worth and societal value. It means hardship if not poverty, and it understandably provokes anger and scorn. So to present programming for diverse audiences while conducting our business affairs as usual is more than inappropriate, and we should not be surprised at a minimal response to our efforts however well-intended. Too often we are giving our communities conflicting messages. On the one hand our programming signals universal welcome, but on the other, our business decisions, where it most auspiciously counts, reflect the "good old boy" network or a passive solicitation of bids from minority firms that "proves" our commitment to diversity and inclusion.

Often we do business with firms and individuals with whom we have developed trusting business relationships or with those who are known and recommended by board members. Based on past experience we know that we will receive good service. This is a logical way to minimize risks, to insure predictable pricing and quality

products, and to relieve worries about delivery or completion sched-
ules. At times all of us have felt obligated to do business with donors
to annual or capital campaigns. When we do solicit bids, we too
often use a relatively small list of vendors known to us from previous
business experience. We assume that with this business philosophy
we are acting in the organization's best interest.

The St. Louis region has two and a half million citizens. I assumed that business practices of the Missouri Historical Society would
be of small significance and little interest in a huge regional economy.
A large population base and our small size relative to the expenditures of the larger business community meant that our own business
practices would be trivial and unnoticed. I was wrong for two reasons. I learned that cultural institutions are symbolic in the community because so many have long been bastions of the community's
elite; they are closely watched because their business dealings are
presumed to reflect the attitudes of their board members and thus
the institution itself. Secondly, although I knew that the number of
minority- and women-owned firms is relatively small, I was unaware
that their low numbers made it easy and even imperative to exchange
information. Thus word about who is serious about awarding contracts travels very efficiently through that communication method
called the grapevine and more formally through the Minority Contractors Association. I realized that business practices are an important indicator of a history organization's genuine commitment to
diversity and inclusivity. I learned firsthand that our organizations
cannot be community-based and continue business as usual, for that
situation nullifies our attempted message of inclusion and alienates
the very audience we seek to attract.

Revising business relationships demands fundamental change,
presents unfamiliar challenges and more risks, and expands the
workload for many of the staff. The problem is compounded when
public history organizations are agencies of government and often
have no control over purchasing policies and implementation. For
these organizations consistency between program messages and
business practices may be at the very least fraught with obstacles.
But appearances do matter, and from the outside, to those in business, especially minority- and women-owned firms, and especially

those who are left out of our business interests, the institution is a closed club. Those business people know that in such situations they rarely get the contract, so if their bids are requested, they are likely to assume that it is just an empty gesture. They have all experienced such gestures; that is, they know that an organization seeks their bids only to demonstrate its good intentions while intending the contract for those vendors whose relationship with the institution is well established. Most of these potential bidders are small firms and find preparing sham bids is too time- consuming and expensive for the feeble results. But the organization can claim solicitation of minority companies. "No bids were submitted. We tried." Perhaps some of these claims are even sincere, but sincerity is no substitute for solutions.

At the Missouri Historical Society we have developed a business system that works. Our process for purchasing is simple but it does demand internal commitment. All of the staff must know, and completely accept, the fact that the distribution of our dollars is a tangible indicator of our commitment to our community-focused mission and consequently purchasing is not a matter of just buying goods and services. Procedurally we require that three bids be obtained for any purchase over five hundred dollars, and if there is a female- or minority-owned vendor available in the region, at least one of the bids must be from such a firm. Necessarily we refer to published listings of what are called "disadvantaged business enterprises," which is bureaucratic jargon for firms certified to be under a certain size owned by a woman or a member of a minority. The result of this simple policy is that more than thirty percent of our purchases are made from "disadvantaged business enterprises."

For smaller purchases not included in the five-hundred-plus category, staff is encouraged to look for minority vendors as well. For instance, we buy most of our film from a camera shop whose owner is an African American. Our staff is committed to this policy in personal ways as well: When her new car was victim of a "fender-bender" accident in a supermarket parking lot, one of our research assistants sought out an African-American-owned body shop for repairs. And she recommended their excellent work to her colleagues.

Purchasing and contracting require different strategies, and contracting is more complicated. Because we have recently been involved in two multi-million-dollar capital construction projects, the dollars involved are significant. We had no experience in this area, and no models were immediately available and hence no ready-made prescriptions for success. We have had to develop our own procedures, often through trial-and-error experimentation. Traditional contracting procedures do not result in high rates of utilization of disadvantaged business enterprises. General contractors and construction managers do not have much experience in these kinds of business practices. They too find it easier to do business as usual, so they are a part of the problem. However, when the client is paying the bills on a large project, as we have been, the general contractor will cooperate to do whatever the client demands. It will not suffice to demand that the general contractor or construction manager set a percentage goal for minority or female participation; the sought-for objective will not be attained with the customary procedures, and most often a general contractor lacks the necessary experience to comply. Typically when the bids are opened very few will be from "disadvantaged business enterprises," and even fewer of these will be a qualified low bidder. The general contractors will explain that they did their best to increase participation from minority- and women-owned firms and the client should not be disheartened because this is just the way it is. This is business as usual, and it will not work.

We no longer set meaningless targets. We mandate that the general contractor or construction manager award an exact percentage of contracts to disadvantaged business enterprises. This tactic has been very successful: On our most recent multi-million dollar project we awarded thirty-four percent of contracts to such qualified firms, which won us recognition from the Minority Contractors Association.

This thirty-four percent is no accident. Most minority- or women-owned firms are small, and small firms prudently do not respond to huge projects' bid packages because of the business risks. They are either undercapitalized relative to the job size, or the package is so extensive that it includes skills, trades, and procedures with which small firms have no experience or lack the required specialists or expensive equipment. Project bids broken down into small parcels are not intimidating or dangerous for small firms, so we structured our bid packages in this more manageable way. In some cases our construction manager even helps to refine bids and interpret speci-fications or calculate costs. We can also lower or eliminate bonding requirements because new and often undercapitalized firms find it very difficult to obtain appropriate bonds. Sometimes we ease cash flow problems for these firms by paying for required materials as they are purchased and by reimbursing payroll every two weeks. As the word gets out that we are serious about awarding contracts to minority firms and that we are fair and willing to help overcome obstacles, higher percentages of minority and female participation become easier to achieve. Yet we remain fiscally responsible. We do not pay premiums, and we get good quality. While our success is praised as a model in local editorials and our efforts were recog-nized by minority contractors, these plaudits are far less important than the changed perceptions of the institution. The Missouri His-torical Society is seen as a model for future business practices not only by women and minorities but also by traditional companies of all sizes that need to achieve similar results. Our mission, our mes-sage of inclusion and diversity, our core values are reflected not only in our programming but also in our contracting and purchasing procedures. This objective is no easy goal, nor is this achievement maintained without effort, but it is crucial to our continued survival in the community.

Staffing is another crucial expenditure of dollars through which we either reinforce or weaken our mission and our image. In my first days on the job in St. Louis I spent time in discussion with each of the staff. At that time we had only one professional-level African American. My meeting with this outspoken woman was an experi-ence. "So," she began, "what kind of racist are you?" Ouch! But as we continued the conversation, I tried to see from her perspective. Like so many well-intended white Americans, I abhorred the notion that I was a racist. I still thought that racism was manifested in bla-tant words and vile behavior, not in subtle habits. (And I still reject the accusation that because I am white, I am a racist.) However, I recognized that I do engage in behavior that perpetuates racial disparities. After all, I, a white male, was the chief executive of an institution that had only one person of color on its professional staff. In this sense the accusation was on the mark. The Missouri Historical Society presented excellent programming for "diverse audiences," including exhibitions and programs that explored very difficult topics, but institutionally we were not truly committed. Individual professionals developed these programs and exhibits with a deep commitment to presenting and exploring the history of all segments of our community, but even they did not represent a genuine and comprehensive institutional commitment. Fundamental organizational change had to take place at the board and executive level before we could begin to claim that.

In our community an institution with an all-white professional staff cannot preach a message of inclusion with a straight face. ("So what kind of racist are you?") Our mission and our core values allow no possibility of neutrality and thus no plausible excuse for taking no action. But other factors compel the development of a diverse staff. The very presence of people of color at all levels of our institution is symbolically and strategically crucial to credibility and to successful pursuit of a community-focused mission. Appearances do matter. We cannot accomplish our mission if all the professional faces are white, for this tells all St. Louisans that our public pronouncements are nice but not sincere, that our words need not be taken seriously. Total "whiteness" contradicts our interpretative message of inclusion and diversity. Thus it diminishes the impact of everything we do. An inclusive message and exclusive hiring practices, no matter the reasons, are incompatible.

Our mission to facilitate inclusive discussion of enduring issues requires us to encompass multiple perspectives and diverse voices on those issues; thus our mission also requires us to develop inclusive community relationships. We cannot effectively pursue our mission with a homogeneous staff; our staff must be as diverse as our community. It is true that white people on our staff have built important relationships and bonds of trust with members of the African-American community, but one-on-one relationships are not the same as an institutional stance, and a white St. Louisan, no matter how sincere, cannot replicate a black St. Louisan's perspective and experience. There is no substitute for a consistent presence within the staff. These kinds of relationships are prerequisites not just in programming, collecting, and interpretation but also for membership development, increased visitation, and fund-raising.

In the midst of a national backlash against affirmative action, it may be unpopular to carry on these discussions. Our efforts are affirmative and aggressively active, but it is not because of any legal requirement, quota, or mandated percentage. We do these things because it is the only way to do our job, because it is consistent with our message of inclusion. Nor do we deny the additional benefits: It radically alters perceptions of the institution throughout the community and creates successful role models both for people of color and people in business.

We are pleased but not satisfied with the results. We have targeted minority recruiting efforts at the professional and managerial level, and we do have significant numbers of people of color in professional positions and in upper management, perhaps more than in any other general museum or historical society in our country. Now our staff is more than thirty percent African American. This has not happened easily, and we have more to do. It requires the same diligence as our contracting process.

I attend many national meetings—the American Association of Museums, the American Association for State and Local History, and many others—and I inevitably notice the scarcity of people of color. Some of my colleagues look around at these meetings and say, "No wonder I cannot recruit people of color to work in my institution; there is such a very small pool of applicants." That attitude justifies the status quo—business as usual. The problem cannot be blamed on the applicant pool, nor can we abdicate the burden of solving the problem. After all, the problem is as much ours as anyone else's. There are few African Americans and Hispanics and Asian Americans and American Indians at professional meetings because we ourselves have built up barriers to minority participation, and we are the only ones who can eliminated them. Several obstacles to minority recruitment and hiring are immediately apparent. Traditionally our organizations have not drawn the interest of many people of color because we have been bastions of the elite. Our work was not attractive because it did not include them, their communities, their histories. The narratives that we have perpetuated were exclusive. For example, the most prominent topics at the Missouri Historical Society in the past were Charles Lindbergh, the Louisiana Purchase Exposition, and the Veiled Prophet organization. The latter was until recent years an all-white male club, secret, elitist, construed as racist. This was not enticing fare for people of color in St. Louis. If not overtly antagonistic to their interests, our organization was at least irrelevant. People we seek to attract to work in our institutions will only do so if they find reflections of themselves. Minority recruitment will not be successful without a visible commitment to institutional change. While many of our organizations have made those commitments, perceptions and habits from the past persist.

The minority recruitment efforts of graduate schools that train people for work in historical organizations and history museums have also been lax. But have we placed rigorous demands on them? Have we really made our desires and requirements known? I do not think so. We have not protested much, and few of us have funded scholarships for minority students. We have even been passive in our own recruitment efforts—the human resource equivalent of blandly soliciting bids and then expressing disappointment at the lack of minority response.

We have to do something differently. We can begin with an internal assessment. Is the commitment to inclusion embedded in the institution, a commitment that is obvious in actions, not just statements? Is the institution committed to those changes that make this an attractive and meaningful place for people of color to work? Do staff in senior management and members of the board incite change, or is it a few committed staff members who cannot establish or alter institutional policy? How proactive are recruiting efforts? Have the most important attributes of a candidate been considered? How does the applicant pool change, for example, if we consider community expertise and experience as equivalent to academic expertise and public history experience?

A rethinking of the necessary qualifications is an appropriate way to increase the pool of qualified applicants and an effective means to establish and maintain community relationships. Often I have re-viewed drafts of job descriptions that require a traditional mixture of education and experience, when these requirements really bear little relationship to the actual job and would create unintended barriers to the hiring of people of color. In a community-focused organization knowledge of the community is vital to satisfactory job performance. Yet these job descriptions continue to place priority on academic background and experience in a public history organi-zation, as if the community part is inconsequential or can be pas-sively absorbed at will, and perhaps indicates a conventional approach to public history practice that is no longer valid. Lack of community experience and knowledge is a deficiency in otherwise qualified candidates, an impediment that is more significant than lack of an academic degree or institutional expertise.

Formal education and training are not to be disdainfully waived. We understand that candidates without them will have an expanded learning curve. But we know that candidates without community expertise and experience will also have an expanded learning curve. While we have not precisely quantified the comparative costs of training in these two different methods, I am convinced that the costs are approximately equivalent between those two types of can-didates. With this premise and a tuition reimbursement program for job-related academic coursework, we have attracted and hired can-didates who would not be considered using the old requirements. The benefits are much broader than the hiring of minority people who contribute immeasurably to our efforts; fundraising and devel-opment, visitation, collecting, programming, and publicity have all profited from our renovation of hiring practices.

The dilemma we faced in minority recruitment and consequently our solution can be traced to the scarcity of minority students in pertinent academic programs, but it is also due to the lack of appro-priate academic programs in collaborative, multi-disciplinary, com-munity-focused public history. But we cannot absolve ourselves. We must take an active role in seeking solutions. The Missouri Histori-cal Society is doing so: We initiated a program in community history with the University of Missouri–St. Louis and together solicited the funds to endow a professorship. The person who fills this position

also heads the program. We have funded scholarships jointly with
the university, and several of our staff teach courses. I know that
graduates of this master's degree course of study are not going to
flock to us and permanently solve our recruiting problems. But the
program will be a laboratory for experimentation with new directions in our profession, and graduates will have an impact on our
work wherever they choose to apply their knowledge and skills.

We must also be aggressive and persistent in our recruiting
efforts. Mainstream newspapers and national publications are not
sufficient. African-American newspapers, black expositions, job fairs,
campus recruiting, are all effective. Word of mouth is also vital
because formal job advertisements are frequently ignored by the very
people we seek to recruit, those who assume that they cannot meet
the qualifications for work at a history organization or museum. We
have used professional recruiting firms with explicit direction that
to include qualified people of color for our consideration. However, one-on-one conversation is even more effective in inviting
applications.

While our recruiting efforts in St. Louis are focused on African
Americans, the issue of workforce diversity is crucial in every public
history organization. There are no absolutely homogenous communities. Again I think of my hometown. People in Ishpeming varied
in the predictable ways: age, gender, income, status, preferences,
appearance, politics, and so forth. But there were also ethnic, religious, language, cultural, and folkway differences. Even in a community of fewer than nine thousand people, long after it ceased to be
a town of first-generation immigrants, neighborhoods were segregated by ethnicity. In the mining economy of Ishpeming there were
deep divisions between labor and management. There were and still
are considerable religious and ethnic differences. Emigrants brought
religious traditions and established churches which in Ishpeming
became centers not only for worship but also for ethnic identity.
Ethnically specific holidays and festivals such as St. Rocco's day in
the Italian community are still celebrated and reinforce cultural
differences. The divide between Catholics and Protestants was especially marked. Even in the 1960s parents and churches discouraged
dating between children of different faiths. While it hardly led to

war, this division did nothing to encourage understanding and appreciation of diversity.

So while in my community of St. Louis the deepest divisions are racial and hence we must concentrate our efforts upon them, there are differences that must be acknowledged and incorporated into public history work in every city and town. These community principles are not only applicable to a racially divided city; they are vital to all public history organizations so that our work does not revert to the exclusivity of the past. The same formulas for contracting, purchasing, and recruiting apply and must be adapted to the distinctive attributes of the community we serve. Public history organizations cannot be successful if they are perceived as representing the interests of only a portion of the community.

This representation must extend to the governing boards of community-based history organizations. Trustees, in performing traditional roles of oversight, fund-raising, policy formulation, and hiring and firing of the director, must be representatives of the community and guarantors of the institutional mission. Board members must understand the mission and the role of history in building community. And this cannot happen unless the board members reflect the multiple perspectives of the community.

The composition of the board is a powerful external symbol of institutional ownership. While not-for-profits do not have shareholders who can claim ownership, we do have stakeholders. Our stakeholders are ideally the entire community. Thus if the goal is to assert community ownership, then the very composition of the board must reflect that objective. Who sits on the board is just as important to public perception as staffing, purchasing, contracting, and programming. A homogenous and exclusive board will undermine the most valiant attempts to present history as an inclusive discussion of enduring issues. In St. Louis this requires adequate representation of African Americans, professional women, and others who, without consideration of race or gender, are individuals known to represent multiple perspectives and capable of articulating diverse points of view. For example, a white male Republican corporate executive may have a much different perspective than a white male Democratic labor lawyer. Both of their viewpoints and experiences are a part of our community. The board must look like the community.

But diversity of points of view is not the only standard for selection of trustees. The many demands placed upon trustees are now compounded, not exchanged. Some traditional roles persist, and paramount among these functions is the responsibility to assume leadership roles in giving and raising money. Corporate and civic elites, and the independently wealthy, are never heterogeneous enough to adequately represent the community. Because the board must fulfill new community-focused obligations and still perform traditional roles, a large number of board members is a necessity. The Board of Trustees of the Missouri Historical Society has more than forty members. This number is not unwieldy, for the real work of the board is done in committees.

There are unanticipated benefits when a board is selected on this model. The board itself becomes a body in which the mission of the institution is implemented. Board and committee meetings become a venue for conversations among shapers of community opinion who would not meet in their normal routines. These conversations reveal multiple perspectives on the past, expose common ground, and inculcate mutual understanding. For instance, I have listened to conversations between a chief executive officer of a major American corporation and a notable African-American physician in which they discussed their adolescent experiences in the years just after World War II. The CEO and the doctor, both native St. Louisans, are about the same age, but their experiences as might be expected are very different and have affected their assessments of what priorities our region should adopt for the future. Their conversations are stimulating and useful for the institution, the community, and their personal lives, and I know that both individuals look forward to trustee meetings precisely because of the opportunity for further expansion of their individual perspectives. The board's heterogeneity makes this unusual opportunity available. It is only a small step to explain to all the trustees that it is precisely these kinds of conversations we seek to facilitate community-wide. And trustees say to me that if this is what history is, they want to be a part of it.

When the board is heterogeneous, conversations like these inevitably take place while others are not likely to ever occur. Because of the composition of the Board of Trustees of the Missouri Historical Society, for example, our policies on contracting, purchasing, and hiring are not called into question. The board's finance committee, which regularly reports to the full board, provides oversight to ensure that resources are spent prudently. As long as we are good wardens of our resources and as long as the processes are fair to all, the trustees have fulfilled their fiduciary responsibilities.

The Board of Trustees, by the nature of its composition, is tolerant of the multiple perspectives expressed in all the forums sponsored by the institution and all the forms of dissemination used by the institution: exhibitions, publications, theater, television, radio, lectures, tours, and others. However, this is not a license for caprice but rather a responsibility to encourage open debate and discussion and to insist upon core values as the bulwark against unbridled relativism. Trustees would properly move to prevent

"Corporate and civic elites and the independently wealthy used to fill our board membership. But the composition of the board is a powerful external symbol of the community–today's boards must look like the community." (Presentation of the newly completed Jefferson Memorial Building in 1913, home of the Missouri Historical Society, Missouri Historical Society, St. Louis)

debate without structure and challenge dialogue that permitted, and hence validated by default, destructive points of view. It is incumbent upon my colleagues and me to understand that we cannot serve either our trustees or the public well if we are unnecessarily provocative, if we alienate both our community and the trustees who represent their interests. This is a delicate balance, requiring constant vigilance on the part of staff. Our mission, our programs, and our success depend upon this balance. While we can lead and guide, we must be certain that we do not lose credibility with our multiple constituencies in the process. Trustees are ultimately legally responsible for the actions of the institution and because they both oversee policy and represent the community, they are our principal constituency fulfilling both internal and external roles.

If the board is constructed on this model, they collectively embody the fundamental axiom in our institution that history is a discussion of multiple perspectives on enduring issues and a search for common ground. Therefore trustees are not distressed at disagreement over the meanings of the past. They understand disagreement in dialogue as a natural step in the process of history. They know that if we discuss important things, things that really matter to people, there will not be instant consensus on the origins and evolution of such issues nor quick agreement on their resolution. Without this understanding and support from the trustees, it is impossible to implement the mission. We all know of many recent instances of destructive debate focused on historical interpretation in public history organizations and history museums. These conflagrations erupt because of perceptions that there is but one orthodox interpretation of the history in question. When a board upholds historical orthodoxy, the struggle for history is lost. When a board supports expression of divergent points of view as the starting gate of history, the process goes on.

The change process described in this and the previous chapter will produce a transformed organization, whether it is a historic site, museum, historical society, or any other type of institution that presents history for the public. The process demands that institutional ownership be transferred to the community at all levels. It requires commitment to internal and external inclusive and collaborative processes. Once undertaken, the process inexorably dissolves barriers between community and history organization, and the process of discussion of burdens and legacies from differing perspectives is lodged where it counts most, within the community itself. Hence it becomes not an institutional process, but rather an integral component of the community's process of going about its most important business. In order to do this, we must reject traditional authoritarian roles in which we were the purveyors of historical truth. We must assume our obligations as facilitators of inclusive community conversations and as responsible custodians of those symbols of the past that reside in our collections.

Last night I walked along the bluffs overlooking Ishpeming, gazing toward Lake Superior and listening for the voices of the loons. How far I seemed from purchasing procedures, minority recruitment, board development. Yet this time too is a part of my own commitment to the process of history and the building of community. The process of becoming a public historian has also dissolved—or at least diminished—some of the barriers between the personal and the professional. The conversation I have been developing through many years and multiple experiences continues whether I am in the urban forum of my present community or upon these shores where I first began to know and feel community.

✍10 ✍

Facing the Future

The connections between memory and public history have been examined in a variety of venues, including the Missouri Historical Society. But I wanted to use my own memory as a personal historical experiment, and so I went to Michigan's Upper Peninsula because it is my formative memory place. Before I even arrived, it was apparent that this would not be an objective procedure, not a controlled laboratory environment and not within scientific standards. I was, after all, both subject and investigator. My experiment was personal and introspective, informed only by my own memory and my own extensive experience as a professional public historian. I make no apologies, for I was seeking a kind of truth that has no space in either laboratory or marketplace. For many years I have poked and probed the memories of other people, some alive and some long gone; but never have I set out to systematically examine my own remembrances and the interactions of those memories with the places to which they are attached.

My intent in this journey was to refine my skills as a public historian by undertaking a personal role reversal, although I knew that setting myself up as both examiner and subject violated the professional standards of nearly every discipline. Perhaps historians are less reflexive than we ought to be. Anthropologists ponder the relationship between examiner and subject and understand that the process of investigation has consequences for both parties. But historians seldom examine how their own personalities and memories influence their interpretations or how studies affect our subjects. Almost never do we examine how the process of history alters our own lives. If history is the way to self-understanding and if we are to credibly advocate it as a tool for others and for our communities, then those of us who practice it must be cognizant of its effects upon us. In the past, history was principally constructed from documentary and artifactual relics, not living informants. Thus historians were not greatly concerned with how the process of history modifies the course of events. But practitioners of community history purposefully intend to modify the course of events. As a result we must now consider the consequences of our actions and consider carefully and cautiously the intended future. So while I now understand the perils of my strategy, I have also discovered it to be extremely useful. While I have not removed my historian's mantle and I have not permanently abandoned Clio, I did try to temporarily set them on the far perimeter of my current work.

Historians have done an inadequate job of defining the intersection of history and personal memory. Too often these are viewed as separate spheres with little in common, one professional and subject to stringent rules of historical evidence, and the other personal, anecdotal, and of suspect accuracy. Certainly oral history makes use of personal reminiscences, but oral history as a discipline has a structured format and a specific research objective, where the personal narrative is of subsidiary interest and the interview is conducted

"The last standing Ishpeming mine shaft headframes. . . a memory anchor for anyone who grew up in Ishpeming in the twentieth century." (Photo by Sue Frisk, 1998.)

in accordance with the historian's research design. The informant is asked to provide information on a predetermined topic selected by the historian. The interview may be biographical, but the personal narrative is seldom accepted at face value. In contrast as I did my work, I accepted my personal narrative as legitimate. It may be inaccurate from the perspectives of others with whom I share experience, or of questionable value for historians without independent corroboration, and even of little significance. But for me, since I base my life on this narrative, it has definite legitimacy and, insofar as I have the ability and capacity to influence the future, substantial power.

Historical accuracy was not my question. Rather, the question was: How do I remember what I remember, and why do I remember it that way? So I have had long conversations with old friends and acquaintances, members of my own family, and others who were living in the Upper Peninsula when I was growing up but whom I did not know then. I have sat in familiar places but I have also visited places that I didn't know although they were here, too, years ago. I have also renewed my remembrances by discovering how the place has changed. Some change is obvious: buildings demolished, strip malls and shopping centers created, old neighborhoods in disrepair, some communities in decline while others in stages of growth, the aging or sadly the disappearance of familiar faces and the arrivals of new ones. I have also investigated what has seemed not changed: Lake Superior, the U.P. climate, flora and fauna and broad patterns of human settlement, and some of the places built by humans. But everything does change. What makes some things seem to me unchanging is just a slower rate of change. Although it appears unchanged and unalterable, in fact Lake Superior is different. I notice where erosion has reshaped the contours of the shore, that paths once safe are now perilously close to cliffs. Decades of waves have inexorably undermined the rocks beneath those cliffs and forced huge boulders and whole hillsides to crash down into the water, eventually to be ground up by the movement of the water and rendered into sand. However, Lake Superior time is not my time; my time has a finite beginning and end, a lifetime we call it, while the geological time of the lake stretches over countless lifetimes.

My earlier suspicion that confirmation of memory and hence of personal identity does not require time to stand still is poignantly apparent to me now. I find an inverse relationship between the pace of change and the anchoring of remembrance—the slower the pace the firmer the anchor. While I cannot prove it objectively, I know intuitively that our health and sense of security depend upon a rate of change in our world that does not too quickly obliterate the objects and places of memory. Public historians are monitors of rates of change. But we do not just measure. We are advocates for the type of change that does not disorient humans whose fragile memories depend upon substantial fragments of the past for recollection, connection, and well-being.

Pickling the past in a historic site does not compensate for disorienting change. Nearly every community has some well-intended efforts to convert portions of the built environment into "historic sites." While this may be wise in some circumstances, it is not preservation of the past. Rather it is a recognition that change has overwhelmed the past and that the past is no longer useful and must either be placed in a special purgatory for obsolete things or disappear entirely. When I was in Montana and supervised the State Historic Preservation Office, ghost towns were a dilemma. There were lots of them in various states of decay and disappearance. Now a ghost town is a special kind of historic relic, by definition in a state of disintegration. I concluded that a ghost town was by its nature a site in the process of disappearance. Their particular attraction is that peculiar nostalgia of decay. A preserved ghost town is no longer a ghost town. Besides, ghost towns are not good sites for mass tourism because they are inherently fragile, deserted, potentially dangerous, and with limited access. Should ghost towns be transubstantiated into historic sites? I personally concluded that they ought to be left to complete their natural process of decay. Preservation of ghost towns destroyed those qualities that constituted their appeal as places of remembrance, mortality, as witnesses to change and tangible proofs of time's passage. Preservation of a ghost town is an oxymoron.

While I was in the Upper Peninsula, a "save the last standing Ishpeming mine shaft headframes" movement commenced when the Cleveland Cliffs Iron Mining Company gave the headframes and associated buildings to a not-for-profit group planning a theme park around the relics. Usually the headframes and other buildings are demolished after the mine closes, but the Cliffs Shaft buildings, venerable Ishpeming landmarks, were left standing when the mine shut down permanently in 1967. "Save the headframes" and the theme park may be a good idea. It might be good for tourism. I have not reviewed the business plan or the marketing strategy. But a mine shaft theme park is not a memory anchor. It is something else. These mines are no longer extant, and the gargantuan headframes straddling the opening to a maze of underground tunnels no longer have a function. The headframes are now artifacts—symbols, not the reality. That past is irretrievably gone. History can no more be preserved than time can be put in a bottle. Efforts to "preserve history" even in successful tourist attractions are often forlorn, always expensive, and may be ill-advised attempts to compensate for disorienting change. We might more productively consider ameliorating the consequences of change too rapid for our own well-being.

If the headframes of the Cliffs Shaft Mine become a mining theme park, my own memories will be further diminished. A theme park on this site, even if it is constructed around the gloomy relics, is a further intrusion into this place which is a memory anchor for anyone who grew up in Ishpeming in the twentieth century. History theme parks are as much a contemporary phenomena as shopping malls and have as little to do with history. Better perhaps to simply stabilize the shafts and let them stand as reminders of what was; let the town's current and former residents attach their own memories to what is now a new place; let these headframes become quiet but eloquent artifacts. Let people who know them talk, and let others ask questions, and let the stories be repeated for as long as they are needed.

Acceleration of change causes individual bewilderment, diminishes identities, and devalues communities because ties of common memory are broken. My historian self may ponder the intersection of personal history and communal memory, but in my personal narrative the boundaries are not distinct, actually irrelevant. It is not just landmarks like the Cliffs Shaft Mine site that are anchors for personal and communal memory, but it is the landscape, too.

Wetmore's Landing is a beautiful stretch of beach on Lake Superior bounded by rocky outcroppings at either end. My favorite spot here is on rough rocks elevated a dozen feet over the lake's waves that sometimes crash against the rocks, sending spray high in the air. At other times the waters gently lap in and out of the rocky interstices creating a gentle sucking sound. When I look to the northwest from this point, I see nothing but rocky tree-lined shore broken here and there by small patches of beach where wave action has ground rock into fine sand. But when I look in the other direction, toward Marquette, I see the high smokestacks of the electric power plant. The power plant is not new; within my memory it has always been there, and although it seems an intrusion, it has always stood in that place. But the beach seems flawed by the line of black coal dust pushed up onto the sand by the waves. Maybe that line has always been there, but now it bothers me. The same boats that carry iron ore down the lakes bring coal up to fuel the power plant, unloading coal onto a long conveyor belt that spews chunks of it into the huge pile that will be gradually burned to provide electricity. Fall is a particularly busy time for building the black pile because in the coldest months ice, bitter cold, and unpredictable weather close Lake Superior to shipping. I do not know exactly how the coal dust ends up on the otherwise beautiful beach, but anecdotally I've been told that coal dust blows off the windward slope of the pile, over its top and into the lake where waves carry and deposit the light black powder here on this beach where it dramatically contrasts with the light-colored sand.

The coal dust is an intrusion into my own narrative. I do not want it here. It is an imperfection, visible pollution in an otherwise perfect place. But the fine black dust symbolizes larger dilemmas, not just my own, that are reflective of community concerns. This dust has focused local debates on environmental issues. Implicitly the dust fuels the debate over the nature of "progress" and the issue of who bears its costs. While the *Marquette Mining Journal* is conservative in many respects, it is emphatically not so on the topic of Lake Superior. I picked up this paper each day, and debates over the lake and its shoreline received more copy than any other topic. One edition included both an editorial on plans to sell Lake Superior water and a letter objecting to a shoreline development plan. "The Nova Group," the editorial concluded, "must be told once and for all to back off from this scheme and the Canadian government should get the message that Lake Superior isn't theirs to give away." The letter, written by Darren Muljo, ended with a personal reflection. "I choose to live in the City of Marquette because of its proximity to Lake Superior and the beauty it has to offer. Delve deep inside you and think what 12-story towers and traffic congestion will do to our shoreline." Just as the editorial considers international and national policy and the letter reflects personal attachment on the same topic, so my personal narrative is also a community narrative. It expresses my personal affront at the line of coal dust, but it also conjoins me with larger communal concerns about the protection of this lake, the future of our planet, and the quality of life that will be left to those who follow us here. Additionally my concerns place me on one side of community, national, and global debates over how we can best secure the future. Clearly I side with those who are convinced that humanity must change its behavior if our species is to survive for the long term and if we are to fulfill our obligations to the future.

But the issue is even more immediate. We are all like Darren Muljo. We all need Lake Superiors. The persistence of such places is central to an environmental debate with future implications, but it is also reflective of a deep-seated need to find refuge from the complexities and insecurities of contemporary life in places that set humans in context, that provide constancy in the midst of profound and rapid change. Certainly these are places of transcendence but they are also a counterpoint to the sterility of subdivision living, the degradation of civic and community life, the chilling isolation of contemporary existence, the vacuity of television, and the looming loneliness of the information age. Here I find hints of another ethic, a reassurance that there is another way, a system of values not measured by the ability to consume, not premised on an illusory conviction that resources are infinite. When I look at the line of coal dust on the beach, my personal narrative and community concerns are conjoined. Not only do personal and communal narratives develop from each other but they embrace both built and natural environments. What is good for me is also good for the places I love.

Historic preservation and ecology are distinct disciplines requiring different professional methodologies and research techniques and encountering different kinds of political obstacles. But my remembrances make no such distinctions between the memory places in a built environment—my hometown of Ishpeming—and those in a natural environment like Lake Superior. Certainly they stimulate different memories, but they are interconnected and my memory does not assign priority to either Lake Superior or Ishpeming. Hence the same deep-seated human need craves preservation of both environments. Without both the natural and the constructed environments we are bereft of those memory places that are crucial to remembering and consequently essential for our own humanity. The precipitous decline of Ishpeming is not just my personal loss; it is also symbolic of our national crisis of family and community. It is not just I who lost something; we are all losing something upon which our common enterprise depends. If public history organizations are to be effective advocates for places, narratives, and relationships, then we must oppose accelerating rates of destruction of our environments. Since we are advocates for shared memory and collective narrative, we must also be advocates for those places that are their nurturing crucibles.

Understanding the character of communal narratives is important for public history organizations because those people who participate in their creation are our community and thus the focus of our efforts. We do not advocate an exclusive narrative but instead one that includes all who share a place, who therefore must acknowledge interests and obligations in common. We do not call for the creation of one master narrative; rather, we advocate sensitivity for disparate narratives, an understanding that the development of community between people who share ties to a place depends upon recognition of common ground. Community requires an acknowledgment of interdependence and mutual obligations that can only develop through a narrative weaving people together in a common destiny.

So how do we define community? Who must participate in the process of narrative construction? Who are our constituents? While this is a crucial question, there are no facile responses. Marketers who demand quantifiable responses to such questions seem to run the world. How else can we define target audiences and spend our marketing dollars wisely? While I appreciate the skills that marketing can provide, I am put off by the notion that surveys of target audiences should determine our actions. We are leaders, not followers. We do not seek the perpetuation of the status quo. Our mandate is to change opinion climates, not to cater to existing attitudes. We advocate change and the evolution of values that enable creation of better communities, good places for people, and improved prospects for the future. Marketing techniques assist in gauging success, but they must not divert us from the task. Most importantly, we cannot define our community through surveys that seek to identify target audiences based on habits and preferences.

In my Montana years I spent too much time meeting with senior staff in planning efforts that wrestled with the critical question of just who was our community. We met weekly over several months. We attempted to define what I now call community, but what we then called audiences, without reference to a clear statement of organizational mission. We also debated the issue without reference to real needs of people but rather with reference to existing institutional activities. Consequently the staff people responsible for publication of our journal defined its audience based on circulation of the magazine. We avoided considering why we published the journal and what it ought to contain; instead we considered how best to increase circulation. The archivist and the librarian logically considered audience to be synonymous with patrons who used the materials, and museum and educational staff regarded the question as simply a matter of attracting and serving larger numbers of people. Because the Montana Historical Society was primarily funded by the State of Montana, we acknowledged our obligation to serve its citizens. But the question of exactly what we would do for the state's citizens was nebulous. We just agreed that because the citizens of Montana paid the bills they needed to be listed as a primary audience. We laboriously debated the exceptions: out-of-state researchers and magazine subscribers, tourists who visited the museum, and the historic preservation office that enforced compliance with federal regulations. Without the clear direction that a precise mission provides, we had no logical way to define our audience or to assign priority to existing audiences. Certainly the discussion could not produce a concise blueprint for future direction. The only resolution was a vague and unsatisfying definition: "we serve all of the interested public." In the absence of a compelling sense of institutional purpose, this was the best we could do.

The same question was on the table when I went to St. Louis in 1988, but it was further complicated by the national significance of the institution's collections and the name Missouri Historical Society which led to an assumption that we had a statewide mandate (we didn't, and don't). The Missouri Historical Society was founded in St. Louis in 1866 by a group of the city's illustrious male citizens. The significance of its collections is principally reflective of St. Louis's preeminent nineteenth-century role in the settlement of the west and its historic dominance as Missouri's metropolis, and not of a conscious, systematic effort to document the history of the entire state of Missouri or the Trans-Mississippi West. So the name of the organization precipitates statewide expectations while the collections attract a national research constituency. The institution's funding base contradicted these expectations. While the Missouri Historical Society continues to hold its private not-for-profit status, since 1987 it has benefitted from a tax on real property levied in the city and county of St. Louis. Most of our substantial philanthropic dollars also come from donors in the same metropolitan area.

Defining audience based on existing programs, collections, publications, exhibitions, or funding base produces unsatisfactory conclusions, indeed a labyrinth of misdirection. It is not possible to precisely define audience, which I now refer to as community. Community cannot be defined by examining what the institution collects or the programs it presents. Community is defined as those who comprise a community. This sounds almost like a tautology; but as I have gained more experience, I have raised my own tolerance for ambiguity. This tolerance does not imply that I evade the question. I know now that community can only be defined through a vision of who will benefit if the institution succeeds in accomplishing its mission. Corollary to this is the requirement that we consider who must participate in the construction of shared narrative in order to ensure that those who have overlapping and intersecting destinies find themselves in the story.

True, all human beings on earth share a common destiny and narrative. Those people who live in the St. Louis region or in Ishpeming have a history and a future with commonalities in a different sense than the human residents of the planet. Community boundaries may be arbitrary but nevertheless necessary. The framework of enduring issues helps. For example, the St. Louis region ranks near the top in national comparisons of urban sprawl and political fragmentation. These phenomena are products of national trends like automobile ownership and transportation policy. However, our dismal ranking is exacerbated by our peculiar history, our particular narrative that has constricted our choices. Nearly 125 years ago the city of St. Louis seceded from St. Louis County in a furious debate over taxation in which city residents objected to taxes used to provide county services. A tradition of political localism was established in the politics of the region that has spawned a proliferation of governmental units. Hence there are impermeable but invisible political membranes that separate hundreds of independent political units. They have persisted despite the expense and complexities, due to racial fears and a tradition that justifies better service for those who can afford to pay more. This tradition infects nearly all aspects of public and private life—education, infrastructure, neighborhood policy, transportation, real estate values, cost of government, de facto segregation. These problems seem intractable because regional fragmentation reinforces the paucity of common narratives while shared memories diminish in a fragmented region. The St. Louis region's lack of a shared narrative is both a cause and effect of fragmentation.

Presented with a map of the St. Louis region, I can draw an arbitrary floating boundary around the geographic area affected by this peculiar history and the consequent contemporary problems. This boundary will roughly coincide with the Metropolitan Statistical Area used by the regional planning agency. Now I know that our world is far too complex and interconnected to support any contention that the St. Louis region is not influenced by and has no impact on the world beyond any boundary on a map; any arbitrary boundary can be questioned and its rationale dismissed. However, we need to adopt some reasonable boundary defining a people and a place, or history will be meaningless and shared narrative pointless. While the line may be subjective, its existence is defined by the past and crucial to the future. Communities do not really exist in cyberspace. If we do not presume that people who share a place have interests in common, then public history is sophistry and we should find something else to do with our time and resources. I know that St. Louis has longitude and latitude, specific geographical features, enduring issues, marvelous human accomplishments and that do define shared interests and permanent bonds. We can debate the boundary, but we do know that St. Louis does exist.

We first acknowledge that St. Louis does not exist in isolation and that the boundaries we use are not permanent but vary both with the topics addressed and the time period discussed. For example, during the heyday of the Rocky Mountain fur trade in the first half of the nineteenth century St. Louis monopolized a commercial hinterland that extended to the Rockies and beyond. Consequently our collections are significant to the histories of most of the states carved from the Trans-Mississippi West. Likewise, we know that the current crisis in urban education or the soaring cost of infrastructure are not just local phenomena but rather are manifested in multiple variants across our nation. Thus to facilitate inclusive discussion of enduring issues in our region we must place those issues in larger contexts as appropriate. So while we know that St. Louis had different boundaries in the past, we focus our current efforts on contemporary boundaries as defined by the enduring issues in the region.

Enduring issues define community boundaries. Those boundaries change through time as issues and circumstances change. That community defined by contemporary enduring issues must be the priority for public history organizations, but public history organizations must also respect past issues and former boundaries as the explanatory antecedents to the present and be willing to reexamine and redefine the boundaries as the future unfolds.

These principles are applicable to all community history organizations that enjoy the opportunity to define boundaries and hence

encompass a community defined and unified by issues and interests. The matter is not so simple for public history organizations
that cannot define boundaries according to enduring issues or those
which serve regions with boundaries defined by laws or have char-
ters that have less coherence. The St. Louis region, for example,
encompasses people and places that straddle the Mississippi River
to include the states of Missouri and Illinois. If the Missouri Historical Society was not a private entity, but instead an agency funded by
the State of Missouri, service delivery in Illinois would not be politically possible. State historical organizations confront state boundaries which may constrain community definition in two ways. The
first is the example of historically defined regions that straddle state
boundaries. The second is the reverse. Sometimes state boundaries
define only enduring political issues at the state level but do not
define areas conjoined by any other history or enduring issues. In
my native state of Michigan, the Bureau of Michigan History located
in the State Capitol in Lansing must serve both the Upper and Lower
Peninsulas which are separated geographically, culturally, and historically. A history of Michigan is really two separate histories because the states' boundaries define a political entity and little else.
The Upper Peninsula has periodically engaged in talk of secession
and separate statehood because of the estrangement that is a consequence of a separate history and a distinct set of enduring issues
that share little with prominent concerns in the Lower Peninsula.

Michigan is an extreme example because of the geographical
separation imposed by the Great Lakes, but this bifurcation exists in
many states. In Montana the eastern two-thirds of the state are high
plains, with an agrarian and ranching history more connected to the
Dakotas in many respects than to the history and concerns of the
western third of the state. The western third of Montana is moun-
tainous with an economy historically based on the mining and tim-
ber industries and now increasingly on tourism. The fissures were
apparent in every legislative assembly. Historical and cultural ties
between the two regions are largely the result of state government
rather than any natural affinity and community of interest. Other
states are further divided between rural and urban interests. States
such as Illinois, New York, Colorado, and many others are divided

along such lines. Modern thinkers suggest that states are artificial
entities and that in the future the cultural and economic engines of
our nation and perhaps of the world will be "city-states" because
they are rational entities bound together historically, culturally, and
economically. Thus state history organizations confront exceptional
obstacles. How can these organizations span state boundaries when
history and issues require it? How can they facilitate a common
narrative in a geographical area differentiated by history and concerns? It is possible to acknowledge that a state is an artificial political construct and that the people and places within its boundaries
may have little in common beyond state politics. Perhaps there is no
coherent narrative other than the political one that stimulates common interest among its citizens. The task then becomes acknowledgment of the disparate communities, separate narratives, and variant
enduring issues without attempting to impose common identity other
than that established by political ties. Likewise, where necessary, state
history organizations must form strategic collaborations that transcend state boundaries. State history organizations will acknowledge
that within their boundaries there may be a multiplicity of enduring
issues and hence that they are obliged to facilitate separate inclusive
discussions and the creation of multiple narratives that may have
few intersections. These are certainly challenges, but not insurmount-
able obstacles.

My Upper Peninsula sojourn and memory experiment required
that I compare my personal perceptions of the past with my professional historian's experience of the past. As I tramped around
Ishpeming and its environs, experienced once familiar places, and
conversed with old friends, I came to view history as analogous to
what I recall as "perspective" in representational art, the notion that
there is some invisible point on the canvas where the picture con-
verges and where the painting ends. The viewer see nothing beyond
that invisible point. I was puzzled in the Negaunee Cemetery where
members of my father's family are buried. I can tell stories about my
Great-grandfather Michael Quinn, and I recognize his three wives,
not because I ever knew them, but rather because they are connected
to Michael. I cannot tell stories about them other than they were
married to Michael and that one of them, Emma, was the mother

of my grandmother. My grandmother, who was also named Emma, could certainly have told many stories about all of these people, for they were her parents and her stepmothers. And her memory extended several generations further back, to include not only my great-grandparents but also at least two generations before them. These were people within her personal memory, and I am certain she either knew them herself or vicariously knew them through stories relayed by her parents. But I only recognize a few family names of relatives who preceded me by more than three generations. The individuals have no meaning to me because I have no personal recollections and no relayed stories to connect to them. Three generations are the historical equivalent of the invisible vanishing point in the painting, but in this case it is not where the picture ends. Instead it is that point where my personal knowledge of the past ends. I have compared my personal vanishing point with those of other people. I find that while personal memory may vary by a generation, few people, unless they are historians or genealogists, have personal recollections or even specific family stories that extend further backward in time. So history as personal narrative has clear limits, no more than roughly one hundred years.

Any historical knowledge that extends back more than one hundred years is either the product of an unusually long life or of historical and genealogical research. Although I am a historian, my knowledge of my own past, my first community's past, and the pasts of people I know and love adheres to this generational rule. Any knowledge of an earlier past is a reconstruction. It is built using those symbols that remain including documents, photographs, paintings, landscapes, buildings, personal effects, literature, all those tangible remains of past human activity and interaction with the world. But the past itself does not stay around awaiting our interpretations. What we can know of the past is only what is left. Some of it is left to us intentionally by humans who wished us to remember them in certain ways, and more of it survives accidentally. These things are the only evidence we possess of times before our own. Yet, what remains is a minuscule portion of the past; and, because so much of it survives serendipitously, we cannot presume it to be either a representative nor comprehensive sample. Despite the obstacles and the paucity of evidence, we persist in assuming that the past is knowable and comprehensible. Many insist that somehow history is precise knowledge of the past, but the past is really inscrutable in many ways, just because there is so much that we can never know and so much more that we can only surmise.

Yet history may be all we can know. My summer in the Upper Peninsula of Michigan startled me with the recognition of how very much I have forgotten. My resumption of a first-hand contemporary relationship with people and places once intimately familiar has stimulated the process of remembering, which is what I had anticipated when I decided to spend time here and experiment with my own memory. I did not spend my time in the Marquette County Historical Society's Library nor in the Carnegie Public Library nor in Olson Library at Northern Michigan University. My libraries were the people and places of my formative years. I was amazed at how extraordinarily selective my memory is, and I am confused as to why I remember what I remember and why I had forgotten so many things that my recent experiences have prompted me to remember. I am left with a profound respect for the mnemonic effects of familiar people and places. Some of my resurrected memories seem trivial: I remember clothes, colors, smells, and minor incidents such as the taste of the hot chocolate we drank after skiing at the Winter Sports Club or going to Homburg Photographic Studio for portraits during my senior high school year. But the memories that now seem most important to me are not memories in the usual sense. Instead they are feelings, the experiencing once again of emotions dormant for thirty years. These marvelously frightening experiences connect me once again to people, places, and events submerged and all but gone until I returned to this place.

On one wonderful evening, visiting with an old friend but in a new friendship, I was overwhelmed by a conviction that at least for a few minutes I absolutely lost awareness of the distinctions between past, present, and future. At that moment a blending took place in my mind as the past exerted a transforming effect upon me, and I knew that I could never be quite the same again. My own narrative of myself was reshaped, my sense of identity refined and expanded, and my connections reinforced. Painful as it was at times, I now believe

that this connection with the past is essential to my own sanity and
health. This was an emotional awareness, but it sharpened my intellectual conviction that the past is implicit in the present and in the
future. But even in three intense months in Michigan I could not
remember everything, certainly not every significant and insignificant detail of my former life there. My sense is that I did not replace
my existing narrative of self; that would be neither desirable nor
possible. But rather my existing narrative acted as a filter, a framework for renewed old stories and once-forgotten experiences. However re-remembering is not the simple process of hanging new
ornaments on old trees, because the process modifies the pre-existing framework and filter. Through this process my understanding of
myself is modified and expanded. History is self-knowledge. History,
personal and communal, is the only way we can know ourselves or
understand the feelings and perspectives of others.

We must dispel the notion that personal memory and history
are infallible records of the past. Both are interrelated methods for
making sense of ourselves and the world that we inhabit. History is
artificial; that is, it consists of ideas and experiences that do not
reside in remembrance of personal experience but instead is dependent upon symbols we call artifacts. However, in other ways history
and personal memory are similar, the boundaries barely discernible.
Both are subjective yet eminently valuable, because they respond to
contemporary concerns and are based on incomplete recall of the
past. History and personal memory are useful maps of the world.
They may not correspond to reality exactly but must correspond to
knowable facts. Interpretations vary because meanings vary according to individual perspective and because there is the question of
which facts are most salient. Reality is a matter of perception. That
is why my memory, narrative, and identity are different from yours.
That is why historical interpretation is never static but rather re-
sponds to the needs of the time and place in which it is created.
Good memory and good history are frameworks that permit us to
respond in the present in logical ways both to conduct our lives and
to solve problems. They are not infallible, but they are what we have.

If public history organizations position themselves as the
venues where individuals and communities engage in inclusive

discussion of enduring issues and if we insist upon the application of core values as the basis for identification of burdens and legacies, then we have expansive roles to play in the communities we serve. We are places to inculcate empathy and respect for divergent points of view. We are places to castigate perspectives that promote injustice, undermine our sense of continuity, obliterate our memories, degrade our places, diminish the spiritual needs of humanity, or foment suspicion and mistrust. We are preeminently places to seek and define common ground, emphasize what we share, and define an agenda for the future.

Our task is urgent. Not only are communities fractured and their identities assailed but traditional sources of community leadership have vanished or become ineffective. Old narratives that justified hierarchical community decision-making are discredited. The great democratizing influences in the post-World War II period have empowered women, minorities, and other previously muted voices. Now those individuals insist that they be included in decisions that will affect their lives. Where they still exist, community elites struggle to find new patterns for participation in community business, for the old ways no longer work. In the future inclusion will provide the model for community business, and inclusion will only work if we create models for facilitating community consensus on a course of action that democratically addresses community needs and establishes priorities.

Radical economic and social restructuring accompanied the post-World War II process of democratization. Struggles to achieve equal legal rights for women, African Americans, and other minorities continued the expansion of American definitions of justice and citizenship to include those previously excluded or relegated to second class status. Simultaneously global economic change detached corporations and corporate executives from community concerns. Once many corporate executives were homegrown, and corporations depended upon local markets and a local labor force. Consequently corporations, their executives, and shareholders had an obvious self-interest in the welfare and health of the communities in which they conducted the bulk of their business. Now no major corporation can confine its interests to a specific community and a local market.

The magnitude of the modern global corporation and global competitive pressures requires all successful and profitable corporations to think and act globally, not locally. Such corporations hire the best professional executives without regard to community attachment and have expanded corporate perspectives on markets and labor forces far beyond the community. Global business and local concerns are now disconnected, and successful executives must attend to global, not local, issues. Executives cannot pay excessive attention to communities that contribute less and less to bottom-line profit percentages.

Despite the disconnection from local issues, business leaders seem to have a persistent commitment to quality-of-life issues in American communities and a willingness to adopt new collaborative civic and business models. Yet in community after community either traditional sources of leadership are now more detached, a response to the changed character of business, or local business leadership is replaced by absentee ownership. In my hometown of Ishpeming the dilemma is not only that downtown is gutted as retail business adapts to an automobile culture, but also that the locally owned businesses are replaced by chain stores that are based elsewhere. Thus the store of choice for consumers is the Wal-Mart or the McDonald's down the highway instead of local hardware and clothing and drug stores and restaurants. Not only is the community rearranged in a manner less conducive to casual sidewalk association, but local business leadership is decimated by stores that have a different perspective on local concerns. In another midwestern town where I have done consulting work for a city-owned cultural center, elected officials cannot yet replace the leadership once provided by local businessmen and are struggling to find new frameworks that rely upon community consensus-building instead of the obsolete hierarchical model of community decision-making.

In my ten years in St. Louis the number of "Fortune Five Hundred" firms headquartered there has steadily declined, reflecting mergers and the growing portability of corporate headquarters that enabled electronic communication and corporate globalization have allowed. In fact some corporate leaders point to portability and detachment from any particular place as definite competitive advantages in the coming century. More than ever before, corporations can hold communities hostage by demanding financial concessions from regions eager to retain or attract new employers. While communities do need to be concerned with job growth and economic opportunity, the time has passed when communities ought to be consumed with retaining or attracting corporate headquarters. While corporate headquarters may bring prestige in some circles, communities must now learn to do business through reinvigorated inclusive democratic processes. The old top-down leadership model is no longer functional for reasons apart from the altered character of American corporations.

In the future history will matter more than ever. In the past we could be mirrors on the margins, but now our skills are demanded by communities pursuing new decision-making processes, seeking new methods of doing civic business. Either public history organizations assume a pivotal role in this process, or we will be sidelined far from where communities do the business that really matters. Inevitably new forms of civic deliberation will use skills that we represent, those skills that facilitate community consensus through dialogues in which multiple perspectives are discussed, habits of mutual trust inculcated, empathy engendered, burdens and legacies agreed upon, and an agenda created. This process implicitly depends upon history, for history is the process of discussing what we have done well, what we have done poorly, and how we can do better. If we do not actively respond to these new demands, our functions will be replicated in other institutions. Planning organizations, elected officials, churches, and community-based advocacy groups will use the process of history to facilitate dialogue and consensus. We are obliged to restructure ourselves to integrally collaborate in the process. If we choose not to do so, just what are we for? How do we justify the investment that society and communities make in us, either by assisting us directly with tax dollars or indirectly through tax incentives? This is the opportunity for public history organizations and practitioners to make a crucial difference. In the future our measurements of success will not be our own prosperity and popularity but instead the health of our communities.

I left the Upper Peninsula of Michigan even more convinced of the intimacy of people and place, even more committed to the principle that if we are to rebuild healthy communities, we must oppose those forces that detach people from place and confine them in a lonely present, truncated from past and future alike, isolated from each other, bereft of connections to each other. In such an environment we truly behave as if there is no tomorrow. Ironically the consequences of our beliefs and actions do impose a mortgage upon the future that may result in metaphorical bankruptcy. From the perspective of the long history of our species on this planet, this is self-destructive behavior that violates the terms of our inheritance from those who lived before and destroys our pact with the future. We are only the living generation in a unknown lineage extending untold generations into the past and a link to generations into a future where the unborn have claims to life's necessities as legitimate as our own. This earth belongs to the future as much as to the past and present. I will not stray into a theological discussion, but I do believe the terms of our existence are bound up inseparably with our place, this earth. We do not know precisely how life here originated and we do not know how or if it will end. We do know that it all had an existence before we were born and will continue to exist after we are gone. We get to add chapters to the narrative. We cannot rewrite it, and if life is really sacred, then we must not engage in behaviors that terminate the story.

While I was in Michigan friends and relatives lovingly chided me for my frequent trips to cemeteries, as if I had some odd fascination with the dead. Yet they have gone with me, and my interest has stimulated their own curiosity about their personal pasts. I have assisted them in finding their own connections; it is as if my interest and my presence enabled others to admit to their own needs to reinvigorate their ties to the past and to their places. Contemporary Americans have a pronounced tendency to dismiss the past as if it ought not to matter. This outward denial of the past is combined with a profound and furtive yearning for the consolation that the past provides. The past is not trivial or silly. The reconnection is central to the most important work that public history organizations can do for people and communities. But to do this well, public historians must do it personally and acknowledge the importance of the emotions that accompany the experience. Acknowledgment of the past requires acknowledgment of the efficacy of emotion and a willingness to feel. This is no esoteric business. It is central to the human heart and to what we hold most dear.

My experience during my summer in the Upper Peninsula wonderfully confirmed the indivisibility of past, present, and future. My long, painful absence from the place made the experience possible, for what I experienced during my three-month sojourn was a confrontation and re-remembering of my own past in this place from the perspective of present time spent there. At first my time with Theresa in Andriacchi's Store was excruciating. Both she and the place were so relic-like, such powerful reminders of time's passage, so painfully and tangibly symbolic of the passage of my own life that they induced in me a mourning for myself and my past youth. On subsequent visits, however, my remembrance was updated, my mourning subsided, and I allowed Theresa and her family store to re-enter the present and there she remains. On my last visit with her before I left she cast me and herself into the future. "I will be ninety-seven in November," she said. "I will remember," I thought. Then she added, "And if I hear that you are in Ishpeming and you do not visit me, I will be disappointed." "I will never do that," I thought. There is no way to adequately explain the sense of ease that I feel _Comfort_ in this reconnection of past with present, this recognition that Theresa exists now and that she has continued to live her life in my absence, this acknowledgment that she is not a relic but a living symbol of all that has happened in my childhood, my long absence, my present, and now a part of my future as well. This brings me a serenity.

Theresa Andriacchi is alive while Great-grandfather Michael Quinn is dead and buried with great-grandmothers, grandfathers, and grandmothers in the Negaunee Cemetery. Although Michael is dead, he continues his work through me in the present. He lives in my remembrances and informs me that this is my place, that I have a past that extends both behind me and ahead of me, that I am one of his, that I belong, that I am alive, and that I too will have an indelible imprint upon those who succeed me. If public historians can inculcate this sense of obligation to past and future in the communities we serve, imagine how we might make decisions differently. Would we tread more lightly, less voraciously on this resilient but fragile planet? Would we build with permanence and relationships in mind? Would we take the long view and would we consider obligations to the future of our species more seriously? Would we place more importance on relationships and less on consumption?

I have Lake Superior on my mind. In my final days in the Upper Peninsula I found myself returning to its shores more often. This was not a conscious act but an irresistible emotional urge. I climbed over the rugged rock, watched the waves crash explosively and spit into the air as they dashed against granite and squirted through crevices. As I approached my necessary departure, the north winds of autumn gradually increased Lake Superior's peaks and troughs into a froth that swept over rocks, breakwaters, and deep into my own soul, rinsing and refreshing my spirit. Astounded and inspired by the majesty of our earth and all else that exists, I am both diminished and expanded by the experience: diminished because I am overwhelmed by my own insignificance, expanded as I merge into something larger, stronger, bigger, timeless compared with the boundaries of human life, and so very different than myself. This is simultaneously a humbling and exhilarating experience. Although different than my interaction with either Michael Quinn or Theresa Andriacchi, it is one more way in which I confront my place in the order of the universe and where I am. It is another way to know who I am.

We all need such places, or analogous ones, just to know who we are. Here is the context of our lives, and yet these places console us and inspire us to exceed the boundaries of our lives. These places too are story places, compelling the attentions and concerns of public historians, for here are the wellsprings of human aspiration. These are the places where we have created our stories, where we find our shared memories, where we can identify our common ground, the places where we have experienced community and where we can learn to create it again. Here we are humbled, yet inspired to overcome what seem to be impossible obstacles.

On one of my final days there I drove by the Ishpeming High School. There is not a teacher or administrator left who worked there during my four years of attendance. The students who attend now are younger than my own children and not many years older than my grandchildren. I can almost see myself entering the front doors more than thirty years younger, a bit leaner. Then life held all possibilities. I did not know then that choices I unwittingly made would shape my life now in unanticipated ways. Now I see students enter the same doors nearly thirty-five years later. I am their past. They are the future. It is the tale of replacement repeated, generation after generation for all time. When I stand in front of this brick school building, I know that decisions matter and that they have consequences. I know that my own decisions matter. They are the material from which I made my own narrative, my own life, and from which I constructed myself. I dreamed myself into who I am. Standing there I know that the past is real, but as I watch the students oblivious to me, I know that the future is real, too. Past, present, and future are not separate. But we who are in the present are now accountable for the story.

✒ A Brief Booklist ✒

It is not possible to list all the readings or even all the books that have influenced this work and informed my thinking on the subject. From the Bible and Shakespeare to the latest edition of Webster's dictionary and the most recent plaque in our local Walk of Fame, I find inspiration, ideas, answers, and perplexities. Further, it seems that the bibliography for history and community lengthens daily. For instance, just after I finished *A Place to Remember*, Roy Rosenzweig and David Thelen published *The Presence of the Past: Popular Uses of History in American Life* (NY: Columbia University Press, 1998), a work I surely could have added had it preceded my writing. My best advice, in addition to the short list below, is that those who are interested in the topic search out their own lists.

David Ashley, *History Without a Subject: The Postmodern Condition* (Boulder, CO: Westview Press, 1997)

St. Augustine, *Confessions* (NY: Book-of-the-Month Club, 1996)

Murray Bookchin, *The Philosophy of Social Ecology: Essays on Dialectical Naturalism* (Montreal: Black Rose Books, 1996)

Peter Calthorpe, *The New American Metropolis: Ecology, Communities, and the American Dream* (New York: Princeton Architectural Press, 1993)

David Carr, *Time, Narrative and History* (Bloomington, IN: Indiana U Press, 1986)

R. G. Collingwood, *The Idea of History* (London: Oxford University Press, 1956)

Antonio Damasio, *Descartes' Error: Emotion, Reason, and the Human Brain* (NY: G. P. Putnam's Sons, 1994)

Paul Davies, *About Time: Einstein's Unfinished Revolution* (NY: Simon & Schuster, 1995)

Paul Davies, *God and the New Physics* (NY: Simon & Schuster, 1983)

Paul Davies and John Gribbin, *The Matter Myth* (NY: Touchstone Books, 1992)

Joel Davis, *Mapping the Mind: The Secrets of the Human Brain and How It Works* (Secaucus, N. J.: Birch Lane Press, 1997)

Michael Delp, *The Coast of Nowhere: Meditations on Rivers, Lakes and Streams* (Detroit: Wayne State University Press, 1997)

Alexis de Toqueville, *Democracy in America*, vols. I and II (NY: Random House, Inc., 1990)

Todd Gitlin, *The Twilight of Common Dreams: Why America Is Wracked by Culture Wars* (NY: Henry Holt and Company, Inc., 1995)

Jeffrey Goldfarb, *The Cynical Society: The Culture of Politics and Politics of Culture in American Life* (Chicago: The University of Chicago Press, 1991)

John Gribbin, *In Search of Schrödinger's Cat: Quantam Physics and Reality* (NY: Bantam Books, 1984)

Eddy L. Harris, *Mississippi Solo: A River Quest* (NY: Nick Lyons Books, 1988)

Stephen W. Hawking, *A Brief History of Time* (NY: Bantam Books, 1988)

James Howard Kunstler, *The Geography of Nowhere: The Rise and Decline of America's Man-Made Landscape* (NY: Simon & Schuster, 1993)

Roger Lewin, *Complexity: Life at the Edge of Chaos* (NY: Collier Books, 1992)

Edward Linenthal and Tom Englehardt, eds., *History Wars* (NY: Metropolitan Books, Henry Holt and Company, 1996)

Barry Lopez, *About This Life: Journeys on the Threshold of Memory* (NY: Alfred A. Knopf, Inc. - Distributed by Random House, 1998)

Russell M. Magnaghi and Michael Marsden, eds., *A Sense of Place: Michigan's Upper Peninsula* (Marquette, MI: Northern Michigan University Press, 1997)

Ray Oldenburg, *The Great Good Place: Cafes, Coffee Shops, Community Centers, Beauty Parlors, General Stores, Bars, Hangouts and How They Get You Through the Day* (NY: Paragon House, 1989)

Oliver Sacks, *An Anthropologist on Mars* (NY: Alfred A. Knopf Inc., 1995), p. 49–50

Carl Schorske, *Thinking With History: Explorations in the Passage to Modernism* (Princeton, NJ: Princeton Univesity Press, 1998)

Jefferson A. Singer, and Peter Salovey, *The Remembered Self: Emotion and Memory in Personality* (NY: The Free Press, 1993)

ꙅ About the Author ꙅ

Robert R. Archibald has just completed ten years as president and CEO of the Missouri Historical Society in St. Louis, Missouri, the public history institution which received the first National Award for Museum Service in 1994. He has been the director of the Montana Historical Society and of the Western Heritage Center in Billings, Montana, and curator of the Albuquerque Museum in New Mexico. An active member of many professional and community organizations, he served as president of the American Association for State and Local History from 1994 through 1996. He writes and speaks on numerous topics from history and historical practice to community building and environmental responsibility.

Archibald spent his first twenty years of life in Michigan's Upper Peninsula, born in Ishpeming and educated at Northern Michigan University in Marquette, where he achieved undergraduate and graduate degrees. He earned his doctorate at the University of New Mexico, an experience he deeply values, and last year received an honorary doctorate of letters from the University of Missouri–St. Louis and the Distinguished Alumni Award from NMU, honors he thoroughly appreciates.